STUDENT MENTAL HEALTH

STUDENT

MENTAL

HEALTH

A GUIDE FOR

TEACHERS, SCHOOL AND DISTRICT LEADERS,
SCHOOL PSYCHOLOGISTS AND NURSES,
SOCIAL WORKERS, COUNSELORS, AND PARENTS

UPDATED AND EXPANDED

WILLIAM DIKEL, MD

W. W. NORTON & COMPANY
Independent Publishers Since 1923

Copyright © 2022, 2020, 2014 by William Dikel

Previous edition published as THE TEACHER'S GUIDE TO STUDENT MENTAL HEALTH

For information about permission to reproduce selections from this book, write to Permissions, W. W. Norton & Company, Inc., 500 Fifth Avenue, New York, NY 10110

For information about special discounts for bulk purchases, please contact W. W. Norton Special Sales at specialsales@wwnorton.com or 800-233-4830

Manufacturing by Lakeside Book Company
Production manager: Katelyn MacKenzie

ISBN: 978-1-324-05214-2 (pbk.)
978-1-324-05214-2 (revised pbk.)

W. W. Norton & Company, Inc., 500 Fifth Avenue, New York, N.Y. 10110
www.wwnorton.com

W. W. Norton & Company Ltd., 15 Carlisle Street, London W1D 3BS

1 2 3 4 5 6 7 8 9 0

Contents

PART III

The Diagnosis and Treatment of Child and Adolescent Psychiatric Disorders

PART IV

School District and School Policies and Procedures

Preface: A Pandemic-Informed Perspective

SHORTLY AFTER THE SECOND EDITION OF *STUDENT MENTAL Health* was completed in 2019, the first known case of COVID-19 was identified in Wuhan, China. The disease has since spread worldwide, leading to an ongoing pandemic. As of this writing (March 2022), there have been 425 million cases of COVID-19 worldwide and nearly 6,000,000 deaths.

Although there are indications that this highly adaptive virus may be weakening its hold, there is the distinct possibility that the virus will continue to mutate, triggering yet another resurgence of the pandemic. Even under the best of circumstances, the consequences of COVID-19 will linger for some time to come. School districts need to have clearly developed plans for both post-pandemic educational programming and for the unfortunate possibility that the pandemic may be far from over.

The pandemic has added another daunting layer of challenges to already overburdened educational and mental health systems. The mental health implications of COVID-19 are complex and not fully understood, especially in children and adolescents. It is clear, however, that COVID-19's impact on student mental health has been devastating.

Prior to the pandemic, mental health disorders in children and adolescents were already pervasive. Disorders of mood and anxiety were common, and generally went untreated. Suicidal behavior was on the rise. The World Health Organization (WHO) declared children's mental health as being in a state of emergency, and the global prevalence of anxiety and depression increased by 25% during the first year of the COVID-19 pandemic, they estimated, with young people disproportionately affected.[1]

COVID-19 CAN DIRECTLY AND INDIRECTLY IMPACT STUDENT MENTAL HEALTH

There is a paucity of data clarifying a direct relationship between the COVID-19 disease and mental health disorders. Studies in adults indicate that people infected with COVID-19 are 60% more likely to develop mental health symptoms including anxiety, depression, and suicidal ideation, as well as opioid use disorder, illicit drug and alcohol use disorders, and disturbances in sleep and cognition.[2] One study estimated the risks of incident mental health disorders in survivors of the acute phase of COVID-19, comparing people who were hospitalized for COVID-19 within 30 days of contracting the infection to those hospitalized for any other cause. The researchers found that mental health disorders were 86% more likely in people hospitalized for COVID-19. The findings suggest that people who survive the acute phase of COVID-19 are at increased risk of an array of incident mental health disorders.[3]

There is also evidence that people who have pre-existing mental health disorders are at higher risk of developing a COVID-19 infection and may have more severe medical outcomes.[4]

While experts still need to study the long-term effects of COVID-19 on the brain, over half of one sample of US COVID-19 survivors reported symptoms of depression months after recovery.[5] Those who had more severe COVID-19 symptoms were most likely to suffer from depression.[6] COVID-19 infections likely have contributed to nearly 3 million new cases of mental health disorders in the US.[7] It has been hypothesized that the virus responsible for COVID-19 can enter the brain and disturb cellular and neuronal pathways, leading to mental health disorders.[8] One study suggested that some pediatric patients who had been infected with the virus developed anti-neural antibodies that can attack brain tissue. This was thought to have contributed to symptoms of anxiety and depression.[9] There is also evidence that symptoms of "long COVID" (COVID-19 cases that result in long-duration symptoms) can include anxiety and depression.[10]

Adverse Childhood Experiences (stressful or traumatic events that children experience before the age of eighteen) are major contributors to mental health difficulties, especially in the realms of anxiety and mood. The direct effects of a COVID-19 infection can be an adverse childhood experience for children and adolescents who have contracted the virus, if symptoms are severe enough.

COVID-19 also has pervasive indirect effects due to the consequences of pandemic-related traumas. These traumas include social isolation, loss of social structure, inadequate household supplies, absence of physical exercise, intrafamilial violence, and limited or no recreational activity. Loss of employment income resulting in difficulty paying for usual household expenses has been a major stressor. Tragically, numerous caregivers have lost their lives to COVID-19.

Thus, the mental health of children and adolescents who have contracted COVID-19 may be directly affected by the disease. But far more pervasively, the pandemic has had indirect but serious implications for the mental health of young people worldwide.

These stressors—which are significantly associated with anxiety, depression, and symptoms of PTSD—have contributed to a marked increase in many students' mental health difficulties. Adolescents with poor emotional regulation abilities are particularly at risk for experiencing increases in all mental health symptoms during the COVID-19 pandemic.

Thus, many students who previously had no mental health symptoms are now suffering from adjustment-related difficulties, particularly in the realm of anxiety and depression. Even more problematic is the fact that students who already had mental health disorders prior to the pandemic are now experiencing the additional negative impact caused by the trauma of COVID-19.

AN OPPORTUNITY TO REIMAGINE MENTAL HEALTH SUPPORTS FOR STUDENTS

This exacerbation by the pandemic of an already acute mental health crisis presents an opportunity for educators to address student needs on a systemwide basis. The topic of student mental health is now widely and openly discussed, and such discussions no longer focus solely on students who require special attention for emotional and/or behavioral problems. This broadening of perspective has the potential to reduce stigmas, and to successfully frame the topic of mental health within a public health context.

This is a crucial moment in time for schools to review and reconsider their practices. Schools can take a two-pronged approach, providing interventions for students who have mental health disorders and also providing universal social emotional learning (SEL) interventions such as developing skills in self-mastery and mindfulness and cultivating a healthy lifestyle for all students.

This approach aids students in recovering from the stress and trauma they have experienced as a result of the pandemic. Learning these techniques can also help students cope with other major life stressors that range from local problems in their community to geopolitical crises.

Self-Mastery and Mindfulness

Children and adolescents have a remarkable ability to self-regulate their bodies and minds.[11] They can easily learn techniques that result in self-relaxation, increased focus and concentration, improved productivity, and overall increases in well-being. Learning self-mastery is especially useful in dealing with the multiple stressors related to the COVID-19 pandemic.

Mindfulness is a crucial component of self-mastery. Students who learn mindfulness demonstrate a reduction in perceived stress and significant improvements in sustained attention. These students also demonstrate a reduced response of the amygdala—a brain structure associated with emotion and stress—to negative stimuli.[12]

School districts are increasingly utilizing yoga as one of their SEL techniques for learning self-mastery. It helps students cultivate competencies in mind–body awareness, self-regulation, and physical fitness.

The utilization of SEL programs and mindfulness techniques to develop skills in self-mastery is further discussed in Chapter 18.

Lifestyle

A healthy lifestyle is a key factor in promoting well-being. Lifestyle behavioral patterns include diet, exercise, adequate sleep, limited use of tobacco, alcohol or other intoxicants, and social connectedness. Especially now, due to the stress of COVID-19, interventions that promote health and well-being are important for vulnerable students. Teaching healthy behaviors through a partnership between parents and schools can aid in the development of healthy students who have optimal coping mechanisms for dealing with life stressors. The importance of lifestyle in promoting mental health is addressed in Chapter 1.

REBUILDING SCHOOL COMMUNITY

As schools struggle to make up for learning loss after long closures, the schools that are the most successful appear to be those that focus first on recreating a sense of school community. In the months and years following the height of the pandemic and mass quarantine—which interrupted crucial periods in children's and adolescents' social and emotional development—it will be essential to foster strong relationships and a sense of safety within classrooms and schoolwide. This will be necessary regardless of the trajectory taken by the pandemic.

The United Nations Children's Fund (UNICEF) has provided a number of recommendations to educators to help them support students' mental health following the pandemic.[13] They encourage listening to students' concerns and demonstrating understanding and empathy. Students should be engaged in making the classroom a welcoming, safe, and comfortable space, and should be given ample opportunities to socialize, play, and interact with peers. If significant changes in a student's behavior are noted that reflect impaired functioning, additional support and guidance should be sought. The UNICEF recommendations also encourage educators to be good role models for students and protect their own physical and mental health: for example, maintain healthy eating and sleeping habits, rest, exercise, and connect with friends, family, and colleagues.

CONCLUSION

While it is abundantly evident that COVID-19 has had negative implications for child and adolescent mental health worldwide, the pandemic can also serve as a catalyst for educators to reconsider their classroom and schoolwide practices when it comes to addressing student mental health. As schools hopefully can return to some state of normalcy, the focus should be on developing healthy behaviors and coping skills that will aid students in processing the stressors they have experienced. Students can learn to self-regulate with techniques in relaxation and mindfulness, while an education in healthy lifestyle habits can bolster students' resilience in the face of stress. Finally, a strong sense of school community can help students recover from long periods of isolation and assist them in reacclimating to the classroom. The COVID-19 pandemic can be viewed as a mental health disaster, or as a unique opportunity to address a mental health crisis that was already pervasive among young people. The support of educators and school administrators—as well as that of counselors, nurses, social workers, psychologists, and parents—will mean all the difference in students' abilities to thrive.

Additional information for schools can be found at:

The National Center for School Mental Health (NCSMH) provides a repository of resources to address school mental health during COVID-19: https://www.schoolmentalhealth.org/COVID-19/. The resource repository includes COVID-specific tools and information for school staff and leadership, students, and families, and on topics related to student and staff wellness and mental health.

The National Center for MH in Schools & Student/Learning Supports provides a special focus on resources during the COVID-19 pandemic: http://smhp.psych.ucla.edu/pdfdocs/centercorona.pdf

The US Department of Education provides the following handbooks:

- Volume 1: Strategies for Safely Reopening Elementary and Secondary Schools: https://www2.ed.gov/documents/coronavirus/reopening.pdf
- Volume 2: Roadmap to Reopening Safely and Meeting All Students' Needs: https://www2.ed.gov/documents/coronavirus/reopening-2.pdf
- Volume 3: Strategies for Safe Operation and Addressing the Impact of COVID-19 on Higher Education Students, Faculty, and Staff: https://www2.ed.gov/documents/coronavirus/reopening-3.pdf

REFERENCES

[1] Mental health and COVID-19: early evidence of the pandemic's impact. (2022, March 2). *World Health Organization.* https://apps.who.int/iris/handle/10665/352189

[2, 3, 6, 7, 8] Xie, Y., Xu, E., & Al-Aly, Z. (2022, February 16). Risks of mental health outcomes in people with COVID-19. *The BMJ.* https://doi.org/10.1136/bmj-2021-068993

[4] Lin, L., et al. (2021, September 8). Mental and neurological disorders and risk of COVID-19 susceptibility, illness severity and mortality: a systematic review, meta-analysis and call for action. *EClinicalMedicine.* 40(101–111). doi: 10.1016/j.eclinm.2021.101111

[5] Perlis, R., et al. (2021, March 12). Association of acute symptoms of COVID-19 and symptoms of depression in adults. *JAMA Network Open.* 4(3), e213223. doi:10.1001/jamanetworkopen.2021.3223

[9] Bartley, C., et al. (2021, October 25). Anti–SARS-CoV-2 and autoantibody profiles in the cerebrospinal fluid of 3 teenaged patients with COVID-19 and subacute neuropsychiatric symptoms. *JAMA Neurology.* 78(12), 1503–1509. doi:10.1001/jamaneurol.2021.3821

[10] Huang, C. (2021, January 8). 6-month consequences of COVID-19 in patients discharged from hospital: a cohort study. *The Lancet.* 397(10270), 220–232. doi:10.1016/S0140-6736(20)32656-8

[11] Dikel, W., & Olness, K. (1980). Self-hypnosis, biofeedback, and voluntary peripheral temperature control in children. *Pediatrics.* 66(3), 335–340.

[12] Shudong, Z., et al. (2021, October 2). Functional connectivity of amygdala subregions predicts vulnerability to depression following the COVID-19 pandemic. *Journal of Affective Disorders.* 297, 421–429. doi: 10.1016/j.jad.2021.09.107

[13] 8 ways teachers can support students' mental health during COVID-19 school returns. (n.d.) *UNICEF.* https://www.unicef.org/coronavirus/8-teacher-tips-student-mental-health

Introduction to the Paperback Edition

THE TOPIC OF SCHOOL MENTAL HEALTH WAS ALREADY GAINING momentum when this book, then titled *The Teacher's Guide to Student Mental Health*, was first published in 2014. The book was well received, but feedback indicated that the focus needed to be expanded beyond teachers in order to reach a wider audience for this important topic.

Thus, this paperback edition is directed towards all educators. Teachers, school and district leaders, school psychologists, school nurses, social workers, and counselors can all benefit from the material covered in this book. It is also directed toward parents in order to provide them with the information required to advocate for their children's needs in school. Since many students are involved with multiple systems, the updated text will prove useful to other audiences as well, including physicians, community mental health providers, school attorneys, and professionals working in the child protection and juvenile justice systems.

As a result of the expansion of the audience, a significant amount of new material has been added to the paperback edition. Much of this was derived from articles that I wrote or co-wrote on a variety of topics related to school mental health. Some of this material was incorporated into the existing text and some was kept complete and placed in the appendix section of the book. Please refer to my website, williamdikel.com, for the full articles.

NEW TO THIS EXPANDED EDITION

The additional material encompasses a wide variety of topics related to student mental health. Evidence-based teaching methods, coordinating mental health services and schools, relationships with outside providers, creating school mental health plans, special education concerns, student violence, healthy lifestyles and mental health, the handling of mental health data in school files, and policy issues related to special education are all covered in detail.

The section on evidence-based educational interventions for students who have emotional and/or behavioral problems can assist educators in tailoring successful programming for students who have a range of mental health disabilities.

Methods of providing mental health services in schools are described in detail, with analyses of the risks and benefits of each model of service. Recommended contractual relationships for mental health services provided in the school setting are described, with an emphasis on how school districts can assist in the provision of mental health services while staying out of the mental health business of diagnosis and treatment.

Methods of successful collaboration with outside systems including county social services and community mental health programs are illustrated with examples.

Although school districts tend to have medical plans when dealing with students who have disorders such as diabetes or asthma, they tend to not have mental health plans outlining specific interventions for students who have mental health disorders such as depression, ADHD, or anxiety disorders. This new edition focuses on methods of creating successful mental health plans to aid school districts in meeting the needs of students who have mental health disorders.

New material on special education provides an in-depth look at the overlap between mental health and special education. This includes the roles of the emotional disorder, autism spectrum disorder, and other health-impaired categories of special education as they relate to students' mental health disorders. The methodology of conducting special education evaluations for students who abuse drugs or alcohol is outlined in detail.

The topic of student violence, including school shootings, is very much in the news these days. The new edition provides an in-depth analysis of the relationship between students' mental health disorders and violent behavior.

Lifestyle and mental health is an important topic, as issues related to nutrition, exercise, sleep, and positive social relationships play an important role in student mental health. The relationship between physical health and mental health is described, and recommendations are made regarding student lifestyles that provide the opportunity for optimal health.

It is not unusual for educators to have some confusion about handling student mental health information in school files. For example, school social workers may believe that their documentation regarding meetings with students is confidential, whereas in fact it is part of students' educational records. Mental health information from mental health providers in the community needs to be handled in a specific manner. Recommendations regarding the handling of mental health data in school files provide direction to educators.

Several policy issues are discussed in detail. They include the need to reevaluate the criteria and the definition of the emotional disorder category of special education, as it is an outdated category that has abysmal outcomes. Also, recommendations are made for eliminating the payor of last resort provision of IDEA, since this provision puts school districts at significant financial liability for potentially having to pay for mental health treatment—including costly residential treatment—for students in special education.

EXPANSION OF NATIONAL CENTERS THAT PROMOTE SCHOOL MENTAL HEALTH

When I first began consulting to schools over 30 years ago, many districts were so reluctant to address students' mental health issues that it seemed that they were forbidden to use the words "school" and "mental health" in the same sentence. Times have changed, and there is now a burgeoning interest in school mental health topics. For example, the University of Maryland's National Center for School Mental Health (NCSMH) had approximately 1400 attendees at its 2018 Annual Conference on Advancing School Mental Health, an increase of over 30% since this book's first edition in 2014. NCSMH has worked with the Health Resources and Services Administration's Maternal and Child Health Bureau to develop a National Census as well as National Performance Measures related to quality and sustainability in school mental health. The NCSMH supports a dynamic, free online portal, the School Health Assessment and Performance Evaluation System (www. theshapesystem.com) that offers schools, districts, and states a workspace and targeted resources to advance high quality school mental health systems. The NCSMH continues to work at local, state, and national levels to advance comprehensive school mental health across a multi-tiered system of support and through a shared family–school–community mental health agenda. Some emerging areas of focus in the field include social emotional learning, trauma-informed care, telemental health, social determinants of health, and school safety and climate.

Meanwhile, on the west coast, the UCLA Center for MH in Schools & Student/Learning Supports has experienced ongoing expansion and interest in school mental health topics. Established in 1986, the School Mental Health Project (SMHP) focused on pursuing theory, research, practice, and training related to addressing mental health and psychosocial concerns through school-based interventions. SMHP staff worked closely with school districts, local and state agencies, special initiatives, and organizations and colleagues across the country. In 1995 the project established the National Center for Mental Health in Schools, and in 2015, the Center established the National Initiative for Transforming Student and Learning Supports. In 2017, the Center name was expanded to be the Center for MH in Schools & Student/Learning Supports. The Center's mission is to improve outcomes for students by helping districts and their schools enhance how they address barriers to learning and teaching and reengage disconnected students. SMHP provides information and links for leaders and practitioners to access a range of no-cost resources that can be used for school improvement, professional development, and direct student/learning support. SMHP also helps districts move away from what typically is a fragmented, piecemeal approach to one of providing student and learning supports throughout the school system.

THE GROWTH OF ON-SITE SCHOOL MENTAL HEALTH SERVICES

The provision of on-site mental health services in schools has been a growing trend since the publication of the first edition of this book. Co-locating mental health services into school districts, through partnerships with community mental health providers, is a model that is expanding across the U.S. This model provides the opportunity to build bridges between school districts and mental health providers while maintaining legal firewalls to protect the districts from legal and financial liabilities. The ideal model of service provision includes services such as teacher consultation, attending team meetings (with parents' permission), providing in-service presentations, and so on. As these ancillary services are generally not reimbursable from insurance, grants are often used to pay for these services and to cover costs for uninsured and under-insured students.

In my home state of Minnesota, school mental health services are in 50 schools in the Minneapolis public school system, in 163 schools and 9 PICA Head Starts across Hennepin County (the state's most populous county that includes Minneapolis), and in approximately 1000 of the 2066 schools across the state of Minnesota. According to Mark Sander, Ph.D., Director of School Mental Health at Hennepin County and Minneapolis Public Schools, this is a significant increase from 10 years ago when there were services in about 11 schools in Minneapolis Public Schools, 45 schools across Hennepin County, and about 400 schools across Minnesota. A large driver in this increase of school mental health services is due to the School Mental Health Grant program beginning in 2007 that is administered by the Minnesota Department of Human Services. The school mental health programs (SMHPs) typically provide on-site mental health services in schools as well as providing treatment-related consultation to teachers and other school staff. In addition, SMHPs provide mental health professional development for school staff and care coordination with other professionals outside of the school. Families' health insurance pays for a large portion of the services (as it would in outpatient settings) and the state grant funds typically pay for the cost of clinical care for the uninsured and under-insured. The grant funds also help pay for the treatment-related consultation and care coordination. In some school districts, the school district is paying for the treatment consultation and care coordination if grant funds are not available. The expansion of school mental health in Minnesota is largely due to the fact that these programs significantly increase access to care for families and provide the opportunity for mental health professionals to collaborate and educate school staff on how to better support students who have mental health concerns. In 2018, the Minnesota Department of Human Services provided funding of $33 million in state grants over the next three years to serve students in Minnesota's public schools. Grants were awarded to

57 recipients of its School-Linked Mental Health program, who collectively will serve more than half of the state's schools. Under the last round of grants, the program reached students in 953 schools, but the state expects that to be up to 1,200 by mid-2021.

Based on my experience consulting on numerous grant-funded programs that lost their grants and were forced to discontinue services, it is my opinion that grants should only be relied upon for startup pilot programs and then transition into self-sustaining models of service provision. School-based mental health services could become self-sustaining if a state increased the Medicaid reimbursement rate, expanded the mental health benefit set to include all ancillary services, allowed Medicaid billing for mental health related services provided to general education and special education students, and made all students who demonstrated emotional disturbances eligible for Medicaid services at no cost to their families.

EXPANSION OF MENTAL HEALTH TRAINING FOR EDUCATORS AND STUDENTS

Over half of the states in the U.S. have mandates for teacher education about mental health topics. For example, in 2018, Iowa passed legislation that requires training to help teachers recognize signs of depression in students and help them seek mental health services. Many states utilize the Mental Health First Aid program, an 8-hour course that gives professionals the skills to help someone who is developing a mental health problem or experiencing a mental health crisis.

In 2018, New York and Virginia became the first two states to enact laws requiring mental health education in schools. New York's law updates the health curriculum in elementary, middle, and high schools to include material on mental health. The New York law does not mandate a specific curriculum. Instead, it updates the health curriculum to include mental health in its definition and purview. The law indicates that mental health "is an integral part of our overall health and should be an integral part of health education in New York schools." Under the law, health education in the state "must recognize the multiple dimensions of health and include the relationship of physical and mental health," according to the New York State Department of Education.

According to the New York law, "90 percent of youth who die by suicide suffer from depression or another diagnosable and treatable mental illness at the time of their death." By emphasizing mental health literacy, schools are making an effort to prepare students with lifelong skills to understand wellness and mental health. By educating children of all ages about mental health, the hope is that they will learn how to recognize early symptoms in themselves and their friends and seek help before a crisis develops.

Virginia's law mandates that mental health education be incorporated into physical education and health curricula for ninth- and tenth-graders, and it mandates the state's Board of Education to update the Health Standards of Learning with mental health material for ninth and tenth grades. The law requires the state's department of education to consult with experts, including the National Alliance on Mental Illness, to develop a more stringent set of standards using the latest research and best practices. The goal is to have a statewide educational program that explains the brain science behind mental illness, in order to help students learn how to improve their own mental well-being, and to reduce the stigma around mental health.

A PUBLIC HEALTH APPROACH TO STUDENT MENTAL HEALTH

The purpose of this new edition is to explain, in lay terms, essential information regarding the educational needs of students who have mental health disorders. The goal is to make schools supportive environments and to improve educational outcomes for this vulnerable population of students.

There is a growing awareness among educators that student mental health issues require at least the same amount of attention as issues relating to physical health. Taking a public health approach, school mental health activities can be incorporated into all aspects of students' education.

Having worked as a school mental health consultant, locally and nationally, for over 30 years, I find it very satisfying that student mental health issues are now receiving the attention that they deserve. I am hoping that this thoroughly updated edition of my book will greatly benefit educators and the students who they serve, and I feel fortunate to be able to assist in this goal.

Acknowledgments

THIS BOOK COULD NOT HAVE BEEN WRITTEN WITHOUT THE help of many outstanding professionals whose work supports student mental health activities. First and foremost, I want to thank all the teachers I interviewed, including those who requested to remain anonymous. Debra Goodlaxon, Donna Harris, Nancy Kurtzman, and Cindy Ralston all shared their knowledge based on years of working with students who have mental health disorders. Mark Weist, Nancy Lever, and Sharon Hoover Stephan, past and present directors of the Center for School Mental Health, and Howard Adelman and Linda Taylor from UCLA's School Mental Health Project have been leading the way in promoting school mental health activities. Jan Mohr and Charlene Myklebust, administrators at Setting 4 programs for emotionally disturbed students, have provided district leadership in addressing these high-risk students' mental health needs. Renelle Nelson from the PACER organization shed light on school mental health from a parent's perspective, and Katy Perry from Education Minnesota shared the perspective of teachers. Mark Anderson, from the Barbara Schneider Foundation, provided insights about violence prevention. Mark Sander shared his extensive experience in overseeing school mental health programming in Hennepin County, Minnesota. Beth Freeman has assisted school districts across the United States in creating sustainable school mental health programs. Gordy Wrobel has worked to incorporate school mental health into school health programming and has advocated for an increased mental health role for school psychologists. Kelly Stern has successfully implemented several mental health programs in the Hawaii School District, following my consultative review of the district's program components. Sheldon Braaten, from the Behavioral Institute for Children and Adolescents, provided insight into the educational system's role in addressing students' behavioral problems in the classroom. Joanne Cashman, from the IDEA partnership, put school mental health activities in the context of communities of practice, which link various stakeholders around a common goal of serving at-risk students. Jan Ostrom, licensed psychologist and behavioral analyst, has provided invaluable assistance in creating a conceptual framework that bridges the gap between behavioral and clinical perspectives, and cocreated the Clinical-Behavioral Spectrum concept with me. Most of all, I want to thank the countless teachers, school psychologists, counselors, social workers, nurses, and school administrators across the country who are dedicated to educating students and preparing them to overcome their challenges and live successful lives.

PART I

Overview of Children and Adolescents' Mental Health

Why Schools Should Be Concerned with Students' Mental Health

THE BANK ROBBER WILLIE SUTTON, WHEN ASKED WHY HE robbed banks, was quoted as saying, "That's where the money is." A similar analogy can be made when asking why schools are an ideal setting for addressing youth mental health issues—that's where the kids are.

THE ROLE OF SCHOOLS AND TEACHERS

In fact, schools are the most common settings where youth who have mental health disorders receive any services: for example, school counseling (25%), followed by mental health specialists (24%), general medical providers (11%), human services (7%), alternative medicine (5%), and juvenile justice (5%) settings (Garland et al., 2001). Schools are also a gateway to additional mental health services, following the recognition of their disorders by school professionals. The President's Freedom Commission on Mental Health, the Institute of Medicine, and the U.S. Department of Health and Human Services all have encouraged schools to enhance their methods of early identification. It is clear that early response to these problems with targeted services provided by mental health professionals has a significant positive impact on both psychiatric and educational outcomes. Educators play a pivotal role in children's mental health. Given the prevalence of mental health disorders in children and adolescents, the odds are that every classroom in America will have at least one student who has a mental health disorder, and many of these students will have severe emotional disturbances. Success in school is a key predictor of later success in life, and students who have mental health disorders are at a significant disadvantage for school success if they do not receive appropriate services. With knowledge about mental health, educators will be more effective in working with all students and their families and ensuring academic success.

Teachers in particular play an essential role in assisting children and adolescents who have mental health disorders. Teachers can identify and address areas of learning difficulties or disabilities that are sources of frustration and that can lead to emotional and behavioral difficulties. They can help students learn valuable life skills that have been undeveloped due to the effects of a mental health disorder. They can identify signs and symptoms of mental health disorders and communicate them to parents and to treatment providers in order to assist the diagnostic and treatment process. They can contribute information and opinions to school teams that strategize methods of helping students who have emotional or behavioral problems, and can institute helpful interventions within the classroom to help students succeed. They can help coordinate services with school social workers, psychologists, counselors, and nurses, and with medical and mental health professionals in the community. They can encourage their administrators to develop mental health procedures and guidelines that clarify protocols regarding the roles of school staff, methods of crisis intervention, and methods of conducting assessments of students who have mental health disorders. They can team with parents to create seamless behavior-intervention plans that are consistent between the home and school environments. Most importantly, they can become more successful teachers, and their students who have mental health disorders will have greater academic proficiency, reduced behavioral difficulties, improved attitudes about school, and improved self-esteem as a result of their success in the classroom. Teachers play a vital role in the field of children's mental health, and it can be said that effective teaching is therapeutic for these students. If teachers are sensitive to the nature of a student's mental health difficulties and are able to separate the student from the disorder, the resulting support and compassion go a long way in assisting the student to feel that the school is a welcoming environment.

Risk factors for the development of mental health disorders are complex and differ for different disorders. Even for disorders that have a strong genetic component, environmental influences play a role. For example, if one identical twin has schizophrenia, the chances are only approximately 50% that the other twin, who has identical genetics, will develop schizophrenia as well. This statistic indicates that other factors contribute to the development of this disorder. Environmental factors such as child abuse, poverty, and chaotic home environments can increase the risk of developing mental health disorders. Environmental factors can also be protective, however. One of the strongest protective influences is a strong positive relationship with an adult. This can be a family member, a concerned adult in the neighborhood, or a teacher—but, in particular, a relationship with a teacher who shows concern, and who provides consistency, structure, and nurturance can help a child or adolescent build resilience to be able to successfully face life's stresses. Many experienced teachers describe being visited by their former students who tell them that they made the greatest difference in their ability to succeed in life. A successful teaching relationship can help prevent mental health problems.

THE NEED FOR MENTAL HEALTH EDUCATION AND THE IMPEDIMENTS TO PROVIDING SERVICES

Teacher education programs are packed with information on, and guidance about, the many subjects students are to be taught and the most effective teaching strategies. Unfortunately, there may be little school time left for adequate attention regarding students' mental health. Despite the impact of mental health disorders within the educational environment, many teachers and school administrators lack basic information about the nature of child and adolescent mental health disorders, how they are diagnosed and treated, how they manifest in the school environment, and what types of school-based interventions will have the greatest likelihood of success with affected students.

Compounding this gap is the wide variation in approaches toward student mental health disorders within school districts across the United States. Even within a district, there may be major differences in approach from school to school. Some school districts have intensive training on mental health issues while others have little to none. Some place mental health treatment as a related service on numerous special education students' Individualized Education Programs (IEPs), whereas others rarely if ever do this. Some districts have on-site mental health diagnostic and treatment services, provided either by school-hired professionals or by co-located community medical and mental health providers, while others have no mental health services available.

Some districts have clearly defined mental health procedures and guidelines while others have none. Some districts encourage a clinical perspective on students' mental health disorders, while others steadfastly maintain a strictly behavioral approach to interpretations of students' problems and to subsequent interventions. It is my belief that four major factors contribute to school districts' failure to adequately address students' mental health issues. The first is the lack of knowledge about mental health disorders and their impact on students and on schools. Second, some schools have a bias against a medical, diagnostic model and toward a behavioral model. This stems from a variety of factors. Most students who have mental health disorders are never diagnosed, and behavioral observations may be the only method that educators feel they can rely on to clarify the nature of a student's disability. In some cases a child or adolescent has received numerous different diagnoses made by different medical and mental health professionals. Given the variability of these diagnoses, educators have found it necessary to focus on reliably observed behaviors. The third major reason is due to potential financial liability for school districts regarding the identification and referral for treatment of a student who has a mental health disorder, if the student is receiving special education services. According to the Individuals with Disabilities Education Act (IDEA), schools are the payer of last resort for services that are necessary to support a student's education. Although school districts are exempt from having to pay for medical treatment provided by physicians, schools may be required to pay for mental health treatment. This situation provides a powerful financial disincentive for schools to address mental health issues. This problem is exacerbated by the underfunded mandates of special education requirements and the lack of adequate services for students in need, especially in poor communities.

A Parable to Ponder

Imagine a world in which meningitis was the major cause of students' emotional and behavioral difficulties in the classroom. In this world, teachers would receive minimal training on recognizing the signs of meningitis and what to do when the signs are recognized. In this world, meningitis screening would not be widely done during routine medical appointments, and physicians would have limited training in the diagnosis and treatment of meningitis. In this world, there would be a great shortage of professionals who are skilled in the diagnosis and treatment of meningitis, and schools could experience significant financial repercussions for recommending to parents that they have their child evaluated for meningitis because the school could be the payer of last resort for the evaluation and subsequent expensive treatment. In this world, student behaviors that are the direct result of meningitis would often be misinterpreted as willful, and students would become demoralized when they feel that they are being blamed for behaviors that they have great difficulty controlling. In this world, specialized educational programs for these students would be expensive and tend to have very poor outcomes. Now, substitute the words "mental health disorders" for "meningitis" and consider the implications of this unfortunate situation.

Mental health disorders are a major public health problem for children, adolescents, and adults. In an ideal world, these disorders would be routinely identified during medical visits, all parents would be motivated to seek effective treatment for their children, an adequate number of skilled professionals would be available to treat these students, and educators would be well-trained to recognize and address the mental health manifestations of these disorders.

THE CONTENTS AND PURPOSE OF THIS BOOK

This book is intended to be a practical reference for a wide variety of individuals who support student development in a variety of roles: teachers, school and district leaders, school psychologists, social workers, counselors, parents, and clinicians including primary care physicians and therapists. It provides a broad range of information about children's mental health issues that can supplement the overlapping knowledge bases of the many professionals involved in children's education and care. Specifically, it reviews the nature of different mental health disorders affecting children and adolescents and how they manifest within school, describes how disorders are diagnosed and treated, and discusses classroom interventions (both academic and non-academic) that have been shown to be effective. It outlines both general and special education issues as they relate to these students, illustrates why educational interventions often fail, and suggests alternative perspectives to increase the rate of success. It is hoped that this guide will provide a strong foundation of practical knowledge for educators who are interested in students' mental health.

In Part I, a brief overview of children and adolescents' mental health sets the stage for Part II, where individual chapters are devoted to a more detailed description of a range of emotional or behavioral disorders, including depression and bipolar mood disorder, attention-deficit/hyperactivity disorders, anxiety and obsessive-compulsive disorders, post-traumatic stress disorder, substance use, oppositional defiant disorder, and autism. Part III explains the diagnostic process and most common psychotherapeutic and psychopharmacological treatments for these disorders. In Part IV the roles of school and district staff, and the optimal coordination of services by educators with community and school mental health professionals, is discussed. Part V outlines evidence-based teaching strategies and interventions for students with emotional or behavioral problems, and offers recommendations for school mental health policies and practices to provide a seamless system of coordinated professionals working together to meet the needs of these students. Vignettes are scattered throughout the book—composite examples drawn from my decades of experience providing individual case consultations and school district consultations—in order to illustrate the nature and types of problems and situations that arise in school mental health. These are accompanied by Reflection Questions that will help to facilitate discussion for book study groups or spur the thinking of individual readers.

The key message in this book is that mental health disorders in children and adolescents are real; that they can be identified, correctly diagnosed, and successfully treated; and that many individuals key to children's development can play a major role in ensuring the success of students who have these disorders. I have specialized in school mental health for over 30 years, working locally (in Minnesota) and nationally with school districts and state departments of mental health and education. At the beginning of my career, in some districts it was nearly taboo to use the words "school" and "mental health" in the same sentence. There has been a major paradigm shift over the years, and schools have become increasingly aware of the need to address mental health issues. This book was written with the hope of extending and deepening that awareness, and of fostering collaboration between educators, parents, and mental health professionals within the school and in the community.

CHAPTER 1

A General Introduction to Students' Mental Health

THE 1999 SURGEON GENERAL'S REPORT ON MENTAL HEALTH and the subsequent 2000 Report of the Surgeon General's Conference on Children's Mental Health clearly established mental health as a major public health problem (U.S. Department of Health and Human Services, 2000). These documents indicated that mental health disorders were common and treatable though they generally went untreated.

THE PREVALENCE AND TYPES OF MENTAL HEALTH DISORDERS

According to the Surgeon General's reports, approximately one in five children, adolescents, and adults are noted to have a mental health disorder, and one in 20 children and adolescents have severe emotional disabilities. Only one in three adults and one in five children and adolescents receive even minimal treatment for their disorders. Treatment is generally provided by primary care physicians rather than by mental health professionals. The impact of mental health disorders on society is noted to be immense, not only in human suffering but in financial repercussions as well. The financial impact on the U.S. economy of just one disorder, major depression, is estimated to be $40 billion per year. Subsequent studies have reported similar findings (Pastor, Reuben, & Duran, 2012), and problems remain severe two decades after the Surgeon General's reports were released. The World Health Organization has identified major depressive disorder as the leading cause of disability among Americans aged 15 to 44 years. The National Comorbidity Survey—Adolescent Supplement found that about 11% of adolescents have a depressive disorder by age 18 years. Girls are more likely than boys to experience depression. The risk for depression increases as children become older.

The Centers for Disease Control and Prevention's report of May 2013 (Perou et al., 2013) estimated that 20% of children and adolescents in the United States have mental health disorders. It also noted that the prevalence of these disorders appears to be increasing. Mental health disorders were defined as "serious deviations from expected cognitive, social and emotional development." The most common mental health disorder was ADHD at almost 7%, followed by conduct disorder (3.5%), anxiety disorders (3%), depression (2.1%), autism spectrum disorder (ASD, 1.1%), and Tourette's syndrome (0.2%). Additionally, nearly 5% of adolescents aged 12–17 years reported having an "illicit drug use disorder" in the past year, and 4.2% had an alcohol use disorder in the past year. Suicide is the second leading cause of death among children and adolescents aged 12–17 years. Among individuals aged 10–19 years, the suicide rate is 4.5 suicides per 100,000 people.

Researchers at the National Institute of Mental Health have found that half of all lifetime cases of mental illness present before the age of 14 years. Mental health disorders are thus very prevalent in the general population of children and adolescents. For example, the Centers for Disease Control and Prevention study quoted above found that approximately 5% of children 4–17 years of age had parental reports of severe or definite emotional or behavioral difficulties during the past 6 months, and 17% had reports of minor difficulties. A higher percentage of boys than girls had difficulties at both levels of severity. Among boys and girls, the percentage reported to have difficulties increased with age. Hispanic children were less likely to have parental reports of difficulties at either level of severity compared with non-Hispanic white or non-Hispanic black children. Non-Hispanic black children were as likely as non-Hispanic white children to have severe or definite difficulties but were more likely to have parental reports of minor difficulties. The percentage of children in mother-only families with severe or definite difficulties was double the percentage reported for children in two-parent families (8% versus 4%). Nearly twice the percentage of poor children had parental reports of severe or definite difficulties as nonpoor children (7% versus 4%). The percentage with severe or definite difficulties was 9% of

Medicaid-insured children compared with 4% of privately insured children and 5% of uninsured children, and 12% of children 4–17 years of age were reported to have been diagnosed with at least one of the following disorders: ADHD, learning disability, mental retardation, autism, Down's syndrome, or developmental delay. Nearly 7% had been diagnosed with ADHD, 8% with a learning disability, and 3% with a developmental delay. The percentage of children with ADHD, learning disability, or developmental delay was strongly associated with a child's level of emotional or behavioral difficulty. Among boys with severe or definite difficulties, 59% had been diagnosed with ADHD, 48% with learning disability, and 21% with developmental delay. Among boys with no difficulties, less than 4% had parental reports of any of the diagnoses. Similarly, among girls, diagnosed disorders were most often reported for those with severe or definite difficulties and least often for those with no difficulties.

Educators are keenly aware of the troubled background of many of their students who display emotional or behavioral difficulties in the classroom. Many students experience multiple stresses in their lives, and stresses can increase their risk of developing mental health disorders. Risk factors include physical problems and chronic illness; intellectual disabilities and cognitive impairments; low birth weights; and prenatal exposure to alcohol, drugs, and tobacco. Additional factors include a family history of mental health or addictive disorders, multigenerational poverty, caregiver separation, neglect or abuse, stressful unsatisfactory relationships, and exposure to traumatic events. Children and adolescents typically experience various emotional upheavals and feelings of frustration, anxiety, and self-doubt as a normal part of growing up. It would be very inappropriate for a mental health professional to diagnose a child or adolescent based on normal behaviors. In fact, this was the case when DSM-III listed a disorder, oppositional disorder of childhood, which included behaviors that were so common in the general population that it was changed in DSM-IV to oppositional defiant disorder, and more stringent diagnostic criteria were added in order to justify the diagnosis (for more on the DSM, see Appendix 3).

A diagnosis cannot be made unless there is evidence of a significant disability that is causing major difficulties in functioning intrapsychically (e.g., constantly struggling with internal emotions of anxiety or depression), within the family, socially with peers, in the workplace, or in the school setting. If a child or adolescent is functioning well in all of these areas, by definition, she or he does not have a mental health diagnosis. The degree of disability, if present, may be mild, moderate, or severe. As school systems are the only systems that cannot exclude children and adolescents from services, some of the most psychiatrically disabled children and adolescents in this country are served solely by school programs. For example, treatment centers can discharge patients for being too violent, and it then becomes the responsibility of the school system to serve their multiple needs.

Some children and adolescents are described as internalizers, in that they keep their problems to themselves and may appear to be functioning well while they are suffering. There are abundant examples of adolescents who are active in sports, popular among peers, and good students, who commit suicide, to the shock of all who know them. These individuals were severely disabled, but their disability was hidden to others. Others are externalizers who have significant behavioral difficulties, often in multiple environments. Many of the externalizers, however, also have internalized problems of anxiety or depression.

FACTORS INFLUENCING MENTAL HEALTH

It is important to recognize that some students appear to have mental health disorders when, in fact, the underlying issues are related to cultural factors, lifestyle issues, physical illnesses and the drugs to treat them, or problems stemming from stressors within the school environment.

Cultural Issues

Cultural sensitivity is essential in correctly formulating mental health diagnoses and in providing mental health treatment. If clinicians do not have cultural sensitivity, they run the risk either of inappropriately diagnosing behavior that is culturally normal for the individual or, conversely, of missing evidence that indicates significant psychopathology. For example, Western assumptions about the need for individuals to gain autonomy from their family are inappropriate when dealing with individuals from many Asian cultures. A belief about the normal need to compete and excel, perhaps at the expense of peers, is very inappropriate for many Native American cultures. It is not surprising that many individuals of color have significant skepticism in regard to being labeled with a mental health disorder. In fact, in the time of slavery in the United States, a psychiatric diagnosis known as "Drapetomania" was given to slaves who ran away from a plantation. It was suggested that they "obviously would have to be mentally ill to behave in such a manner."

There is a significant concern that children who are behaving in a culturally appropriate manner may be inappropriately identified as having a mental health disorder, and thus may be placed in programs where they are isolated from their peers and have less chance to be academically successful. Ironically, there is clear evidence that children of color in the United States who have the same types of problems as European American children are more likely to be placed in correctional facilities, whereas the European American children are more likely to be placed in mental health treatment programs. This is evidence of significant underrecognition of mental health problems in communities of color. School professionals need to be aware of these issues when communicating concerns about children of different cultures.

It should also be noted that a significant stigma is associated with mental health problems in the mainstream culture as well. Many children and adolescents would prefer to be seen as bad rather than as sick, so they may mask their mental health or substance use problems through disruptive, acting-out behaviors, ultimately being diagnosed with oppositional defiant disorder or conduct disorder while their underlying problem goes undiagnosed and untreated.

Mental health problems, like medical problems in general, affect children, adolescents, and adults of all races and cultural backgrounds. They may manifest differently in individuals of different cultures, but they can be effectively treated when clinicians have appropriate cultural sensitivity. If teachers are aware of cultural or lifestyle issues that have the potential to impact a student's diagnosis, they can be helpful by communicating their concerns to the parents and to the professional who is performing the diagnostic evaluation.

Physical Illnesses and Medication

Medical disorders frequently mimic mental health disorders and often go unidentified by mental health clinicians. Research indicates that at least

10% of patients being treated by mental health professionals do not have mental health disorders at all; they suffer from undiagnosed medical conditions. Vitamin deficiencies, infectious diseases, metabolic abnormalities, tumors, degenerative disorders, endocrine dysfunction, neurological disease, cardiopulmonary disorders, toxins in the environment, medication side effects and alcohol and illicit drugs can mimic clinical depression, anxiety disorders, dementia, and psychosis. Moreover, significant differences in brain anatomy and brain functioning have been noted for many psychiatric disorders, and genetics plays a significant role in autism, mood disorders, ADHD, anxiety disorders, and so on. Indeed, many disorders that were previously thought to be "psychiatric" are now correctly diagnosed as medical disorders. As medical diagnostic technology and research advances, many of the disorders now thought of as being "psychiatric" will some day be identified as being "medical."

Complete physical examinations and appropriate laboratory testing are essential to rule out medical causes of psychiatric symptoms in children, adolescents, and adults. (Dikel, 2013).

Medication used to treat medical or psychiatric disorders can have side effects that can mimic medical and psychiatric disorders. Examples of psychiatric side effects from medical treatments include steroid treatment causing organic mood disorders such as depression or mania and asthma medications causing hyperactivity and irritability. Psychiatric medications can also cause other psychiatric symptoms, such as antipsychotics causing agitation and stimulants causing irritability. Psychiatric medications can also cause physical disorders, such as antipsychotic medications contributing to the development of type 2 diabetes.

Lifestyle Issues

Lifestyle issues can impact a student's mental health. If these issues are not addressed adequately in a mental health evaluation, problems that could be remedied through changes in lifestyle are likely to be misconstrued as major mental health disorders that warrant psychotherapy and possibly psychiatric medication. Therefore, a mental health diagnostic evaluation needs to address these issues. Lifestyle issues can impact mental health in children and adolescents in either positive or negative ways, and many lifestyle issues result in symptoms that can be mistaken for mental health disorders.

The typical American diet includes at least 30% empty calories in the form of nutrient-poor foods and beverages, and 37% is made up of fats. There is an epidemic of obesity in the United States, and obesity rates are two to three times the rates seen 20 years ago. Over 90% of obese children and adolescents have a sleep abnormality, most often sleep apnea, which is characterized by abnormal pauses in breathing during sleep and can lead to inattentiveness at school. These attention difficulties may be misdiagnosed as ADHD, which may result in the use of medications that can exacerbate the sleep disorder.

Other dietary issues include poor nutrition and deficiencies in vitamins and essential fatty acids. Vitamin deficiencies can lead to depression and irritability (B6), insomnia or confusion (B3), and musculoskeletal pain (D). Low blood levels of essential omega fatty acids have been found to correlate with behavior and learning problems. Foods containing artificial colors have been found to produce symptoms of hyperactivity in some children. Refined sugar has been found to result in cognitive functioning difficulties, and high-protein breakfasts are preferable to high-sugar or carbohydrate breakfasts. Mercury, lead, and many pesticides have neurotoxic qualities that can affect cognition and behavior. Bisphenol A, a chemical used to make plastic baby bottles, has been linked to damage in developing brain tissue.

Many students drink excessive amounts of caffeine, and symptoms of caffeinism and caffeine withdrawal are common. Caffeinism generally can occur with the intake of over 250 milligrams of caffeine a day, which is the equivalent of two 8-ounce cups of coffee. Symptoms of caffeinism include insomnia, confusion, anxiety, dizziness, gastrointestinal problems, and irritability. Symptoms of caffeine withdrawal include headache, irritability, sleepiness, and lethargy.

Many adolescent students smoke cigarettes and may experience nicotine withdrawal during the day. Symptoms include impaired concentration, tenseness, irritability, disturbed sleep, and drowsiness as well as significant craving for nicotine, which can distract a student from schoolwork. Both the intoxicating effects and the withdrawal symptoms of alcohol and tobacco clearly impact an individual's mental health, and the effects of these substances on the respiratory, neurological, cardiovascular, and immune systems are well documented (Dikel, 2013).

Environmental influences can result in mental health symptoms as well. Many students who have autism spectrum disorder experience significant anxiety in classrooms lit with fluorescent lighting, especially the type with large-diameter bulbs and magnetic ballasts. These students respond negatively to the flickering of the lights and may have significant behavioral acting-out responses as a result. Fluorescent lighting can also trigger panic attacks in susceptible individuals. Noise pollution (excess or disturbing background noise) can cause annoyance and aggression, high stress levels, tinnitus (ringing in the ears), sleep disturbance, and even hypertension.

Many students' lifestyles are also notable for poor sleep. The typical adolescent has a sleep-wake cycle that is not in accordance with early school start times, and many students are significantly sleep deprived. As a result, some school districts have moved start times to later in the morning. Sleep deprivation can lead to problems with cognitive functioning, problems with working memory and attention, impaired motor abilities, alterations in endocrine functioning, automobile accidents, obesity, and poor school performance.

Lack of exercise is a major problem among today's "video game" youth. Regular exercise can reduce the risk for obesity and can also improve cognitive performance and reduce the risk of depression. Physical education has been eliminated from some schools, adding to the problem of the lack of exercise in children and adolescents.

Clearly, lifestyle issues affect students' mental health. Schools can promote improved lifestyle choices and thus improved student health and mental health in a variety of ways. School breakfast and lunch choices can be improved with additional fruits and vegetables; adequate vitamins and essential fatty acids; and reductions in sugar, salt, and fats. Soda machines can be removed from schools. (This is a major financial issue for schools that gain income from sales of soft drinks.) Soft drinks can be replaced with 100% juice drinks. Schools can also reduce environmental stressors of excess noise and of the effects of artificial lighting. Architectural plans for new school buildings can focus on access to daylight through the use of skylights and expanded window space. School health classes can emphasize the effects of lifestyle on health and mental health, and this information can also be distributed to family members. Through a focus on healthy lifestyle change, many students will improve not only their physical health but their mental health as well.

Mental health problems that result from lifestyle choices are best addressed through positive lifestyle changes rather than through psychotherapy and psychiatric medication.

School Environment Stressors

It is important for mental health professionals, physicians, and school staff to recognize that, for some students, factors within the school can contribute to or even cause mental health disorders. When these stresses are effectively identified and addressed, these vulnerable students will experience a significant reduction in their emotional difficulties. If these issues are not recognized at the time of a mental health diagnostic evaluation, then treatment interventions are unlikely to be successful.

Bullying

Bullying is a major cause of suffering for many students. It may be physical, verbal, or written (as in cyberbullying), and may be perpetrated by a single individual or by a group. Boys tend to bully physically and girls tend to bully verbally, but there is overlap in methods between the sexes. Victims of bullying may experience significant anxiety and depression, may have suicidal thoughts, may display suicidal behavior, or may even commit suicide. They may have academic difficulties and significant absenteeism.

According to the American Psychological Association (Graham, 2013), 40–80% of students experience bullying at some time during their school careers, and 5–15% are victims of constant bullying. Disabled students are often very vulnerable to being targeted by bullies. This includes students who have learning disabilities, speech and language difficulties, and significant emotional disabilities. It is important for teachers to recognize that bullying may be pervasive in their schools and to be sensitive to this possibility when talking with their students. The presence of an adult in areas where bullying often occurs (e.g., unstructured times in recess, hallways, bathrooms, on school buses) can reduce the incidence of bullying. Since most students who are bullied do not tell their parents or teachers about it, their symptoms of anxiety or depression may not be correctly identified as stemming from this toxic abuse. As a result, interventions such as medication management may be initiated, while no one is addressing the root cause of the problem.

Curriculum Issues

Students may be off-task, giving the impression that they have ADHD when in fact they are simply bored with a curriculum that is not interesting or challenging. The same students may have no difficulties with attention when they are engaged in learning topics that hold interest for them. Of course, lessons at school cannot always be fascinating and highly engaging, and students need to learn to do schoolwork that may not be very interesting. Nonetheless, students who do not have mental health disorders may simply tune out what they perceive to be irrelevant, boring material.

Teacher–Student Interactions

Good teachers have rapport with their students, engage them in the topic at hand, are encouraging, and use positive behavioral reinforcement techniques. Fortunately, most teachers are dedicated to their work and are continuing to improve their teaching abilities. Unfortunately, a few teachers, for a variety of reasons, have significant deficits in their teaching abilities. Students in their classrooms may respond with off-task behaviors or even symptoms of anxiety or depression. If a teacher is emotionally abusive with students or is making demands that cannot be met, students are likely to experience the classroom as a toxic environment. Although this is a sensitive topic, it needs to be mentioned as one of the causes for students' school stress–related mental health symptoms. I have evaluated several children over the years who were reported to have multiple symptoms of ADHD in their classroom, whose symptoms disappeared when they were moved to a different classroom. Prescribing medication to these children would have been the wrong intervention.

Fortunately, most teachers are hardworking and dedicated to their students. However, when teachers lack understanding of the nature of mental health disorders, students who have these disorders may experience additional mental health difficulties as a result of the teacher's misperception of the nature of their disabilities. For example, a student who has significant difficulties with organization, attention span, and distractibility whose teacher views these problems as willful attempts to avoid doing schoolwork may become demoralized, may feel powerless, and may eventually engage in power struggles and be labeled as oppositional. When teachers understand the nature of a student's mental health disorders, they are able to effectively work with the student and see the disorder, rather than the student, as the problem. Teachers have the opportunity to identify and work with other school professionals to address school-related stressors. It is important for mental health diagnosticians to have a sense of teacher–student interactions in order to clarify whether they play a role in the student's classroom difficulties.

The Mental Health of Adults Working with Students

Although the focus of this book is on helping educators work with students who have mental health disorders, learning about these issues can also help educators find ways to optimize their own mental health. Reading this book may result in the recognition by some educators that they themselves suffer from an untreated mental health disorder, prompting them to seek effective treatment for themselves. They may also recognize symptoms in friends or family members, which can result in effective treatment for an otherwise disabling disorder.

Being an educator can be a very stressful profession, and it is made more so when educators are working with students who have significant emotional or behavioral problems. The demands of the profession are great, and in schools where students do not perform well, the media often blames educators when numerous other factors are major contributors to the problem. Students may be very oppositional and defiant, disruptive in the classroom, and not responsive to interventions that have proved effective with other students. Adjustment-related stress is a common problem for educators and is especially problematic for special education teachers who serve the emotionally disabled population. It has been estimated that the typical teacher of emotionally disturbed students works in the field for an average of 3.5 years, less time than she or he spent training for that position. It is important for educators to keep a balance in their work with students, especially with those who can be very challenging. If an educator is overly involved with the stresses (e.g., poverty, homelessness, social services involvement) and general emotional turmoil experienced by some students and their families, she or he runs the risk of emotional burnout. Some educators do the opposite; they become emotionally disconnected when dealing with these students and their families. These educators do a disservice to the students and themselves, as they are not giving of themselves in the way that educators need to in order to inspire their students to learn. The middle path of affectionate detachment, with compassion for troubled students and families while maintaining good personal boundaries, is the one taken by the educators who excel in the profession.

Even in the best of circumstances, dealing with the multiple challenges facing educators can be very stressful. Lifestyle management is an important component of maintaining educators' mental health. It includes positive social relationships; a support system consisting of administrators, colleagues, and family and friends; and a healthy well-balanced diet. Despite the best lifestyle management, some educators experience significant mental health difficulties. Just as mental health disorders affect approximately one in five children and adolescents, they affect a similar percentage of adults. Clinical depression is common, especially in women, and affects one in five women sometime in their lives. Only one in three adults who experiences depression receives any treatment, and those that do generally see primary care physicians who may have limited knowledge and skills in diagnosing and treating the disorder. Individuals who suffer from depression may not recognize that they are suffering from a mood disorder and may attribute their problems to their jobs, families, or other factors. Depression can cause an individual to believe that students whose problems are within the normal range have mental health problems, due to the fact that depression (like a toothache) increases the perception that everything in the environment is worse than it is.

Other disorders such as bipolar mood disorder, panic disorder, PTSD, obsessive-compulsive disorder, and so on may be experienced by educators as well. Since most adults who have mental health disorders receive no treatment for them and often are unaware that they have a treatable disorder, many educators are experiencing significant untreated mental health disorders that are adversely affecting their personal and professional lives. The stigma associated with mental health disorders makes it difficult for many people to reach out to others for help, and many do not seek help even when they are aware that they have a treatable disorder. It is hoped that this book, in addition to helping educators understand student mental health issues, will provide both the information and the inspiration for educators who have mental health disorders to recognize this fact and to seek treatment accordingly.

PART II

Types of Mental Health Disorders Affecting Children and Adolescents

CHAPTER 2

The Clinical-Behavioral Spectrum

BEFORE I GO INTO DETAIL ABOUT THE DIFFERENT WAYS THAT mental health disorders may manifest and may be addressed within the school setting, it is important to examine the underlying assumptions about the causes of students' behavioral difficulties. Using a model of behaviors that stems from medical disorders can be helpful in this regard. If a student has diabetes, and has a low blood sugar level that leads to irritability in the classroom, teachers and other school staff can rationally assume that the student's irritable behavior is a direct manifestation of the medical disorder. The primary response in this situation would be to communicate concerns to the parents who would then work with the student's physician to adjust the insulin dose. No one would conclude that the function of the student's irritability was to seek attention from others, to avoid schoolwork, or to gain some reward. Yet, during educational assessments and functional behavioral analyses, these functions are routinely assigned to behaviors that stem from students' mental health disorders. If in fact the behaviors are purely due to the mental health disorder, then the behavior has no function. However, students who have mental health disorders may also have behavioral difficulties that are planned and volitional and that do not stem from their mental health disorders. In these instances, a behavioral approach that identifies antecedents to the behaviors through a functional analysis and includes behavioral interventions can be very effective. The behavior of many students has a mixture of causes, both clinical and behavioral, and the sources of students' behavioral difficulties in the classroom can thus be very confusing for educators.

Behavioral problems are common in the student population, and for some students they are severe and chronic. Clinical disorders such as depression, ADHD, autism, and anxiety disorders are also common, and they may have behavioral manifestations. On one end of the spectrum of problematic behaviors is planned and volitional misbehavior by a student who has no evidence of any clinical disorder. On the other end are behaviors that are direct manifestations of psychiatric disorders (e.g., the agitation of mania) that are not under the student's control, and that are not likely to respond to traditional behavioral interventions. In order for educators to effectively target their interventions to have maximum success, it is important for them to recognize where a student is on the Clinical-Behavioral Spectrum, and to intervene accordingly. The difficulty of identifying appropriate and effective interventions may be confounded by a lack of communication and collaboration among the providers of student services and supports, especially between mental health and behavioral practitioners.

Behavioral practitioners use many terms to describe behavior profiles and problems. The word "behavior" refers to one's responses and the ways that one acts or conducts oneself. The term "behavioral," however, when used in the formal context of analysis of behavior change, refers to the scientific approach of dealing with assessment and intervention. An assessment of a student's behavior hypothesizes about the function of the behavior (why the behavior occurs) in an effort to identify appropriate interventions. This practice, based on operant conditioning, requires an orderly correlation between the student's behavior and environmental influences. Such an approach to behavioral assessment renders little opportunity to address the effects of emotions and mood on behaviors. Although behavioral practitioners understand that emotions may play a role in behavior, they focus their attention on measurable, quantifiable behaviors, rather than on internal emotional states that are difficult to define or measure.

Conversely, mental health professionals refer to a "clinical disorder" as a specific diagnostic category of abnormal thinking, emotion, or behavior that is beyond the realm of normal functioning and causes significant dysfunction for the affected individual. Thus, people suffering from major depression have a constellation of symptoms (e.g., disturbance of sleep, appetite, energy, concentration, self-worth, mood) that significantly interferes with their ability to function. The diagnosis of clinical disorders is partially based on internal emotional and cognitive states, which are inferred from direct observation, patient self-report, and corroborative information.

The term "emotion" refers to feelings (e.g., anger, joy, fear) that are distinguished from cognitive states of mind. Both mental health and behavior practitioners understand that emotions may manifest in physiological changes (e.g., increased heartbeat, respiration, crying) and may accompany a student's misbehaviors. However, while emotional states frequently accompany behaviors, the existence of emotions would not be considered clinical unless the emotions were a manifestation of a psychiatric disorder. Although both medical and mental health professionals make clinical diagnoses, medical diagnoses often have correlates of physical signs and symptoms, and abnormalities of laboratory tests, x-rays, EKGs, and so on. Unfortunately, although there is clear evidence of the biological basis of many psychiatric disorders, medical tests have not yet been developed with adequate sensitivity and specificity to confirm psychiatric diagnoses.

Mental health disorders are often invisible to others, despite the suffering and dysfunction that they can cause for those who are afflicted with them. It may be difficult for educators to recognize how these seemingly invisible disorders are influencing students' behaviors and how an understanding of this process can lead to more effective educational interventions. This can lead to an overreliance on traditional behavioral approaches, even for students whose mental health disorders are severe and are the direct cause of the problem behaviors. If educators appreciate that behaviors may have causes that span a spectrum, then successful interventions can be tailored to each student's specific situation.

THE SPECTRUM CATEGORIES

The Clinical-Behavioral Spectrum is a conceptual model that assists the process of providing successful interventions. I developed it in partnership with Jan Ostrom, a licensed psychologist and applied behavioral analyst, as a useful tool for conceptualizing and addressing behavioral difficulties in children, adolescents, and adults. It has five categories that can be visualized along a continuum:

Behavioral
Predominantly Behavioral
Mixed
Predominantly Clinical
Clinical

These categories are useful in identifying the nature of a student's behavioral difficulties and in identifying interventions that are most likely to be successful.

THE ENDS OF THE SPECTRUM

In general, students who have behavioral difficulties would not typically be placed at either extreme end (purely behavioral or purely clinical) of the spectrum, but such situations do occur.

Behavioral

This student's behaviors are clearly functional and are not related to any mental health clinical disorder. The behaviors are planned, volitional, and serve a function such as gaining tangible rewards, attracting attention, avoiding work, and so on. Medication interventions are not effective, as medications are useful for disorders of attention, mood, thinking, and anxiety, and these are not present in this type of individual. Feelings-oriented psychotherapy is also ineffective. Behavioral interventions are the interventions of choice, and these students require "a narrow path with high walls" of contingency.

EXAMPLE: **Jason**

Jason is a 14-year-old student in the ninth grade. He has a history of stealing, lying, destruction of property, setting fires, and aggression toward others. The behavioral profile is pervasive, dating back to early childhood. He was raised in a home by antisocial parents who encouraged him to engage in antisocial behaviors such as shoplifting. Jason has a probation officer, and, under the threat of incarceration, Jason has demonstrated the ability to refrain from disruptive behaviors.

Clinical

An individual classified as Clinical has no history of behavioral problems prior to the onset of a mental health disorder. Psychiatric symptoms such as the delusions and hallucinations of schizophrenia or the agitation of the manic phase of bipolar mood disorder are severe and not under the student's control. The symptoms are the direct cause of the behavior, and there is no function to the behavior any more than there is a function of the irritable behavior of a diabetic whose blood sugar is low. Behavioral interventions are generally not effective. Appropriate clinical treatment can result in the amelioration of not only the psychiatric symptoms but of the accompanying behaviors as well.

EXAMPLE: Mark

Mark is an 18-year-old high school senior who was recently diagnosed with schizophrenia. He had no history of behavioral difficulties and had done well academically through tenth grade. In the past year, he has had deterioration in his grades, social isolation, unusual interpersonal interactions, and poor personal hygiene. His mental state deteriorated to the point that he was experiencing auditory hallucinations and paranoid delusions. He was hospitalized after threatening a school bus driver whom he believed was kidnapping him. Mark demonstrated improvement with medication treatment but has had poor compliance. When he doesn't take medication, he becomes hostile, paranoid, and agitated. Behavioral interventions have not improved the behavior, and his parents have gone to court to file commitment papers for hospitalization.

THE INTERMEDIATE COMPONENTS OF THE SPECTRUM

The majority of students will fall in the intermediate parts of the spectrum. It is important for school personnel to recognize the complexity of the mixture of behavioral and clinical contributors to behavior and to respond accordingly.

Predominantly Behavioral

An individual who has a mental health disorder, but whose behaviors are, for the most part, not due to the disorder would be in the Predominantly Behavioral part of the spectrum. This student may use the disorder as an excuse for inappropriate behaviors, saying that he or she cannot control them, for example, "because I have ADHD." In fact, the student's behaviors tend to be planned and volitional, and the student is well aware of the impact of the behavior on others. For some students, the behavioral problems predate the onset of mental health problems.

EXAMPLE: **Jerrod**

Jerrod is a 10-year-old fifth grader who has a long history of behavioral problems in the home, school, and community. He recognizes the consequences of his behaviors, but believes that they are justified if he doesn't get caught. He has been on various medications for ADHD that have improved his on-task behavior when he is interested in a subject, but the behavior problems have continued. When asked, for example, why he hit a child on the playground one day, he said, "I decided when I was walking to school this morning that he needed to be taught a lesson." Essentially, given his antisocial tendencies, medication for ADHD will not reduce behavioral problems, but will, instead, "help him plan his crimes better." The Predominantly Behavioral student primarily needs a behavioral approach to address his problems. Searching for the ideal medication to extinguish behavioral problems will be in vain, given that these problems do not stem directly from the mental health disorder. This is not to say that the mental health disorder should not be treated, but rather that professionals, both in education and in mental health, should avoid the misconception that the disorder is the primary causal factor in his or her behavioral difficulties.

Predominantly Clinical

Individuals in the Predominantly Clinical portion of the spectrum have some component of behavioral contributors to their acting out, in that their behaviors have some identifiable antecedents and some degree of function. However, these are overshadowed by the presence of a clinical disorder that is a far greater contributor to the behavioral problems. In some students, mild oppositionality or conduct-disordered behavior was present prior to the onset of the mental health disorder, and the symptoms of the disorder greatly magnified the behavioral difficulties. For these students, clinical treatment is the predominant component that produces behavioral improvement. Behavioral principles should be applied as needed, but by themselves, they are not likely to extinguish dysfunctional behaviors that stem directly from the core symptoms of the student's mental health disorder.

EXAMPLE: Kim

Kim is a 16-year-old 11th grade student who recently began having symptoms of bipolar mood disorder. She has started taking mood-stabilizing medication, but symptoms of mania are not fully under control. She demonstrates rapid shifts in mood, anger outbursts, agitation, impulsivity, and irritability, and she has been verbally intrusive. Prior to the onset of her illness, she had demonstrated some teenage rebellious behavior with mild oppositionality toward her parents, and she had violated curfew on two occasions. Overall, she had been a good student. Behavioral interventions need to focus on recognizing the source of her behavioral difficulties and should provide her with enough safe space to be able to avoid situations where these behaviors could be problematic. As her medication response improves, her behavioral problems would be expected to improve as well.

Mixed

Students in the Mixed category pose significant challenges to both mental health clinicians and educators. They have both major psychiatric disorders and significant behavioral contributors to their behavioral difficulties. It is not uncommon for students in the Mixed category to be placed in self-contained school settings for students who have severe behavioral problems (e.g., diagnosed as "emotionally disturbed," "seriously emotionally disturbed," or "emotionally or behaviorally disturbed"). Often, their mental health disorders, such as ADHD, depression, bipolar mood disorder, and post-traumatic stress disorder (PTSD), are unrecognized and untreated, even when they had been diagnosed in the past. In fact, many of the students evaluated for special education and qualifying for services in the Emotional Disturbance special education category fit this Mixed category. This population often has poor outcomes in education, employment, and rates of arrest. They pose a challenge to mental health professionals who may tend to focus on the mental health disorders without fully recognizing the impact of volitional behavior. Conversely, education professionals may not recognize the underlying contributions of these students' mental heath disorders and may become frustrated when traditional behavioral approaches are used with little or no success. These students are often viewed by school staff as having behavioral problems, with minimal understanding by staff of the role of clinical contributors. Many of these students are not being treated for their mental health disorders, or they may be inappropriately treated or misdiagnosed by medical or mental health professionals. School professionals are often frustrated by the challenges of addressing these students' clinical disorders, given that schools are educational and not clinical settings.

This Mixed category population poses significant challenges to all professionals, and successful intervention requires collaboration, communication, and shared perspectives from professionals in all fields of service and support: education, corrections, mental health, medical, and social services.

EXAMPLE: **Nick**

Nick is a 14-year-old ninth grade student in a Federal Setting Special education program, in which students receive special education services at separate school facilities for more than 50% of the school day. He has a multitude of disabilities and a long history of delinquent behaviors. His mother used drugs and alcohol during her pregnancy with him and neglected him during his infancy. After living with his mother until age 6 years, when she was arrested for selling drugs, he was placed in multiple foster homes and was sexually abused in one home by a foster brother. He has a full-scale IQ of 78 and has been diagnosed with fetal alcohol spectrum disorder, PTSD, ADHD, reactive attachment disorder, and "mood disorder not otherwise specified." Antisocial behaviors date back to age 3 years, and have included fire setting, cruelty to animals, stealing, lying, aggression, and destruction of property. He has benefited from medication for his ADHD and mood disorder but continues to engage in significant delinquent behaviors. He has a county social services mental health case manager and a juvenile corrections probation officer. Nick will require a great deal of services from multiple systems for many years. He is not an "either-or" student, but rather "both-and," in terms of the clinical and behavioral contributors and the combination of clinical and behavioral solutions to his acting-out behaviors.

THE IMPORTANCE OF THE CLINICAL-BEHAVIORAL SPECTRUM CONCEPT

Understanding where an individual falls on the Clinical-Behavioral Spectrum is an important first step in designing interventions that are most likely to be effective. The spectrum can also contribute to a common understanding among the professionals providing services and support, especially if they are viewing the student from vastly different perspectives. For example, if a school social worker sees a student as Clinical or Predominantly Clinical, whereas the teacher sees the student as Behavioral or Predominantly Behavioral, the recognition of this discrepancy can be the first step in understanding why interventions have not been successful to date and in creating more effective accommodations and modifications for the student. Similarly, parents who see their child's behavior as being solely due to a diagnosed mental health disorder may be at odds with a teacher who recognizes significant behavioral contributors and volitional behaviors. Or, parents may see their child as delinquent and may have been unaware of evidence of mental health problems until they met with a school social worker who had identified evidence of a problem such as major depression. By briefly describing the concept of the Clinical-Behavioral Spectrum at a team meeting and by asking the various members of the team to identify where on the spectrum they believe a student to be, major areas of disagreement about the nature of a student's problems can be identified. This can be the first step in ensuring effective interventions for the student.

While clinical disorders may seem to be invisible, behaviors are obvious and observable. As such, there can be a tendency to overemphasize behavioral versus clinical contributions to the spectrum. This problem can be magnified if school staff feel constrained in addressing mental health issues. For example, there may be pressure not to identify mental health problems due to potential concerns that the school is the payer of last resort, or there may be a pro-behavioral, anti–medical model bias within the school environment. Given the substantial research indicating the very poor outcomes of special education for emotionally disturbed individuals, and the fact that poor outcomes are often associated with the lack of attention to students' mental health, it is important to encourage an emphasis on the continuum of student support needs that includes mental health components.

HOW TO IDENTIFY THE CORRECT CATEGORY

The Clinical-Behavioral Spectrum provides a perspective that allows educational staff the opportunity to broaden their conceptions about students' behavioral difficulties and about the interventions that will most likely be successful. As school professionals are not clinicians, they may feel uncomfortable assigning a category to a student, especially given the fact that many students who have mental health disorders have not been diagnosed and that many have been incorrectly diagnosed. The spectrum should be viewed not as a diagnostic tool but as a working hypothesis. It is useful to consider, especially when educational interventions have not been successful for students who have been diagnosed with, or have evidence of, mental health disorders.

Given the clinical aspects of the Clinical-Behavioral Spectrum, in my opinion school mental health staff (social workers, psychologists, counselors, and nurses) should take the lead in the process of hypothesizing a student's position on the spectrum. Teachers can assist this process by providing information to the school team that describes a student's observable classroom behaviors. Some guidelines that can be helpful in the process of assigning a category are as follows, for the Clinical end of the spectrum:

- Has the student been diagnosed with, or is there evidence of, a mental health disorder other than conduct disorder or oppositional defiant disorder?
- If so, do the DSM-5 (American Psychiatric Association, 2013) criteria for that disorder match the behaviors observed?
- Were behavioral problems absent prior to the onset of the mental health disorder?
- Is there a previous history of treatment in which behavior problems were reduced or disappeared as a result of treatment?
- Is there no evidence of volitional, planned misbehavior?

For the Behavioral end of the spectrum:

- Is there no evidence of a mental health disorder besides oppositional defiant disorder or conduct disorder?
- If a mental health disorder is present, do the student's misbehaviors not reflect the criteria of the diagnosis?
- Is there evidence that behaviors are planned, volitional, and under full control of the student?
- Is there clear evidence of antecedents or social functions to the behaviors?

- Is there evidence that behaviors have responded to behavioral-based programmatic interventions in the past?
- Is there a chronic history of behavioral problems dating to early childhood?
- Does the student lack remorse for misbehaviors?

For Mixed:

- Is there clear evidence of both a clinical mental health disorder and behaviors that are functional and that have clear behavioral antecedents?

ADVANTAGES OF USING THE SPECTRUM CONCEPT

- It creates a common language, bridging the gap between various educational disciplines.
- It raises mental health awareness, encouraging educational teams to reframe their thinking about behaviors that stem from internal, clinical symptoms of mental health disorders.
- It helps educational teams unify their approaches and recognize when viewpoints of team members or parents regarding the source of a student's behaviors are polarized.
- It helps mental health staff reconsider situations where behavioral issues were thought to be due to a mental health disorder when, in fact, they were planned and volitional.
- It directs educational interventions to be maximally effective, achieving the best academic and behavioral outcomes.

Understanding the nature of the diagnostic criteria used to diagnose the various mental health disorders can shed light on how these disorders will manifest in the classroom. It is important to recognize that some of these disorders tend to be chronic (e.g., ADHD, autism spectrum disorder) whereas others may have had a more recent onset. The ways that disorders may manifest are significantly related to the student's mental health history. A student who has a chronic mental health condition will generally not display symptoms that are dramatically different from those seen in the past, unless the symptoms have significantly worsened. On the other hand, a 10th grade student who previously had been outgoing and gregarious, and who recently developed a first episode of major depression, might have a dramatic shift in behavior, becoming withdrawn and reclusive.

The development of a disorder is not always obvious, though. Another student of the same age, whose temperament had been introverted and quiet, may not have very observable symptoms of major depression when it occurs.

Note: As dramatic shifts in behavior can also stem from recent trauma (e.g., sexual abuse or bullying), it is important to identify trauma if it is occurring.

Some disorders have obvious symptoms, while others have more subtle or even unrecognizable symptoms. Some disorders are externalizing, meaning that the student may act out, have few behavioral inhibitions, or may be hyperactive, disruptive, or even aggressive. Students who have ADHD, combined form, may demonstrate significant externalizing symptoms. On the other hand, students who have internalizing disorders tend to direct their symptoms inward rather than displaying them externally. Depression and anxiety disorders are often considered internalizing disorders. However, they may also manifest externally, as is illustrated in the chapters describing mental health disorders and their manifestations in the classroom.

Even under the best of circumstances, it is not always clear where the source of a student's difficulties lie on the spectrum from purely Behavioral to purely Clinical. If excessive accommodations and modifications are provided to a student who in fact is behaving purely volitionally, then the consequence may be that the student will "get away with misbehavior" and not learn to take personal responsibility. On the other hand, if school staff believe that behaviors that are the direct manifestation of clinical symptoms (e.g., disorders of attention, mood, anxiety) are due to willful behaviors (e.g., attempts to avoid doing schoolwork), students are likely to respond to this by feeling demoralized and powerless. This can lead students to engage in power struggles, to have a lack of motivation, or to be perceived by teachers as being oppositional and defiant.

For students who have been diagnosed with a mental health disorder, there is a good rule of thumb to follow. When the degree to which a student's behaviors are more volitional than clinical is not clear, staff can clarify whether the observed behaviors are listed in the criteria of the disorder with which the student is diagnosed. School psychologists, social workers, counselors, and nurses can be very helpful in determining this, with the teacher's assistance. For example, distractible behavior would be identified for ADHD; mood changes, agitation, and irritability are criteria of bipolar mood disorder; and withdrawn behaviors are noted in social phobia. It is best to give the benefit of the doubt to students who have been diagnosed with, or have evidence of, mental health disorders when designing educational interventions.

The Clinical-Behavioral Spectrum concept addresses the gray areas of behavior and encourages school professionals and parents to avoid black-and-white, all-or-nothing approaches. When a parent says to a teacher, "My child has ADHD and therefore can't control his behavior," there is an opportunity to explore the fact that the child has some degree of control, and that it is important to identify and encourage that control in order for the child to gain mastery skills and become a responsible adult. If a school staff member says about a student, "I don't care what diagnostic label has been given this student; she needs to control her behavior," a discussion of the effects of the disorder is needed. This provides an opportunity for developing interventions that address the disorder and thus improve behavioral control.

The Clinical-Behavioral Spectrum concept can be confusing due to the many interpretations of the term *behavioral*. This term can refer to any observable activity in an individual—from specific principles of behavioral analysis, to interventions that provide rewards and consequences, to behavioral treatments of clinical disorders. Applied behavioral analysis focuses on antecedents of behaviors and the functions of those behaviors. Although students who have behavior predominantly driven by an underlying mental health disorder may have antecedents to and functions of their behaviors, the Clinical-Behavioral Spectrum still would view these behaviors as clinically driven. The behaviors would be viewed as being a direct manifestation of the underlying mental health disorder.

EXAMPLE #1: **John**

John is a 16-year-old student who has high-functioning autism spectrum disorder with intact language skills (previously termed Asperger's disorder). Because of his intense need for predictability and routines in his environment, he feels a need to sit in the same lunchroom chair every day. One day, he is carrying his tray to the table, only to see a classmate sitting in the chair. John stands rigidly, orders the other student to vacate the chair, and when the other student doesn't oblige, he pushes the student out of the chair. The lunchroom monitor intervenes, and John is sent to the principal's office. Although there was an antecedent to the behavior (a peer sat in the chair), John's behavioral response stemmed directly from his autism spectrum disorder. The function of the behavior was related to his desire to be able to sit in "his" chair, but the felt need to sit there was directly related to the disorder. Clearly, this situation differs significantly from a typical lunchroom confrontation between two students regarding their choice of seating.

EXAMPLE #2: **Jill**

Jill is a 17-year-old student who is starting treatment for bipolar mood disorder. She has been having intense mood swings at school, and these are at times manifested by extreme irritability. As she is walking down the crowded hallway, she is accidentally bumped on the shoulder by another student. She responds angrily and turns around and punches the peer. Although the antecedent to the punching was being bumped, the reason that she responded with violence was due to her underlying agitation and irritability stemming from the bipolar disorder. When the bipolar disorder symptoms are effectively treated, Jill will no longer display this type of reaction.

Neither John nor Jill displayed behaviors that had predominant functions of seeking attention, avoiding work, or gaining tangibles. The behaviors were direct manifestations of their mental health disorders. It would be appropriate for school staff to work together to clarify the types of interventions that would prevent further occurrences of problems, including considering a specific lunchroom spot for John and of reducing highly stimulating environments (e.g., busy and bustling hallways) for Jill. These interventions would be based on an understanding of each student's underlying mental health difficulties. It is my opinion that addressing behaviors without recognizing the underlying causes of those behaviors often has failed results. This is especially true when the underlying cause is a mental health disorder. Some educators strongly disagree with this opinion. They believe that diagnosis is not relevant and that behaviors need to be addressed with behavioral interventions that are based on behavioristic principles. The remarkably poor outcomes of students in typically behavior-oriented emotional disturbance special education programs suggest otherwise.

However, as accurate diagnoses of students who have mental health disorders is the exception rather than the rule, educators are left with the challenge of recognizing underlying clinical causes of behavior for students who have not been diagnosed or students whose parents choose not to share diagnostic information with school staff. A basic understanding of mental health disorders and their manifestation in classroom environments will aid educators in designing successful interventions for their students. By gaining an appreciation of the relative contributors of clinical versus behavioral factors, teachers and other school staff will have an improved ability to design effective adaptations for disabled students.

FOR DISCUSSION

VIGNETTE: Jim

Jim is a 12-year-old student who has been treated for ADHD since the age of 9 years. He did well in school up to his seventh grade year, at which point he started associating with antisocial peers. In the classroom, he is disruptive, often seeking attention and approval from his friends. When a meeting is held with his parents, the parents strongly oppose disciplinary interventions, saying, "Jim has a mental illness and should not be held responsible for his behavior."

VIGNETTE: Travis

Travis is a 7-year-old student who has been diagnosed with ADHD but is not receiving any treatment. He has significant difficulty in the classroom settling down and focusing on schoolwork. He benefits from playground activities where he can run around and work off his excess energy. Lately, his teacher has been keeping him in class during recess in order to finish assignments that other students have been able to finish during class time. (Failure to finish tasks is one of the criteria of ADHD.) The teacher maintains that Travis is able to do the work, and that keeping him inside will teach him to be responsible. Travis is becoming increasingly demoralized, and his parents are upset.

REFLECTION QUESTIONS

In both cases, school staff met with the students' parents. How could they use the concept of the Clinical-Behavioral Spectrum to find common ground between school professionals and parents? What would be the role of the teacher on the team? What would be the role of the school mental health staff (e.g., social worker, counselor, or psychologist)? What information would need to be presented to the team in order to seek an agreement regarding each student's placement on the spectrum? How could this help the educational process?

CHAPTER 3

Mood Disorders

DISORDERS OF MOOD AFFECT CHILDREN, ADOLESCENTS, and adults. Their symptoms interfere with functioning socially, within the family, and in the workplace and school environments. Such disorders include those in which one's mood is abnormally low (e.g., major depressive disorder) or abnormally high or agitated (e.g., bipolar mood disorder). Some disorders manifest symptoms that persist for long periods of time, whereas others change from week to week, day to day, or even hour to hour. This chapter describes the mood disorders commonly encountered in the classroom, symptoms that manifest in the school environment, and different types of treatment methodologies.

MAJOR DEPRESSION

It is unfortunate that the same word, "depression," is used to describe the feelings of sadness that everyone experiences on occasion (e.g., "This weather is depressing," "I'm depressed about my checkbook balance") as well as being the name of an often severe and potentially devastating psychiatric disorder. Clinical depression is as different from ordinary sadness as pneumonia is from a common cold.

The diagnosis of depression dates back several centuries, and many different names have characterized it. In the time of Aristotle (384–322 BCE), human emotional difficulties were thought to stem from what was termed an "imbalance of the humors." The humors were sanguine (blood), leading to an optimistic and courageous character; phlegm, leading to a phlegmatic or unemotional character; choleric (yellow bile), leading to a bad-tempered character; and melancholic (black bile), leading to depression, despondency, irritability, and sleeplessness. Thus, the word "melancholy" originally referred to depression as an imbalance in the black bile humor. Over the centuries, other causes of depression were posited, from belief in demonic control in the Middle Ages to the Freudian hypothesis that depression resulted from an unconscious process of anger turned inward. Through the mid-20th century, it was thought that children could not suffer from clinical depression. This was based on the belief that children did not have a functioning superego that could facilitate the unconscious processes leading to the development of depression. Psychiatry textbooks up to the early 1960s did not address childhood depression. There were considerations that behavior problems such as fire setting or aggression might be "depressive equivalents" in childhood, but no clear criteria were proposed to differentiate them from simple behavioral problems.

Following the mid-20th century, it became increasingly clear that there was a strong biological basis to clinical depression, with significant genetic and biological evidence to support this theory. Genetic studies have indicated that depression has significant heritability. Individuals who have parents with this disorder are two to four times as likely as the general population to develop depression. Biological abnormalities have been noted in individuals who have major depression, including increased latency of sleep onset, decreased rapid eye movement latency during sleep, and abnormalities of brain volumes and ratios in structural imaging studies. Individuals who have depression frequently have abnormal responses to steroid challenge testing (the dexamethasone suppression test) compared to the general population. It also became clear that cardinal signs of depression are noted across all cultures, including physical symptoms of abnormalities of sleep, appetite, energy level, and activity level, as well as symptoms of concentration difficulties, lack of enjoyment, low self-esteem, sadness, and frequent thoughts of death. Research with children and adolescents indicates similar symptoms of depression for them as well, with some exceptions (e.g., irritability might be noted rather than sadness). It became clear over time that children who experience major depression often have a parent who has this disorder (often untreated). Child and adolescent depression is a serious disorder, causing significant impairment in multiple aspects of living (e.g., school, family, social). It tends to be more chronic than depression that begins in adulthood and often severely interferes with activities of daily living.

Surprisingly, feelings of sadness are not necessary for making the diagnosis of clinical depression. Some patients are surprised when they are diagnosed with depression, believing that they cannot be depressed because they are not sad. These individuals may have difficulty feeling any emotion at all. Unlike individuals who experience the normal ups and downs of mood that result from life events, children and adolescents who suffer from depression do not respond to environmental cues that would normally result in an improved mood in others. Depression is associated with significant functional impairment, and symptoms tend to interfere with a child or adolescent's ability to engage in social, family, and academic activities. Depression exists on a spectrum, with major depression being the most severe manifestation. Milder forms include adjustment disorder with depressed mood, which is related to life events and which resolves over a relatively brief period of time. Persistent depressive disorder (previously called dysthymic disorder) is a chronic condition that does not have all of the symptoms of major depression and lasts for at least one year in children and adolescents and at least two years in adults.

The diagnosis of major depression in children and adolescents requires the presence of either a generalized sad or irritable mood or anhedonia (the inability to experience pleasure from activities usually found to be enjoyable). Both symptoms may be present, but at least one is necessary to make the diagnosis. At least four other symptoms must also be present. They include weight gain beyond normal levels or failure to make expected weight gains, insomnia or hypersomnia (sleeping too little or too much), psychomotor retardation or agitation (moving too slowly or appearing agitated), generalized fatigue or loss of energy, feelings of worthlessness or excessive or inappropriate guilt, difficulty concentrating, and recurrent thoughts of death or suicide. Depressive symptoms need to have been present for at least 2 weeks, be present at least nearly every day, and represent a change from one's previous level of functioning. If major depression is severe enough, an individual may experience psychotic symptoms of delusions or hallucinations.

Depression often occurs in the context of other mental health disorders. Frequently seen comorbid disorders include substance abuse, conduct disorder, ADHD, and anxiety disorders. The ratio of females to males with mood disorders is up to 3:1. Mood disorders are uncommon in prepubertal children (1–2%), but their prevalence significantly increases with age. Approximately one in five adolescents experience depression.

In addition to the genetic risk factors of having a parent who suffers from major depression, there are family environmental risk factors as well. These include parental substance abuse, parent-child conflicts, lack of family cohesion, child maltreatment, and parental criminality. Having a genetic predisposition to depression plus life stressors puts an individual at significant risk for developing this disorder.

Major depressive episodes tend to last for several months, but around 20% of adolescents have depressive episodes of two or more years' duration. Depressive episodes have a high risk of recurrence—up to 70% within five years. Some individuals whose first episode of a mood disorder is major depression subsequently experience a manic episode, and their diagnosis then changes to bipolar mood disorder.

Depression is a major cause of suicide. Suicide is the third leading cause of death (following accidents and homicide) for individuals between the ages of 5 and 24 years, with 4600 completed suicides per year in that age group. It is the second leading cause of death among children and adolescents aged 12–17 years. Suicide is the sixth leading cause of death for ages 5–14 years. Suicide rates are, for children ages 10–14, 0.9 per 100,000; for adolescents ages 15–19 years, 6.9 per 100,000; and for young adults ages 20–24 years, 12.7 per 100,000.

A national study of 9th to 12th grade students indicated that 16% reported seriously considering suicide, 13% had created a plan, and 8% reported trying to take their own life in the previous 12 months. Males are more likely to commit suicide, and females are more likely to make attempts that are not successful.

Suicide risk factors include a history of depression or other psychiatric disorders, a history of previous suicide attempts, a family history of suicide, alcohol or drug abuse, stressful life events or loss, easy access to lethal methods, exposure to the suicidal behavior of others, and incarceration. The top three methods of suicide used by young people include firearm (45%), suffocation (40%), and poisoning (8%). Children tend to use suffocation most frequently. Clearly, suicide is a major public health problem, and its major cause, depression, requires treatment intervention.

Manifestations of Depression in the Classroom

The symptoms of a student who is suffering from major depression may be very obvious or may be completely hidden in the classroom environment. Depression tends to be an internalizing disorder, in that the symptoms are often directed inward and therefore are not easily observable. There is wide variation in the manifestations of depression, however. Children and adolescents who have depression may experience significant feelings of sadness. They may look very unhappy, have downcast eyes, may cry easily, and may make statements about their sadness. Some depressed children and adolescents experience significant irritability rather than feeling sad. The irritability may manifest in angry outbursts, oppositional behaviors, or even aggressive behaviors.

Low energy is commonly seen in depression, and a student may appear tired much of the time. Psychomotor slowing may occur, which manifests in significantly slower movements. Concentration problems are common in depression. They may manifest in confusion, difficulty staying on task, difficulty with memorization and mastery of schoolwork, and problems with work completion. Students who have depression may have inadequate or excessive sleep. They may sleep in the classroom, or may remark that they have not been sleeping well at home. Appetite abnormalities may be observable. Some students who have depression lose their appetite, may not eat lunch at school, and may be observed to be losing weight. Others who have depression eat excessively and gain significant amounts of weight. Depression can cause lack of interest in and lack of deriving pleasure from previously enjoyable activities. A depressed student may not want to play with peers on the playground, may call previously fun activities boring, and may become reclusive. Low self-esteem may manifest in statements such as, "I'm no good," "I'm stupid," or "I can't do anything right." A student who has feelings of low self-worth may be reluctant to try new activities, due to the belief that she or he will not succeed and that trying would simply be a waste of time.

Of course, the most concerning manifestations of depression in the classroom are frequent thoughts of death and, especially, thoughts of suicide. A suicidal student may report suicidal thoughts to the teacher or may tell a peer about such thoughts. It is important for the student's peers to recognize that these statements are to be taken very seriously and reported to a teacher, school administrator, counselor, psychologist, nurse, or social worker. A depressed student may write notes about suicidal thoughts or plans or may make drawings that have suicidal content. Parents need to be contacted, and in an emergency the student may require immediate transfer to a psychiatric hospital for further assessment. For students who are experiencing severe depression, especially when there is evidence of suicidal thoughts, intentions, or plans, it is essential for teachers to work with the student's parents and with other school staff (e.g., social workers, counselors, psychologists, nurses, principal) as well as with medical and mental health professionals in order to address this potentially life-threatening condition.

Treatment of Depression

Treatment of major depression may include psychotherapy, or antidepressant medication, or both. Research indicates that a combination of therapy and medication has the highest percentage of success for individuals who have significant major depression.

Talk Therapy

Cognitive-behavioral therapy (CBT) and interpersonal therapy have been shown to be helpful in the treatment of child and adolescent depression. CBT focuses on assisting individuals in recognizing their distortions in thinking that result in an overly negative perception of life events, and interrupting this negative cycle through learning a combination of cognitive techniques and behavioral skills. Behavioral changes follow the philosophy "Just do it," in that the client is encouraged to participate in rewarding activities even if he or she doesn't feel like doing so, in order to experience the positive effects on mood that result. Interpersonal therapy for adolescents focuses on an adolescent's relationships with peers and family with the goal of improving relationships, reducing interpersonal conflicts, and improving depressive symptoms as a result.

Medication

In cases of childhood or adolescent major depression, antidepressant medication can be of significant benefit, especially when combined with psychotherapy. Although antidepressants were initially developed to treat clinical depression, they are now used to treat a wide variety of psychiatric disorders including obsessive-compulsive disorder, panic disorder, PTSD, and generalized anxiety disorder.

The Food and Drug Administration has approved fluoxetine (Prozac) for the treatment of major depression in children age 8 years or older, and escitalopram (Lexapro) is approved for children ages 12 and older. The antidepressants Prozac, sertraline (Zoloft), fluvoxamine (Luvox), and clomipramine (Anafranil) have been approved for the treatment of obsessive-compulsive disorder in the pediatric population. A Food and Drug Administration "black box" warning has been attached to antidepressant medication information materials due to research that indicates an increased risk of suicidal thoughts or behavior for children and adolescents on antidepressants (4%) versus those on placebos (2%). This indicates the need for close monitoring for suicide risks in children and adolescents taking these medications. The risk of potential suicidal thoughts or behaviors needs to be understood in the context of the reduced risk of suicides as a result of effective treatment of major depression. Suicide rates decreased with the increased use of these medications and increased following a reduction of their use after the FDA ruling, which suggests that these medications have a significant positive effect regarding suicide risk. Clearly, though, medication effects and potential side effects need to be monitored closely by prescribers.

Students may be prescribed a variety of types of antidepressant medication. Selective serotonin reuptake inhibitors (SSRIs) work by inhibiting the return of the neurotransmitter serotonin at a neuron's presynaptic cleft. As a result, serotonin builds up in the brain. Medications such as fluoxetine (Prozac), escitalopram (Lexapro), citalopram (Celexa), fluvoxamine (Luvox), and sertraline (Zoloft) are in this category. SSRIs are the most commonly used antidepressants prescribed to children and adolescents. They can usually be given once a day and are generally well tolerated. Prior to the introduction of fluoxetine (Prozac) over 30 years ago, tricyclic antidepressants and monoamine oxidase inhibitors were the antidepressants available for treating major depression. Both types have significant side effects (e.g., dry mouth, constipation, and drowsiness for tricyclics and hypertensive crisis for MAO inhibitors) and toxicity in overdose, and neither has demonstrated effectiveness over placebo in treating depression. One tricyclic antidepressant, clomipramine (Anafranil), has demonstrated efficacy in the treatment of obsessive-compulsive disorder, but is considered a second-line treatment due to its side effect profile (e.g., dry mouth, nausea, upset stomach, loss of appetite, constipation).

Bupropion (Wellbutrin) is an antidepressant that affects both the noradrenergic and the dopaminergic neurotransmitter systems. It has been shown to be effective for the treatment of ADHD, but the response is not as robust as with stimulant medications. Venlafaxine (Effexor) is an antidepressant that inhibits the reuptake of both serotonin and norepinephrine at the neural synapse. It has not been approved for the treatment of child or adolescent depression, but may be used off-label (used for purposes other than those approved by the Food and Drug Administration).

Mirtazapine (Remeron) is a tetracyclic antidepressant used for the treatment of depression in adults. Some of your students may be prescribed this medication off-label. It has shown promise in several anxiety disorders. Side effects include sedation, increased appetite, dry mouth, joint and muscle pain, dizziness, and blurred vision. Antidepressant medication can have significant side effects, including anxiety, nausea, sleep disruption, gastrointestinal distress, headaches, increased risk of bruising, and agitation.

Antidepressants can take up to 8 weeks before demonstrating a significant clinical effect. Treatment generally begins with a low dose of medication (generally half the typical dose), which may then be increased to the typical dose within a week. (However, some individuals are very sensitive to medication and may have a positive response using less than the typical dose and significant side effects at the typical dose). The dose should then remain unchanged for another month, in order to give it time to work. If that dose is ineffective, it might be increased somewhat. If this doesn't work, another antidepressant can be considered. In cases where medication does not appear to be effective, it is important to assess for other factors such as substance use, severe environmental stresses, contributing medical illnesses or medications, or other coexisting psychiatric conditions.

Alternative Treatments

Some students may be taking alternative treatments for major depression or other mood disorders, including omega-3 fatty acids, which are essential fatty acids that are found in fatty fish (salmon, tuna, herring, sardines), walnuts, and flaxseed. They have been found to be helpful for the treatment of adult depression and bipolar mood disorder, generally as adjunctive treatments. The fatty acids are EPA (eicosapentaenoic) and DHA (docosahexaenoic). Generally, fish oil capsules are used, with the EPA dose at or exceeding 1000 mg per day. Some child and adolescent studies have demonstrated positive effects as well. Given that omega-3 fatty acids are essential for health, it is prudent to ensure that all children and adolescents (and adults) have adequate amounts of them in their diets. Students may be taking these nutrients for ADHD or autism spectrum disorder as well.

S-adenosylmethionine (SAM-e) is sold as an over-the-counter dietary supplement in the United States but is a prescription medication in Italy, Spain, and Germany. Controlled studies have demonstrated its effectiveness in the treatment of depression in adults. SAM-e is a compound found in the body naturally that aids in metabolic pathways of biochemical reactions such as transmethylation, transsulfuration, and aminopropylation. Gastrointestinal upset is the most common possible side effect.

St. John's wort is an herb that has demonstrated benefit in the treatment of mild-to-moderate depression in adults. Its main potential side effects are dizziness, gastrointestinal symptoms, tiredness, sedation, and photosensitivity.

BIPOLAR MOOD DISORDER

Bipolar mood disorder and its related conditions (bipolar II disorder, cyclothymia, substance/medication-induced bipolar disorder, and bipolar disorder due to a medical condition) are characterized by significant instability of mood. This disorder was recognized by the ancient Greeks. Just as depression was thought to be due to an excess of black bile (melancholia), mania was considered to be due to an excess of yellow bile, or a mixture of black and yellow bile. In the mid-1800s, Jules Baillarger described to the French Imperial Academy of Medicine a mental health disorder characterized by recurrent oscillations between mania and depression. The German psychiatrist Emil

Kraepelin noted that patients with this disorder tended to have symptom-free episodes between their episodes of depression and mania. He named the disorder manic-depressive psychosis. In 1952, DSM-I referred to it as manic depressive reaction, and in 1957 the terms "unipolar" (for depression only) and "bipolar" (for patients who had mania) were introduced.

Manic symptoms are, in some ways, the other side of the coin from depressive symptoms. However, although many individuals feel joyful or elated during manic episodes, others feel agitated and irritable. The situation is complicated by the fact that some individuals experience mixed bipolar symptoms, with both manic and depressive symptoms manifesting simultaneously. The 12-month prevalence of bipolar mood disorder is 0.6%. Most people who meet criteria for bipolar disorder experience a number of episodes, on average 0.4 to 0.7 per year, lasting 3–6 months (Angst & Sellaro, 2000). The disorder is considered to be very uncommon in children. Concerns have been raised about the overdiagnosis of bipolar mood disorder in children and adolescents.

Bipolar mood disorder is characterized by a full-blown manic episode. Although it is possible for an individual to have repeated manic episodes without any episodes of depression, this is rare. Bipolar II disorder is characterized by hypomania (symptoms not at the level of severity or intensity of mania) alternating with clinical depression. Cyclothymic disorder is characterized by mood swings that never reach the severity of major depression on the low end or of mania on the high end. Normal, everyday moods in individuals who do not have mood disorders are characterized by fluctuations from happy to sad, content to irritable, calm to upset, loving to angry, and so on. Normal mood shifts are experienced in response to life events, with positive emotions following fortunate events (e.g., getting a raise, meeting an attractive person) and negative emotions following stressful ones (e.g., losing one's job, marital conflicts). The difference between the mood swings of the bipolar disorders and those of normal life is characterized by their severity, intensity, and chronicity. Although mood swings in mood disorders may be intrinsic to the individual and unrelated to life events, life stressors may trigger mood swings in an individual who has bipolar mood disorder. Also, having symptoms of depression or mania can lead to problem behaviors (e.g., difficulty at work, problems relating to one's spouse) that can lead to unfortunate consequences (losing

one's job, divorce). The life stressors that resulted from having the mood disorder then exacerbate the individual's mood difficulties, causing a vicious cycle
that increasingly worsens. These disorders can be conceptualized by visualiz-
ing different types of roller coasters. Bipolar mood disorder would be a roller
coaster with high peaks and low valleys; bipolar II disorder would be one with
moderate highs but significant lows; cyclothymic disorder would have moderate highs and lows; persistent depressive disorder would have only moderate
lows; and depression would have low valleys, generally alternating with periods of normal height.

The diagnosis of bipolar mood disorder requires the presence of a
manic episode. Manic episodes are characterized by a distinct period of persistently and abnormally expansive, irritable, or elevated mood as well as
persistently and abnormally increased energy or goal-directed activities. The
symptoms need to be present most of every day for at least one week (or any
duration if symptoms lead to psychiatric hospitalization). During the period of
mood disturbance, the individual displays at least three symptoms of mania.
These include grandiosity (inflated self-esteem), decreased need for sleep, pressured speech or excessive talking, racing thoughts, significant distractibility,
increased goal-directed activities (e.g., socially, at work, school, in sexual relationships) or physical agitation, and excessive involvement in activities that
have a high potential for painful consequences (e.g., buying sprees, indiscrimi-
nate relationships). If the individual only has an irritable mood with no expansiveness or elevation of mood, then four of the above symptoms of mania are
necessary for diagnosis.

The most significant risk factor for bipolar mood disorder and bipolar II disorder is a family history of that disorder. There is an average 10-fold
increased risk among adult relatives of individuals who have these disorders,
with risks being higher relative to the closeness of kinship. Although there is
clearly a genetic component, an identical twin of an individual who has bipolar mood disorder only has a 40% risk of developing the disorder. The mean
age of onset for bipolar mood disorder is 18 years. Although the disorder can
occur in adolescence and even in childhood, it is essential for the diagnostician not to label behaviors that may be developmentally normal (e.g., irritability with authority figures, passionate relationships, poor judgment) as being
signs of a severe mood disorder, unless they represent significant pathology.

It is also important not to miss true manic symptoms, assuming that they are normal for the individual. It is important for the diagnostician to get a clear picture of the child or adolescent's baseline behaviors, personality characteristics, energy level, socialization patterns, and so on, in order to compare symptoms that are seen at the time of the assessment. Corroborative information from family members and teachers can be helpful in this regard. The earlier that bipolar mood disorder is treated, the more successful the prognosis.

It is important for clinicians to recognize that at least 60% of individuals who have bipolar mood disorder also have problems with alcohol or drugs. Treatment of the mood disorder is unlikely to be effective unless the substance use problem is also treated. Although most adolescents who have drug or alcohol problems do not have mood disorders, for the ones who do have them, it is essential that they receive comprehensive assessments that ensure that they will receive treatment for both conditions. Unfortunately, individuals who are experiencing manic symptoms are generally unaware that they have a problem, and they may adamantly refuse treatment, even if they have had previous episodes that led to major negative life consequences. As a result, ongoing treatment is recommended.

Approximately 90% of individuals who have a manic episode go on to have recurrent episodes, generally lasting 3 to 6 months in duration. Typically, episodes (in which predominant symptoms are depressive, manic, hypomanic, or mixed) occur less than once a year. If an individual has at least four episodes per year, this is called rapid cycling. There are even instances in which individuals have cycling from day to day (ultrarapid) or even within a day (ultradian cycling). Several researchers believe that children and adolescents who have bipolar mood disorder do not present with the typical adult pattern; instead they tend to have mixed symptoms (depression and mania simultaneously) with rapid shifts in mood, even throughout a day. There continues to be significant disagreement among clinicians about the nature of child and adolescent bipolar mood disorder.

Bipolar mood disorder can be a very disabling condition, affecting one's family life, work, or school and relationships with peers and significant others. It is difficult enough for adults to come to terms with the fact that they have a disabling disorder that requires lifelong treatment, and this is all the more difficult when the disorder begins in childhood or adolescence. Psychotherapeutic interventions need to be supportive and educational, assisting the patient and his or her family in understanding the nature and implications of having this disorder. The issue should be framed in a public health context, as bipolar disorder should be viewed as being a medical and not a mental disorder (as should depression, panic disorder, obsessive-compulsive disorder, ADHD, schizophrenia, and many other mental health disorders). Individual therapy can be helpful in improving coping skills, stress reduction, skill-building, and in addressing self-esteem issues. Family interventions can be helpful in assisting parents and siblings in being supportive of the child or adolescent who has the disorder, while also addressing their own needs for dealing with their own related stresses. CBT and interpersonal therapy for adolescents can provide these types of interventions.

Manifestations of Bipolar Mood Disorder in the Classroom

Students who are having symptoms of bipolar mood disorder will display mood swings. These swings may not alternate between feeling very happy and very sad; the student may be agitated, may be very irritable, and may experience highs and lows simultaneously. Students may have rapid mood swings, even occurring multiple times within a school day. They may appear to be exhilarated one moment, only to then appear depressed the next. Their mood lability (switching from one mood to another) may appear dramatic and may alienate them from their classmates. If episodes of depression and mania last for weeks or months, their mood swings would vary accordingly.

Symptoms of mania can have a dramatic presentation in a classroom. A student may make grandiose statements that he or she has immense abilities, powers, or potential. A student may be observed to have pressured speech, talking excessively, interrupting others, and speaking at a rapid rate. The student may act very impulsively without thinking of the consequences of the act and may make sexual statements or act in a sexually provocative manner. The student may appear to be very agitated, moving quickly and having difficulty settling down. Whereas some of these symptoms overlap with ADHD, in an individual who has bipolar mood disorder and not ADHD, the symptoms would generally tend to be episodic and not continuous. As there is a significant degree of comorbidity between the disorders, many individuals who have bipolar mood disorder also have ADHD. In that case, the baseline ADHD symptoms of impulsivity, distractibility, poor attention span, and so on, would remain constant whereas the mood symptoms (e.g., irritability, grandiosity, expansiveness) would fluctuate, dependent on the student's shifts in mood. As many individuals who have bipolar mood disorder also engage in problematic substance use, these students may also display symptoms of intoxication (e.g., smoking cannabis before school "to take the edge off") or withdrawal.

Treatment of Bipolar Mood Disorder

Psychotherapy can be used to reduce stress, both for the individual who has the disorder and for family members. Life stress is a known risk factor in triggering episodes of mood disorders, and stress management can be a helpful intervention. Unfortunately, there is no psychotherapy that can effectively prevent all future manic or depressive episodes. The treatment of choice for bipolar mood disorder is a combination of psychotherapy and medication. Medication treatment for pediatric bipolar disorder can be challenging. Many of the medications used have significant potential side effects, some require laboratory monitoring, and many individuals who have this disorder require more than one medication in order to have a significant symptom response. Generally, for an individual who has bipolar mood disorder or mixed bipolar disorder without psychotic symptoms, it is recommended that monotherapy (use of one medication) be the initial treatment of choice. Medication options would be lithium, a mood-stabilizing anticonvulsant (antiseizure) medication, or an atypical antipsychotic medication.

Lithium has been shown to treat the manic phase of the disorder, as well as being a treatment and prophylactic agent for its depressive phase. Lithium is actually an element, like sodium, rather than a manufactured medication. It had been used as a substitute for table salt before its toxicity was recognized. It was also provided in low doses in sodas, including 7UP (which was originally called "Bib Labeled Lithiated Lemon-Lime Soda," with the slogan, "Takes the ouch out of the grouch"). Lithium's modern use in the treatment of mania began with the discovery in 1949 that it acted as a tranquilizer in laboratory rats. Further research showed it to be effective in treating bipolar mood disorder.

Unfortunately, lithium has a very narrow therapeutic index, meaning that the toxic dose is not much higher than the therapeutic dose. It has significant toxicity if taken in too high amounts, or if an individual taking lithium restricts sodium or has an illness that results in fluid and electrolyte losses. Routine baseline and follow-up blood levels need to be drawn to ensure that the dose is in the therapeutic and not the toxic range. Blood levels need to be drawn more frequently when the medication is initiated and then at less frequent intervals when stable. Toxicity symptoms include nausea, vomiting, diarrhea, confusion, unsteadiness, lethargy, seizures, and coma. In addition to obtaining laboratory tests for lithium levels, tests for electrolyte imbalance, kidney, and thyroid functions need to be done as well. An electrocardiogram is also recommended to rule out abnormalities of cardiac conduction.

Lithium can have a number of side effects including weight gain, fine tremors, nausea, headache, frequent urination, dry mouth, and gastrointestinal difficulties. Lithium has been approved for the treatment of pediatric bipolar disorder, but there continues to be a need for more comprehensive research to clarify ideal dosing strategies and its effectiveness in acute mania versus long-term maintenance treatment. Lithium is available in short-acting (lithium carbonate, lithium citrate) and long-acting (e.g., Lithobid) forms. Despite its potential toxicity and side effect profile, its effectiveness has warranted it an ongoing place in first-line treatment of bipolar mood disorder. It is FDA-approved for adolescents ages 12–17 years.

Anticonvulsant medications were initially used to treat seizure disorders such as epilepsy. Their efficacy in producing mood-stabilizing effects in bipolar disorder was later recognized. The mechanism of action is not fully understood, but may be due to the stabilization and reduced excitability of the cell membrane. Several different anticonvulsant medications have been used for bipolar disorder in adults. Unfortunately, the pediatric literature is sparse compared to treatment studies on adults with this disorder. The anticonvulsants divalproex sodium (Depakote), lamotrigine (Lamictal), and extended release carbamazepine (Carbatrol) have been approved for adult bipolar mood disorder. Many youths who have bipolar disorder are treated off-label with anticonvulsants.

Divalproex sodium (Depakote) is more widely used than other anticonvulsants. It was first approved for adult bipolar disorder in 1994. It has a number of potential side effects (nausea, abdominal distress, tremor, headache, sedation, hematological, hepatic, and endocrine) and can cause birth defects. Divalproex sodium may increase testosterone levels in teenage girls and is associated with polycystic ovary syndrome. A thorough medical workup is necessary prior to starting the medication. It is available in an enteric-coated form, which reduces the risk of gastrointestinal side effects. Other medications that may be used, but that have limited research to support them, are carbemazepine, lamotrigine, topiramate, and oxcarbazepine. Lamotrigine can cause a severe or even life-threatening skin rash, and rashes are more common in children than adults.

Antipsychotic medications were first developed for the treatment of the psychotic symptoms of schizophrenia. The newer generation of antipsychotic medications, known as atypical antipsychotics, are now commonly used for the treatment of bipolar mood disorder as well. The first antipsychotic medication, chlorpromazine (Thorazine), was developed in the 1950s, and other medications such as thioridazine (Mellaril), fluphenazine (Prolixin), trifluoperazine (Stelazine), and haloperidol (Haldol) followed. These first-generation antipsychotic medications had significant side effects, including inducing symptoms similar to Parkinson's syndrome, as well as dry mouth, dizziness, constipation, sedation, and the potential for permanent neurological damage in the form of tardive dyskinesia, a chronic movement disorder.

By the 1990s, second-generation or atypical antipsychotics began to replace the first-generation antipsychotics for the most part, due to the perception that they had improved side effect profiles. Medications such as aripiprazole (Abilify), olanzapine (Zyprexa), quetiapine (Seroquel), risperidone (Risperdal), lurasidone (Latuda), and ziprasidone (Geodon) are atypical antipsychotics that may be used, either FDA approved or off-label in children, adolescents, and adults. Atypical antipsychotic medications have been shown to have mood-stabilizing properties and have been used alone or in combination with other medications for treating bipolar mood disorder.

Aripiprazole (Abilify) is FDA approved for the maintenance treatment of manic and mixed episodes associated with bipolar mood disorder in patients ages 10–17 years. It has a number of potential side effects including nausea, emesis, headache, sedation, and weight gain. Olanzapine (Zyprexa) is approved for manic or mixed episodes in adolescents ages 13–17 years. Unfortunately, it is associated with the potential for very significant weight gain and endocrine dysfunction (glucose intolerance). Quetiapine (Seroquel) is approved for the treatment of acute manic episodes in pediatric patients ages 10–17 years with bipolar mood disorder. It has potential cardiovascular (elevated blood pressure), central nervous system (sedation), and visual (cataracts) side effects as well as the potential for significant weight gain. Risperidone (Risperdal) is approved for 10–17-year-olds with acute mania or mixed episodes. It may cause sedation, headaches, glucose intolerance, elevation of prolactin, and weight gain. Ziprasidone (Geodon) may have side effects of sedation, motor restlessness, elevated heart rate, and abnormal electrocardiogram findings.

Research indicates that excessive dopamine release is associated with psychotic symptoms. Antipsychotic medications generally block the dopamine receptors in the brain. Some, such as risperidone, block serotonin receptors. The exact mechanisms of antipsychotic medications are unknown, and research continues to focus on developing medications with greater efficacy and more favorable side effect profiles. The atypical antipsychotics were developed in part because of concerns about significant side effects that the earlier generations of antipsychotic medications were known to produce, including permanent neurological damage in the form of tardive dyskinesia. This disorder is characterized by abnormal, repetitive body movements, most often in the face, but which also may be in the limbs, torso, and fingers. Although tardive dyskinesia appears to be less likely with the atypical antipsychotics, it still can occur.

As is noted in the section on major depression, omega-3 fatty acids are an alternative treatment for bipolar mood disorder in adults. When used, they are generally taken in combination with conventional treatments. Some students may be taking these supplements, generally in the form of fish oil capsules. It is clear that bipolar mood disorder is a severely disabling mental health disorder that has very adverse consequences in all aspects of an individual's life. It is also clear that treatment has very significant risks as well. The decision to initiate medication treatment needs to be based on a thorough, comprehensive diagnostic evaluation that ensures a correct diagnosis, followed by a careful analysis of the potential risks and benefits of treatment. It is hoped that future treatments will have greater efficacy and fewer side effects and that someday a cure for this disorder will be found.

DISRUPTIVE MOOD DYSREGULATION DISORDER

Disruptive mood dysregulation disorder (DMDD) is a new diagnosis introduced in DSM-5. It applies to children and adolescents ages 7–18 years who have chronic irritability and severe, recurrent temper outbursts that are grossly out of proportion (either in duration or intensity) to the situation. This diagnosis was developed in part to respond to concerns about the overdiagnosis of bipolar mood disorder in children and adolescents. A 2007 study found that the diagnosis of bipolar disorder in youth had increased 40-fold in the previous decade (Archives of General Psychiatry, 2007). DMDD shares some characteristics with bipolar mood disorder but lacks the episodic nature of bipolar disorder, does not have symptoms of elevated mood or grandiosity, and has a much better long-term prognosis.

Some children and adolescents who had this array of symptoms were previously diagnosed with bipolar mood disorder, some with mood disorder not otherwise specified, and some with depression not otherwise specified. Whereas youths who have major depression or bipolar mood disorder tend to have continued problems as they age, youths with DMDD tend to demonstrate improvement over time. This is one reason why there is a controversy about whether this diagnosis is appropriate, or whether it inappropriately labels youths who have irritable temperaments and repeated tantrums as having a psychiatric disorder rather than a variant of normal behavior.

In order to receive this diagnosis, symptoms need to begin prior to 10 years of age. However, the diagnosis cannot be made prior to the age of 6 years or after the age of 18 years. The child or adolescent needs to have severe, recurrent (averaging three or more times per week) verbal or physical outbursts that are grossly out of proportion to the situation. Outbursts may include verbal rages or physical aggression toward people or property. In between the outbursts, the youth has an irritable or angry mood most of the day. The outbursts are out of proportion to the youth's developmental level, and these behaviors need to have been present for at least 12 months, with no more than a 3-month period where all of the criteria may not have been present. Outbursts and irritable or angry mood need to be present in at least two of three settings (school, home, with peers), and be severe in at least one of these settings. The 6-month to 1-year prevalence of this disorder is estimated to be between 2%

and 5% of children and adolescents, with higher rates expected in males and in children prior to the age of adolescence. Children and adolescents who have DMDD have low frustration tolerance and tend to have difficulty succeeding in school, have difficulty interacting in activities with peers, and have chronic conflicts with family members. Their level of dysfunction, due to their irritability or anger and outbursts, is estimated to be similar to that of children and adolescents who have bipolar mood disorder.

Manifestations of DMDD in the Classroom

Students who have this diagnosis may have significantly disruptive temper outbursts in the classroom, on the playground, and in the lunchroom. They may have verbal rages or may demonstrate physical aggression toward people or property. As these outbursts tend to be frequent (averaging three or more times a week), it is likely that they will occur at school. The student will generally appear irritable or angry most of the time in between episodes. The temper outbursts are grossly out of proportion in duration or intensity to the situation that led to the outbursts.

Students diagnosed with this disorder tend to have significant difficulty with relationships with both peers and adults at school. Peers tend to shy away from them, due to their extremely low frustration tolerance and their generalized irritability. Students who have this disorder may have great difficulty engaging in playground activities, school sports, or other social activities. Parents may share with teachers their difficulties dealing with them in the home environment. Although students who have this disorder may appear oppositional, it is the mood disorder and not a pattern of oppositionality per se that is driving the behavior.

Teachers will generally have no difficulty recognizing symptoms of this disorder in their students. DMDD differs from the behavior outbursts of conduct-disordered delinquent students, as it has the key feature of generalized anger or irritability. Because the behavior stems from the mood disturbance, the behavioral problems tend to not respond well to typical behavioral interventions.

Treatment of DMDD

It is not clear yet what types of treatments will prove to be most successful with these youths. Behavioral interventions, family therapies, individual cognitive therapies, and, for younger children, play therapy, will likely become the major psychotherapeutic options. Pharmacotherapy interventions will likely mirror the treatments for bipolar mood disorder or depression, with the use of mood-stabilizing medications such as lithium, antiseizure medications, and atypical antipsychotic medications.

FOR DISCUSSION

VIGNETTE: Kate

Kate is a 16-year-old who previously had been doing well in school. Within the last 6 months, her grades plummeted, and she appeared unhappy, irritable, and withdrawn from social interaction. A psychiatric evaluation was requested. She was diagnosed with major depression with suicidal thoughts. Following treatment, symptoms remitted and she once again excelled in school.

REFLECTION QUESTIONS

Is there a process in your district for identifying students like Kate? Is there an educational team that meets regularly to discuss at-risk students? How are concerns shared with students' parents? Are recommendations made for parents to seek a mental health evaluation for these students? What are the roles of school staff in the process of identification and referral? Are there impediments that make this process difficult? How is this process different from situations in which a medical disorder (e.g., diabetes or asthma) is suspected?

CHAPTER 4

Attention-Deficit/ Hyperactivity Disorder

CHILDREN WHO HAVE ADHD PRESENT PREDOMINANTLY WITH symptoms of inattention, hyperactivity, and impulsivity, or a combination of these symptoms. The disorder has had numerous names over the last several decades: minimal brain damage, minimal brain dysfunction, hyperkinetic reaction of childhood, attention-deficit disorder with or without hyperactivity, and, since 1987, attention-deficit/hyperactivity disorder (ADHD). The disorder is not a manifestation of modern civilization. In 1775, a German physician, Melchior Adam Weikard, published a medical textbook in which deficits of attention were described (Barkley & Peters, 2012):

> An inattentive person . . . studies his matters only superficially; his judgements are erroneous and he misconceives the worth of things because he does not spend enough time and patience to search a matter individually or by the piece with the adequate accuracy. Such people only hear half of everything; they memorize or inform only half of it or do it in a messy manner . . . .They are mostly reckless, often copious considering imprudent projects, but they are also most inconstant in execution.

Weikard recommended the following treatment: "The inattentive person is to be separated from the noise or any other objects; he is to be kept solitary, in the dark, when he is too active." Over 200 years later, these symptoms continue to be noted in individuals who have ADHD. It is the most common specific psychiatric diagnosis in children and adolescents and is frequently seen in students referred for special education services in the emotionally disturbed category. It is a neurobehavioral disorder, is diagnosed two to four times more frequently in boys than girls, and affects at least 3–5% of children globally. Up to half of individuals who are diagnosed in childhood continue to display symptoms in adulthood, but many adults who have ADHD have learned coping strategies to help them function in society. The DSM-5 estimates the prevalence in most cultures as being 5% of children and 2.5% of adults.

Significant concerns have been raised about the overdiagnosis of ADHD in children and adolescents. The Centers for Disease Control and Prevention (CDC) published data in 2013 indicating that nearly one in five high school–age boys in the United States and 11% of school-age children overall have received a medical diagnosis of ADHD (Perou et al., 2013). This was a 41% increase over the previous decade. Approximately two-thirds of the individuals who were diagnosed received prescriptions for stimulant medication. ADHD has historically been estimated to affect between 3% and 7% of children and adolescents. The CDC data showed that 15% of school-age boys and 7% of school-age girls had received an ADHD diagnosis. For high school–age children, the percentages were 19% and 10%, respectively. Approximately 1 in 10 high school boys were taking medication for ADHD. Rates of ADHD diagnosis varied from 23% in southern states such as Arkansas, Kentucky, and Tennessee to less than 10% in Colorado and Nevada. According to the health care information company IMS Health, sales of stimulant medication to treat ADHD more than doubled from $4 billion in 2007 to $9 billion in 2012. Based on this information, concerns about overdiagnosis are warranted. It is important to recognize that many if not most of these children did not receive a comprehensive mental health diagnostic evaluation; they were seen relatively briefly for an assessment by a primary care professional.

DIAGNOSING ADHD

Symptom lists that are used for the diagnosis of ADHD are split into inattentive and hyperactive-impulsive criteria. If an individual has six or more symptoms from both lists, he or she would be diagnosed with ADHD, combined presentation. If an individual has six or more symptoms in one list but not the other, he or she would be considered to have ADHD, predominantly inattentive or ADHD, predominantly hyperactive-impulsive form.

Symptoms of inattentive ADHD include poor attention to details, difficulty sustaining attention, not seeming to listen when spoken to, failure to finish tasks, disorganization, avoidance of work that requires sustained mental effort, a tendency to lose things, significant distractibility, and forgetfulness. Symptoms of the hyperactive-impulsive form include frequent fidgeting, difficulty remaining seated, running and climbing excessively (or restlessness in adolescents and adults), difficulty playing quietly, frequently being on the go, talking excessively, blurting out answers to questions before the questions are completed, difficulty waiting one's turn, and interrupting and intruding on others' activities. The symptoms need to have been present for at least 6 months, to be developmentally inappropriate, and to have a significant negative impact on social and academic or occupational activities. Several symptoms need to have been present prior to the age of 12 years. Symptoms need to be present in two or more settings (e.g., at home, school, work, with peers).

The criteria in DSM-5 are mostly the same as those in DSM-IV. However, the cutoff for the age of onset has been increased from 7 years to 12 years, and the subtypes of inattentive, hyperactive, and mixed are replaced with presentation specifiers. Also, the threshold for diagnosis in adults was adjusted to five symptoms in either domain to reflect the evidence-based research about ongoing impairments in adults.

MANIFESTATIONS OF ADHD IN THE CLASSROOM

ADHD is a commonly occurring mental health disorder affecting many students. Children and adolescents who are hyperactive and impulsive are easy for teachers to identify as having classroom difficulties. They tend to be boys (there is a 3:1 ratio of males to females in this group, compared with 2:1 or less in the nonhyperactive group), and they may become impatient, frustrated, and disruptive. The symptoms of students who exhibit a combination of hyperactivity, impulsivity, and distractibility are often most pronounced in the classroom where they are required to sit still for extended periods of time, focusing on a specific task. These students are very noticeable to teachers, as they tend to fidget, have difficulty remaining seated, appear to be unfocused, and, at times, may be disruptive. They may act without thinking, and their impulsivity may cause them to make significant errors in their schoolwork and to have significant difficulties with behavioral control. They may have difficulty being quiet in the classroom and may become bored easily.

ADHD may manifest in a student rushing through schoolwork, having difficulty paying attention to details in class, and appearing not to be listening to the teacher. Tasks are often left unfinished, and the student may be very disorganized and forgetful. The student's desk may appear chaotic, and the student may have difficulty finding class assignments. It may be very difficult for students who have ADHD to keep track of assignments that are due, and to pace themselves to study for tests, complete homework, and to allot the time necessary for various schoolwork demands.

Some children who have ADHD, combined type or hyperactive/impulsive type, become less hyperactive as they grow older, but continue to have symptoms of distractibility, poor attention span, disorganization, and other symptoms of inattention. Thus, a high school student who has ADHD may appear to be work avoidant and oppositional to following through on assignments when, in fact, he or she may be having great difficulty attending to the work, organizing written work, and so on.

Another group, the predominantly inattentive students, is easy to miss. While they are not disruptive, they often have poor study skills, are inattentive in the classroom, are disorganized, and tend to achieve at a level significantly below their potential. They are often seen as being lazy, lacking motivation to do schoolwork, and simply being poor students. This is especially true for girls and young women, and their peers may describe them as scatter-brained, spaced out, flaky, ditsy, or social butterflies who lack interest in schoolwork, finding it boring. Meanwhile, their underlying difficulties in remaining focused and on task go unrecognized. Their ADHD is frequently not diagnosed, and they, their families, and their teachers are often unaware that they suffer from a treatable disability. Hyperactive and impulsive children and adolescents comprise the majority of those diagnosed by mental health professionals, but the nonhyperactive ones with ADHD may comprise an equally large number of students.

TREATMENT OF ADHD

Behavioral and focused cognitive-behavioral interventions can be very effective in the treatment of ADHD. In fact, three-fourths of children and adolescents respond to intensive behavioral interventions without the use of medication (MTA Cooperative Group, 1999). If medication is used in conjunction with behavioral treatments, lower doses than would be used if the student were not receiving behavioral therapy can often be effective.

Most children and adolescents who are treated for ADHD receive only medication, generally from a primary care provider. This is helpful for some of them, but may prove to be ineffective if the patient is not actively involved in the treatment process.

Psychotherapy

Psychotherapeutic interventions for ADHD are most effective when they provide practical, skills-focused interventions that help the student understand the nature of his or her disorder and to learn methods of effectively dealing with its manifestations. Children and adolescents often have difficulty appreciating how ADHD affects themselves and those around them. They tend to recognize that they have difficulties in the academic setting, but often mistakenly believe that these problems are due to being "stupid." They are often surprised to discover that many intelligent and successful adults have ADHD. Initially, treatment needs to focus on educating the child or adolescent about the nature of his or her disorder, including the fact that it is neurologically based and not caused by laziness, intellectual deficits, or a bad attitude. Methods of recognizing situations in which ADHD symptoms are likely to be more problematic are discussed, and youths are taught strategies of either avoiding those situations or adapting to them. By adolescence, they need to start thinking about how they will be able to succeed in dealing with life challenges once they reach adulthood. Being part of the treatment process, rather than a passive recipient of a daily pill, makes a significant difference in treatment outcomes.

Behavioral interventions that focus on reinforcing functional behaviors include the use of star charts that reward appropriate behaviors and clearly defined rules and expectations in the home and at school. It is important to have ongoing communication with teachers in order to identify academic or behavioral problems, such as ongoing off-task or disruptive behaviors before they get out of hand, and to ensure that there is consistency in home and school interventions. Parental involvement in treatment is important, especially when power struggles are interfering with progress.

Sometimes parents have ADHD as well, and first recognize this in the process of their child's diagnostic evaluation. The parent may choose to receive treatment, too, and if this occurs, it makes consistent reinforcement more likely in the home environment. Cognitive-behavioral interventions geared to the child or adolescent's developmental stage can assist in the process of mastery. Skills training that focuses on socialization, organization, impulse control, and behavioral management is a helpful intervention that can be provided in the clinical setting or the school environment.

Medication

Medication management generally involves the use of stimulant medication. Stimulants promote the release of the neurotransmitter dopamine and block the return of dopamine at the presynaptic dopamine transporter sites. They also affect the norepinephrine system. The prescriber needs to be aware of the significant variability in response to medication among youths, so as not to prescribe doses that are either too high or too low. Longer-acting forms of medications are preferable, as they do not require a visit to the nurse's office at lunchtime and provide a more even dose of medication throughout the day.

The most commonly prescribed stimulants are dexmethylphenidate (Focalin), DL-methylphenidate (Methylin, Metadate ER, Ritalin SR, Metadate CD, Concerta, Ritalin LA, Quillivant liquid form, and Daytrana sustained-release skin patch). ER refers to extended release, SR to sustained release, CD to extended release capsule, and LA to long acting. Other stimulants are dextroamphetamine in short-acting and long-acting (spansule) forms, and amphetamine mixed salts (Adderal, Adderal XR extended release, and Vivanse).

Hundreds of randomized, placebo-controlled studies of stimulants over the past 40 years have demonstrated their effectiveness in the treatment of ADHD, at least in the short term. Research indicates that, to achieve the best outcome, it is important to have ongoing communication between teachers and the prescriber of the medication. Stimulants should be prescribed at the lowest effective dose. Typically, the starting dose of methylphenidate (short acting) is 0.3 mg per kg of the child's weight. This would translate into 5 mg per dose for an early grade school child. Dosages can be increased if necessary, generally not to exceed 0.8 mg per kg per dose. Amphetamines such as Dexedrine should be started at half the dose of methylphenidate, as they are twice as potent.

Common side effects include appetite suppression, abdominal pain, insomnia, headaches, and tics. As individuals who have tic disorders such as Tourette's syndrome also often have ADHD, it is not always clear whether a tic was caused by the stimulant or whether it would have occurred regardless of whether medication had been prescribed. The vast majority of prescriptions for stimulants are for the treatment of ADHD. They may be useful in treating narcolepsy (sudden, uncontrollable brief episodes of deep sleep), as well as in some youths who have autism spectrum disorder. Stimulants are controlled substances, due to their significant potential for abuse. This raises the obvious question of whether prescribing these medications to children and adolescents causes them to become addicted.

Research indicates that children and adolescents who have ADHD have a higher risk of chemical dependency, whether or not they are treated with these medications, but that there is no increased risk of chemical dependency if the medications are used. However, given studies indicating that high percentages of students are being prescribed these medications (Perou et al., 2013), there is justified concern about overdiagnosis and about the diversion of these medications for illegal drug use.

Although stimulant medications tend to have the most robust effect on ADHD symptoms, for a variety of reasons (history of side effects from stimulants, poor response to stimulants, and parental preference) nonstimulant medications are also used to treat ADHD. Other medications that may be used include atomoxetine (Strattera), clonidine, and guanfacine. Atomoxetine (Strattera) is a selective norepinephrine reuptake inhibitor. It was initially developed as an antidepressant but is currently prescribed for the treatment of ADHD. It can be given once a day, and does not cause insomnia if given in the evening. Approximately 5–10% of individuals who take this medication are slow metabolizers, and they have a higher risk of side effects. Atomoxetine side effects include nausea, tiredness, and decreased appetite. Liver injury is a rare side effect. There is also a possible association with increased suicidal thoughts, as has been noted with antidepressants.

Bupropion (Wellbutrin) is an antidepressant that affects the noradrenergic system. Some studies noted effectiveness, but in general it is less effective than stimulant medication. Clonidine is an alpha-2 presynaptic receptor agonist that is used for the treatment of hypertension. For some children and adolescents, clonidine reduces hyperactivity and aggression. It has potential side effects, including changes in blood pressure. Guanfacine is another alpha-2 presynaptic agonist that is also sometimes used as a second-line medication, or in conjunction with stimulant medication when stimulants alone are not effective for the treatment of ADHD symptoms.

FOR DISCUSSION

VIGNETTE: Jenny

Jenny is a 14-year-old ninth grade student who has been having increasing difficulty mastering her school assignments. She is a bright student and was able to succeed in the past when school demands were less intense. She has been having problems organizing her work assignments in order to finish papers, be prepared for tests, and keep up with school demands. She has become increasingly frustrated, and her school counselor has wondered whether she is depressed. She was seen in psychiatric consultation. Her parents noted that she has never been disruptive or hyperactive, but has a long history of difficulty focusing, distractibility, and disorganization. She was diagnosed with ADHD and responded well to a combination of medication treatment and skills training for study skills and organizational skills.

REFLECTION QUESTIONS

Although the combined form of ADHD in males (inattentive and hyperactive/impulsive symptoms) is the most common form seen in clinics, the inattentive, nonhyperactive type often seen in females is frequently underidentified. What red flags are present in predominantly inattentive ADHD that educators can be on the lookout for in students who have this problem? Looking back, were there students with whom you have worked who, in retrospect, had evidence of predominantly inattentive ADHD? What would you do differently now, in working with students who have this profile?

CHAPTER 5

Anxiety Disorders, Obsessive-Compulsive Disorder, and Post-Traumatic Stress Disorder

ANXIETY DISORDERS

ANXIETY IS A NORMAL HUMAN EMOTION AND HAS HAD EVO-lutionary advantages. Cave dwellers who had no anxiety about predators that might be lurking outside of their caves had a good chance of meeting an untimely death. Those with anxiety and subsequent caution were more likely to survive and to reproduce. In our modern world, some degree of anxiety is useful, prompting preparation for upcoming tests or presentations, for example. However, some individuals experience anxiety that is disabling. Anxiety interferes with their ability to function effectively in social situations, with family members, at work, or at school. When anxiety is this severe, it is considered a disorder.

Anxiety disorders can affect children, adolescents, and adults. They are especially problematic in the pediatric population, as they can interfere with the normal developmental process. An adolescent with disabling social anxiety may not involve him or herself in normal developmental activities such as dates and other social experiences. A child with severe phobias may avoid activities that would normally contribute to healthy development. Anxiety disorders, as a whole, are the most common psychiatric disorders experienced by children and adolescents, yet they are frequently overlooked by medical and even by mental health professionals. They are often mistaken for aspects of normal development, when in fact they account for significant and at times debilitating disabilities.

Their prevalence is estimated to be between 10% and 20% of youths. They are often associated with other mental health problems such as major depression and substance abuse. Some children who have significant behavior problems have underlying anxiety that contributes to their conduct difficulties. Many youths who have anxiety disorders continue to experience them into adulthood. Anxiety disorders can lead to significant problems in school, including an increased risk of academic failure. In the previous diagnostic manual, DSM-IV-TR, separation anxiety disorder and selective mutism were listed in the category of disorders that usually began in childhood or adolescence. The other anxiety disorders (social anxiety disorder, obsessive-compulsive disorder or OCD, generalized anxiety disorder, PTSD, panic disorder, and specific phobias) may begin in childhood, adolescence, or adulthood. DSM-5 places Post Traumatic Stress Disorder (PTSD) and Obsessive Compulsive Disorder (OCD) in separate categories.

Anxiety disorders, OCD, and PTSD tend to be internalizing disorders and, as such, are often not easily recognizable. However, an astute educator who is sensitive to students' thoughts, emotions, and behaviors may recognize the manifestations of anxiety disorders. Manifestations of anxiety depend on the age of the student. For example, anxious children may tend to complain of physical problems (e.g., stomachaches, headaches) and may ask to go home or to visit the nurse's office. The child may be feigning a physical problem in order to avoid the stress of the classroom, or the student's anxiety may cause a psychosomatic (mind-body) reaction that manifests in actual physical symptoms.

Although physical complaints due to anxiety are more common in younger children, they can be problematic in adolescents as well and can reflect a variety of anxiety disorders. The numerous disorders that have anxiety as their common feature encompass a wide variety of mental health problems and thus tend to manifest in different ways under different conditions. It is important to recognize that caffeine can exacerbate symptoms of anxiety and to reduce or discontinue its use if this is the case.

There is a wide range of treatments for anxiety disorders, OCD, and

PTSD. In general, when psychotherapy is used, medication is a backup treatment in case the psychotherapeutic interventions are not successful. However, as many children and adolescents are not receiving psychotherapy and are treated by primary care physicians, medication may be a first intervention. If medication is used for the treatment of anxiety disorders, antidepressant medication tends to be the first choice. Generally, SSRI antidepressants would be considered first.

Generalized Anxiety Disorder

Generalized anxiety disorder is characterized by ongoing symptoms of anxiety that occur in multiple situations and that have worrying as a prominent feature. The anxiety is present most of the time and worrying is generalized to multiple issues. Someone who has generalized anxiety disorder may be restless, easily fatigued, have sleep difficulties, muscle tension, concentration problems, or irritability. (Three or more of these are required criteria in adults, whereas only one is required in children.)

Symptoms need to have been present for at least 6 months and cause significant distress or impairment. This disorder has a prevalence of approximately 1% in adolescents, and the prevalence increases to approximately 3% among adults. There is a 2:1 ratio of females to males with this disorder.

Children and adolescents who have generalized anxiety disorder may worry about their performance in academic subjects or in sports. They may have physical symptoms, including stomachaches and headaches, and may manifest nervous habits. It is important for the diagnostician to do a thorough evaluation to ensure that the child or adolescent doesn't have another disorder in which worrying is common, such as OCD, panic disorder, or phobias.

Manifestations of General Anxiety Disorder in the Classroom

Students who have generalized anxiety disorder may appear tense and nervous, "tightly wound," and unable to relax. They may ask many questions about schoolwork, due to anxiety about doing poorly on a test, getting a bad grade in the class, and so on. They may display nervous habits such as biting their nails or cracking their knuckles. They may express their constant worries during class discussions or may reveal anxiety about topics ranging from their own personal safety to fears of failure or worries about the environment.

Classroom performance and grades may suffer due to constant preoccupation with anxiety-producing topics.

Treatment of Generalized Anxiety Disorder

Psychotherapies that can be helpful include cognitive-behavioral interventions in which the child or adolescent examines the irrational basis of excessive fears, of catastrophizing, and of overgeneralizing. Relaxation techniques can be very helpful as well. Yoga and mindfulness practices can reduce symptoms of anxiety, build self-mastery, and contribute to physical fitness. If medication is to be used, it generally is in the SSRI category. Other medications that may be prescribed by physicians include benzodiazepines and buspirone.

Benzodiazepine medications have been used to treat adult anxiety since the 1960s. They activate the inhibitory neurotransmitter gamma-aminobutyric acid (GABA), which results in the slowing of neural activity in the brain, causing sedation and reduced anxiety. Although these medications may have short-term benefits, there is significant concern about long-term use due to potential for dependence and abuse. Benzodiazepines include alprazolam (Xanax), clonazepam (Klonopin), lorazepam (Ativan), triazolam (Halcion), and diazepam (Valium). Sedation is the most common side effect of benzodiazepines.

Buspirone (Buspar) is a medication that is approved for generalized anxiety disorder in adults. Its mechanism of action is presumed to be due to its properties as a serotonin presynaptic agonist and a serotonin receptor partial agonist. It was introduced as an alternative to the benzodiazepine medications, due to their abuse and dependence potential. It can cause drowsiness, nausea, headaches, dry mouth, fatigue, and insomnia. Although it is not approved for pediatric use, students may be treated with off-label prescriptions.

Social Anxiety Disorder

Social anxiety disorder, which has also been referred to as social phobia, usually begins in childhood or adolescence, with a mean onset at ages 10–13 years (Nelson et al., 2000). It has the characteristic feature of intense fear in social situations. The individual has persistent fears in social or performance situations where there is exposure to unfamiliar people or to scrutiny by others. The individual fears public embarrassment or humiliation caused by his or her appearance or actions. He or she becomes very anxious when in such situations and tends to avoid them whenever possible. The avoidant behavior leads to significant interference with occupational or academic functioning or to relationships with others. Adults who have this disorder recognize that the fear is unreasonable, but children may not. Anxiety in social situations may trigger physical symptoms of trembling, blushing, nausea, sweating, or even a full-fledged panic attack.

This disorder has been recognized since ancient times. Hippocrates, around 400 BCE, described an individual who "will neither see, nor be seen by his good will. He dare not come in company for fear he should be misused, disgraced, overshoot himself in gesture or speeches, or be sick; he thinks every man observes him."

Social anxiety disorder is on the extreme end of a continuum of shyness. Typically, ordinary shyness does not lead to major disabilities in interpersonal, workplace, or academic functioning. Shyness reflects an individual's temperament and is common in the general public. When symptoms are disabling, a mental health diagnosis is warranted. Social anxiety disorder has a lifetime prevalence of approximately 12% and is considered to be the most common anxiety disorder. It has significant comorbidity with major depression, and substance abuse is a high risk due to self-medication with drugs or alcohol for the anxiety symptoms.

Manifestations of Social Anxiety Disorder in the Classroom

A student who has social anxiety disorder will tend to avoid situations in which he or she is exposed to unfamiliar people, due to fears of embarrassment or humiliation. This disorder may manifest, for example, on the first day of school when the student is encountering many new classmates, on field trips, on the playground, or in other social situations that trigger significant anxiety. The anxiety tends to manifest in avoidant behavior. The refusal to go to school can be a very significant manifestation, and anxiety disorders are a major cause of mental health problems leading to missed days at school.

Treatment of Social Anxiety Disorder

Psychotherapy, in the form of cognitive-behavioral therapy (CBT), can be effective in social anxiety disorder. The cognitive component helps the individual examine his or her perceptions of constantly being observed and judged by others and the accuracy of the multiple worries and fears that are experienced in the context of social situations. The behavioral component utilizes gradual exposure to social situations, similar to the systematic desensitization techniques used to treat specific phobias. Relaxation techniques can assist the process of encountering the feared stimuli of social situations. Interpersonal therapy can also be of help. Medication, specifically the SSRI antidepressants, can be helpful for some patients who have social anxiety disorder. No medication has FDA approval for the treatment of this disorder in children and adolescents, so treatment would be off-label.

Specific Phobias

Phobias (from the Greek phobos meaning "fear") are very common anxiety disorders. They are persistent fears of situations or objects that the phobic individual attempts to avoid, even if the avoidance requires significant time and effort. If the situations or objects cannot be avoided, the phobic person experiences significant distress. The avoidance, the anxiety related to anticipation, and the anxiety caused by encountering the phobic situation interfere with both social and occupational activities. In adulthood, the person recognizes that the fear is irrational or excessive, but this may not be the case with children or young adolescents. There are many types of specific phobias, including fears of heights (acrophobia), water (aquaphobia), enclosed places (claustrophobia), flying (aviophobia), spiders (arachnophobia), and crowded places (agoraphobia). There is even a phobia of the number 13 (triskaidekaphobia), which must be widespread, given the absence of 13th floors in most U.S. hotels. Some phobias result from traumatic life experiences (e.g., suffering a dog bite in early childhood and subsequently having a morbid fear of all dogs). Some appear to result from hardwired instinctual responses (e.g., fear of heights), and some appear to have no logical explanation (e.g., coulrophobia, fear of clowns).

Students who refuse to go to school have been referred to as suffering from "school phobia." In fact, few of them have a specific phobia of schools. They tend to suffer from other mental health disorders, most commonly major depression or anxiety disorders such as separation anxiety disorder or social anxiety disorder.

Manifestations of Specific Phobias in the Classroom

Phobias are common in children and adolescents and may be problematic in the classroom under certain conditions. For example, a student who has an intense fear of heights may have significant difficulty sitting near a window on an upper floor of a school building. A student who has claustrophobia may become very anxious and agitated if required to be in an enclosed space, for example on a field trip to a cave. A student with a phobia of snakes may have a panic attack if the classroom has a terrarium with lizards and snakes. Students are often embarrassed by their phobias, and educators need to be astute observers to identify these problems when they occur.

Treatment of Phobias

A psychotherapeutic technique that has been helpful in treating phobias is called systematic desensitization. This technique uses gradual exposure to the feared object or situation. First, a hierarchy of fears is established. For example, if one has a fear of snakes, then the least anxiety-producing situation might be to see a picture of a snake, followed by being on the other side of a window from a live snake, followed by being in the same room with a snake, followed by touching a snake. The patient learns methods of self-relaxation in a calm environment, and then uses this learned relaxation to confront the phobic stimuli. Gradually starting from the least stressful situation and moving to more severely stressful situations as each one is mastered, the phobic individual can eventually learn to cope with a phobia.

Psychotherapeutic interventions can be very effective in the treatment of phobias. If therapy is not successful, medications may be considered. In general, for this and other anxiety disorders, the SSRI antidepressants tend to be prescribed with the greatest frequency.

Separation Anxiety Disorder

Separation anxiety disorder is characterized by excessive fear and anxiety when an individual is separated from those to whom he or she is attached. It is a major cause of school refusal, and children and adolescents who have this disorder may be significantly disabled while at school due to their ongoing anxiety about potential terrible things that may occur to themselves or their family members.

Symptoms include physical complaints when separated, worry about harm befalling attachment figures, significant distress when experiencing or anticipating separation, worries about harm befalling oneself, reluctance or refusal to sleep away from home, repeated nightmares with themes of separation, fears about being alone, and reluctance or refusal to go to places such as school or work due to fears of separation. At least three of these criteria are necessary to make the diagnosis. Symptoms need to be present for at least 4 weeks in children and adolescents and need to be significantly disabling for the diagnosis to be made. Separation anxiety is developmentally appropriate in infancy (e.g., fear of strangers in 1-year-olds). The diagnosis is made when the symptoms are not developmentally appropriate.

The 12-month prevalence for children is approximately 4%, which drops to 1.6% for adolescents. The disorder can occur in adulthood as well, but the prevalence tends to decrease as individuals age. It is a very significant problem for some children, and it is the most prevalent anxiety disorder in children under the age of 12 years.

Manifestations of Separation Anxiety Disorder in the Classroom

Separation anxiety disorder is especially noticeable in younger students who have great difficulty separating from their parents and going to school. Although some separation anxiety is a normal phase of development, students who have this disorder may refuse to go to school, may have severe anxiety when brought to school, and may appear significantly anxious or withdrawn after arriving at school. They may cling to their parents or to other people to whom they are attached. They may verbalize fears that something terrible may happen to them or to their parents during the time that they are separated. In some circumstances, the child may have a parent who suffers from separation anxiety, and the child's symptoms may be reflecting the parent's anxiety.

Treatment of Separation Anxiety Disorder

Psychotherapeutic interventions depend on the age of the individual. Play therapy can be helpful for young children who are unable to verbalize their thoughts and feelings. Older individuals can benefit from cognitive-behavioral interventions. Family therapy can be helpful to assist parents in setting appropriate limits on issues such as school refusal. A child with separation anxiety who has a parent with the same problem will not improve until the parent addresses his or her own anxiety and the behaviors that stem from it.

Medication interventions tend to favor the SSRI antidepressants. Benzodiazepines (e.g., Valium, Klonopin) may be prescribed, but have significant risks of tolerance and dependence in long-term use. Buspirone may be prescribed, but few studies support its use in children and adolescents.

Panic Disorder

Panic disorder is characterized by unexpected panic attacks that come on suddenly, tend to last for approximately 15–30 minutes, and then subside. The attacks are very uncomfortable, and when they clear, its sufferer feels shaken, exhausted, or very anxious about the prospect of the occurrence of another attack. Symptoms include dizziness, trembling, fear of losing control, palpitations, sweating, derealization or depersonalization, numbness or tingling, shortness of breath, chest discomfort, feelings of choking, fear of dying, nausea, and chills or heat sensations. Four or more of these symptoms are required for the diagnosis, and individuals who have panic disorder will have ongoing concerns about a recurring panic attack or will change their behavior in ways that are not adaptive in order to attempt to prevent a future attack.

Panic attacks can occur in other anxiety disorders, but in these situations they follow exposure to anxiety-producing situations. For example, someone who has a phobia of heights may experience a panic attack when climbing a tall ladder. Individuals suffering from panic disorder, on the other hand, have attacks that are unexpected, coming from out of the blue. However, they tend to associate the attacks with the situation they were in at the time of the attack, and they will often do their best to avoid a similar situation in the future.

Panic disorder is uncommon in children (the prevalence under the age of 14 years is less than 0.4%), but the rate increases during adolescence, especially in females, and the 12-month prevalence in older adolescents and adults is 2–3%.

Manifestations of Panic Disorder in the Classroom

Students who have panic disorder may present with a variety of problems in the classroom. If they have a panic attack in class, they may feel an urgent need to leave the room and be in a safe, secluded environment. If they remain in class, they may appear very anxious and thus may be distracted from their assigned work. Following a panic attack, they may appear shaken and disoriented and anxious that another attack will occur.

Students who have had several attacks, and who have developed symptoms of agoraphobia, may appear very anxious in crowded environments. They may feel a need to sit at the end of a row of chairs in order to make a quick exit if necessary. They may be so anxious about being at school that they develop school refusal symptoms. This is especially likely if they have had a number of panic attacks in the school environment.

Treatment of Panic Disorder

Psychotherapy first needs to focus on educating the individual about the nature of this disorder. Many individuals with panic disorder have felt that they were experiencing life-threatening symptoms, only to be evaluated in the emergency room and told that it was "all in their head." There is abundant evidence that panic disorder has biological roots, and individuals who experience it need to understand that it is a disorder that is not simply in their minds. Some individuals are able to practice relaxation techniques that assist them in riding out a panic attack. These techniques can be helpful, but panic attacks often continue despite the practice of self-relaxation activities. Panic attacks can be mild, moderate, or severe, and may occur frequently, after long periods of absence, or both.

Individuals who have panic disorder often develop secondary symptoms, including agoraphobia, in which they are afraid to go to places that are crowded, or from which they might not be able to escape, should they have another attack. Often the avoided places are similar to the places where they experienced a previous attack. This is a classic case of operant conditioning, and if panic attacks continue unabated, the secondary symptoms can remain disabling even when the panic disorder is effectively treated.

Some individuals are so disabled that they become housebound, unable to leave their homes to go out in public. Others remain highly anxious most of the time, in ongoing anticipation of having another attack. SSRI antidepressants have proven to be very helpful in the treatment of panic disorder, often resulting in a total amelioration of attacks. Early intervention is very important in order to limit the disability that can be caused by this disorder.

Obsessive-Compulsive Disorder

An individual with OCD is disabled by obsessions or compulsions. It was previously considered an anxiety disorder, but in DSM-5 it is listed in the section "Obsessive-Compulsive and Related Disorders." Obsessions are persistent thoughts, images, or impulses that are recurrent and intrusive and that cause significant distress or anxiety. These obsessions are not simply excessive worrying about an individual's actual problems. The obsessions are unpleasant, and the individual who suffers from them tries to extinguish or at least suppress them, sometimes through the use of specific behaviors. Trying to not have obsessional thoughts usually makes the thoughts even more prominent. Adults who have OCD recognize that these obsessions are a product of their own minds, but children may not.

Compulsions are either actions or mental activities that are repetitive, and the individual who has OCD feels compelled to perform them. They may follow obsessional thoughts or be part of a framework of rigidly applied rules. Examples of mental compulsions include counting or other mathematical activities such as dividing numbers or repeating words in one's mind. Examples of behavioral compulsions are excessive hand washing, repetitive checking (e.g., whether the door is locked, or whether the stove was turned off), touching objects (e.g., compulsively touching all of the light switches in a room), or putting objects in a specific order (e.g., alphabetical, or by color, shape, or size). Adults recognize that these obsessions or compulsions are unreasonable or excessive, but children may not.

Subclinical obsessions or compulsions are typical for much of the population. (How many of us check the mailbox after we put a letter in it, just to make sure that the letter went in correctly? How many of us have had a song run through our heads repetitively that we cannot extinguish?) When obsessions or compulsions reach the clinical level of a disorder, they are significantly disabling, and an individual may spend over an hour a day engaging in them. They can severely disrupt one's social, academic, or work activities.

Because many people who have OCD are ashamed of their symptoms, for many years OCD was considered to be a rare disorder. Once effective treatments were available, it became clear that it actually affects at least 1% of the general population. At least a third to half of adults who have this disorder report that it began during their childhood or adolescence. One out of five children who have OCD have a family member with this disorder. The ratio of boys to girls is 2:1. It can occur as early as the preschool years. Although some compulsive behaviors are normal in the prepubertal period (e.g., avoiding stepping on cracks in the sidewalk), OCD symptoms are significantly more severe and are disabling.

Manifestations of OCD in the Classroom

OCD may remain completely hidden from teachers or may manifest in observable compulsive behaviors. For example, a student may have a compulsion to touch a light switch when entering the classroom. Fear of contamination may cause a student to avoid shaking hands with others, or to wash his or her hands so frequently and vigorously that dermatitis develops. The student may repetitively pick at his or her skin or may engage in compulsive hair pulling. The student may have an intense need for orderliness, and may be observed straightening pictures, arranging desk space, and so on. The student may demonstrate perfectionistic tendencies. An example of this would be crumpling up and throwing away an assignment sheet because of a small mistake in handwriting.

Although obsessions are thoughts rather than behaviors, they may manifest indirectly in difficulty with work completion. Although the obsessions tend to remain hidden, they adversely affect schoolwork by preoccupying the student's mind. Hidden compulsions can interfere with schoolwork as well. For example, a student who feels compelled to count the number of ceiling tiles in a classroom will have difficulty focusing on classroom materials.

Treatment of OCD

Treatments include cognitive-behavioral therapy (CBT) and medication. A type of CBT called ERP (exposure and ritual prevention or exposure and response prevention) involves having the patient not engage in the compulsive behavior (such as checking a front door lock repeatedly after leaving the house, or washing one's hands after touching a doorknob), and then to learn to tolerate the anxiety that comes from not carrying out the compulsive behavior. As there is considerable evidence of a biological basis of OCD, it is not surprising that medication can be very helpful in its treatment. The antidepressants fluvoxamine (Luvox), Sertraline (Zoloft), and clomipramine (Anafranil) are approved for the treatment of OCD in children and adolescents. Medication does not tend to eliminate all of the symptoms of OCD, but can significantly reduce their severity.

Post-Traumatic Stress Disorder

Post-Traumatic Stress Disorder stems directly from experiencing a traumatic event. It can occur in childhood, adolescence, or adulthood, and can occur in individuals who have no previous history of mental health difficulties. It can cause severe anxiety and has significantly disabling symptoms that interfere with interpersonal, school, and work activities. PTSD was categorized as an anxiety disorder in DSM-IV-TR, but in DSM-5 it is now categorized as a Trauma-and Stressor-Related Disorder. This change was made because some individuals will experience feelings of anger, detachment, dysphoria, or dissociation, rather than experience anxiety symptoms following a traumatic event.

For individuals over age 6 years to be diagnosed with PTSD there must have been exposure to accidental or threatened death, serious injury, or sexual violence. They may have directly experienced the events, witnessed the events, learned that the events involved a close family member or friend, or experienced repeated or extreme exposure to traumatic details of the events. They experience one or more intrusive symptoms such as recurrent and intrusive memories of the traumatic event, recurrent nightmares related to the event, dissociative reactions in which the individual feels that the events are recurring (e.g., flashbacks), intense or prolonged distress when exposed to issues related to the trauma, and significant physiological reactions when exposed to issues related to the event. They also persistently avoid stimuli associated with the traumatic event, having two or more symptoms such as avoidance of distressing memories, thoughts, or feelings about the event or avoidance of external cues that remind them of the event. They experience negative alterations in thoughts and mood, with either inability to remember key aspects of the event, persistent negative feelings about themselves, blaming themselves for the event, persistently experiencing negative emotions, having significantly diminished interest in activities, feelings of detachment from others, or ongoing inability to experience positive emotions such as happiness, satisfaction, or loving feelings.

In addition, they have significant alterations in their level of arousal and reactivity, with two or more symptoms such as irritable behavior or angry outbursts, reckless or self-destructive behavior, hypervigilance, an exaggerated startle reflex, difficulty with concentration, or a sleep disturbance. Symptoms need to be present for more than 1 month, and cause significant distress or impairment.

Some individuals who have PTSD also experience depersonalization (feelings of being detached from, or outside of, their body or their mental processes) or derealization (feelings that their surroundings are unreal). If the full array of symptoms does not manifest until at least 6 months following the trauma, then the individual has PTSD with delayed expression. Children age 6 years and younger have similar symptoms, but some of them often manifest differently. For example, intrusive memories may not appear distressing, and may manifest in the content of their play. Their nightmares may not clearly indicate the content of the traumatic stressor.

Not all children who experience trauma will develop PTSD. In general, the more severe the stressor, the more likely one is to develop PTSD. Other risk factors include lack of parental support, prior exposure to trauma, trauma caused by a caregiver, and the presence of a preexisting psychiatric disorder. PTSD is associated with other mental health disorders in childhood and adolescence including conduct disorder, major depression, and substance use.

Manifestations of PTSD in the Classroom

A student who has PTSD that was caused by repeated physical or sexual abuse in the home environment may have symptoms of severe anxiety triggered by classroom discussions about protecting oneself from abuse. If a teacher or other adult staff member resembles an individual who abused the student, the student may experience severe anxiety when in proximity to this person. The response to other traumatic events (e.g., automobile accidents, witnessing violence in the home or community) can also affect the student at school. PTSD can cause significant numbing to the environment, to the point that a student may appear overly quiet, withdrawn, and not engaged in classroom activities. Younger children may repeat the themes of their trauma in their play activities, drawings, and conversations.

Treatment of PTSD

Therapy is focused on helping the child or adolescent gain mastery over the traumatic memories and be able to feel safe. Relaxation training can help a child deal with exposure to the traumatic memories. The child or adolescent needs to learn that his or her experiences are typical responses to trauma and not a sign of weakness or irreparable damage. CBT can assist this process. If medication is prescribed, the SSRIs are generally the first to be used. They may help with the symptoms of anxiety and depression, with intrusive recollections, and with avoidant behaviors. Other medications that may be used include the alpha-adrenergic agonists such as clonidine or guanfacine, as they may help reduce the state of hyperarousal. Mood stabilizers may be used for unstable mood, and antipsychotic medication may be used in very severe cases.

FOR DISCUSSION

VIGNETTE: Ron

Ron is a 14-year-old who has had a long history of school failure despite his high IQ. He was noted to spend excessive amounts of time on schoolwork, to leave his seat to sharpen his pencil multiple times per day in his classes, and rarely to hand in finished work. He appeared to school staff to be avoiding his schoolwork. A psychiatric evaluation was requested, and he was diagnosed with severe obsessive-compulsive disorder. This disorder was causing him to be highly perfectionistic to the point that he could not complete his assignments. He received treatment, which resulted in alleviation of symptoms and a straight A average in high school.

REFLECTION QUESTIONS

Individuals who have OCD often tend to not reveal their obsessions and compulsions to others. Ron's behavior was misinterpreted as oppositionality rather than as a manifestation of a significantly dis-abling psychiatric disorder. Sometimes there are observable clues that a student has OCD, such as reddened hands that result from excessive hand washing. What other clues might you look for when working with students who may have OCD? How might you broach the topic with a student you suspect has this disorder?

CHAPTER 6

Substance Use Disorders

THE HISTORY OF DRUG AND ALCOHOL USE DATES BACK thousands of years. Initially, through experimentation with plant products and naturally fermented substances, our ancient ancestors experienced the mind-altering effects of these substances. Ancient cave paintings in Spain illustrate psychedelic mushrooms. Chemical tests of ancient pottery reveal that 7,000 years ago, beer was produced in the Middle East. Through the millennia, individuals have used mind-altering substances for religious and recreational purposes. The use of these substances is partly related to cultural distinctions regarding which ones are considered acceptable or unacceptable.

For example, in Western cultures today, alcohol is permitted while cannabis (marijuana) may be illegal, whereas in some Middle Eastern countries the use of alcohol is forbidden.

Distinctions about a "good drug" that a society deems legal versus a "bad drug" that is made illegal are not necessarily based on data regarding the addictiveness or dangerousness of substances. In fact, nicotine is considered the most addictive drug, and tobacco smoking kills 440,000 people, causing nearly one out of every five deaths, each year in the United States. More deaths are caused by tobacco use than by the HIV virus, alcohol use, motor vehicle injuries, illegal drug use, suicides, and murders combined.

Many adults use substances responsibly, within the context of their societal norms. In the United States, for example, moderate use of alcohol and caffeine is the norm, when they are used. Unfortunately, approximately 10% of individuals have significant problems using drugs or alcohol. Attempts to forbid substances through prohibition have not solved this problem and have resulted in the criminalization of use and in the lucrative criminal enterprise of selling drugs. The issues related to societal approaches to substance use are complex and beyond the scope of this book.

It is clear that children and adolescents are particularly vulnerable to problems related to substance use. Their use can interfere with normal developmental stages and their ability to effectively cope with life stressors. It is also clear that drug and alcohol use is pervasive in the adolescent population. The National Institute of Drug Abuse tracks illicit drug use among teenagers. By far, the most popular drug is marijuana. Its use was in decline, but it has been increasing in the last few years. In 2012, 7% of 8th graders, 17% of 10th graders, and 23% of 12th graders had used marijuana in the past month. Fewer teens smoke cigarettes than smoke marijuana, with 17% of seniors reporting current cigarette smoking. Nearly 7% of 12th graders reported daily use of marijuana. Synthetic marijuana is a new and major concern, and is mistakenly considered by some youths to be a safe alternative to marijuana. Marijuana use within the previous year was reported by 36% of high school seniors, and synthetic marijuana by 11%. All other drugs, illicit or pharmaceutical, were reported at less than 8% for the previous year. Illicit drugs include hallucinogens, salvia, MDMA (Ecstasy), inhalants, and cocaine. Alcohol use has dropped to historically low levels, but continues to be a very significant problem as 4% of 8th graders, 15% of 10th graders, and 28% of 12th graders reported getting drunk in the past month. Also, 2.5% of 12th graders reported daily use, and 24% of 12th graders reported binge drinking in the past 2 weeks.

Nonmedical use of prescription and over-the-counter medications is a significant part of the teen drug problem. The most commonly abused drugs are the stimulants Adderall and Ritalin, the opioids Vicodin and Oxycontin, cough medicines, tranquilizers, and sedatives. Given that Adderall and Ritalin are both used for the treatment of ADHD, their illicit use suggests noncompliance for legitimate use and possibly inappropriate prescribing activities.

Prior to DSM-5, drug and alcohol issues were categorized as use, abuse, or dependence. These terms have been replaced in DSM-5 as substance use disorders, with severity designated as mild, moderate, or severe, depending on the number of criteria that are met. The term "addiction" is no longer used, due to its uncertain definition and potentially negative connotation. Intoxication criteria are also listed for each substance. Of course, not all substance use leads to intoxication. Many adults will go to a party, have one drink socially, and display no evidence of intoxication. Some substances, however, tend to be used by many adolescents for the express purpose of becoming intoxicated. The hallucinogen LSD is a good example. Also, because of its potency and its typical method of use, marijuana users tend to experience symptoms of intoxication. Adolescents who use drugs often do so with the goal of becoming intoxicated, which is often the first step toward problematic use.

Although each substance has unique characteristics of intoxication, the symptoms of problematic substance use are remarkably similar across substances. Individuals who have substance use disorders have a pathological pattern of behaviors related to the use of one or more substances. Despite behavioral, cognitive, and physiological symptoms, the individual will continue to use the substance. In individuals who have significant substance use problems, there is an underlying change in brain circuitry even when substance free. This leads to intense cravings when exposed to drug-related stimuli.

SYMPTOMS AND DIAGNOSIS OF A SUBSTANCE USE DISORDER

There are four groupings of criteria for substance use disorders: problems of impaired control, problems of social impairment, risky use, and pharmacological criteria. Symptoms of impaired control include problems such as using larger amounts over longer periods of time than originally intended; attempting unsuccessfully to reduce or discontinue use; spending a great deal of time obtaining, using, or recovering from the substance; and significant craving. Symptoms of social impairment include a failure to fulfill role obligations at home, work, or school; continued using despite the development of social or interpersonal problems; and giving up social, occupational, or recreational activities due to the substance use. Symptoms of risky use include using the substance in physically hazardous situations (e.g., drunk driving) and continued use despite having psychological or physical problems that are substance related. Symptoms of pharmacological criteria include tolerance, which is the need for increasing amounts of the substance to experience intoxication, and uncomfortable withdrawal symptoms upon discontinuation of use. Some substances (e.g., hallucinogens and inhalants) do not produce tolerance or withdrawal symptoms. The diagnosis of substance use disorder is made if there are at least two or three of the symptoms noted above. Two or three symptoms result in the diagnosis of mild substance use disorder, four to five is moderate, and six or more is severe.

There are problems with the diagnostic criteria of substance use disorders when applied to adolescents. The illegal use of drugs can mimic mental health disorders, including mood disorders (such as major depression and bipolar disorder), anxiety disorders, and even psychotic disorders, thereby causing an incorrect diagnosis that will lead educators to mistakenly conclude that a student meets the eligibility criteria for special education under the category of Severe Emotional Disorder (SED) or Other Health Impairment (OHI). Such an error can have serious consequences for the student because neither the adverse emotional effects of intoxication nor the effects of withdrawal will improve from special education and related services. Indeed, the introduction of special education and related services in response to a student's chemical use will compound the problem, and may even be harmful, because such services ignore the real problem and may enable the student to hide the chemical use for a longer period of time (Waldspurger & Dikel, 2010).

Adolescents who have substance use problems will nevertheless tend to demonstrate evidence of other difficulties. It can be argued that any adolescent's use of illicit drugs, of prescription drugs for the purpose of intoxication, or of alcohol is by its very nature problematic. The DSM does not distinguish between adolescents and adults in terms of diagnosing substance use disorders; it uses the same criteria for both groups. However, it is clear that use starting in childhood or early adolescence is a major risk factor for the development of substance use disorders. Further, many adolescents who have substance use problems have not tried to cut down on use, have no difficulty obtaining substances, have a social network of peers who are also abusing substances, and may not have access to automobiles that would lead to risky driving.

TYPES OF SUBSTANCES SUBJECT TO ABUSE

Following are descriptions of various substances that can lead to problem use and the symptoms of intoxication and withdrawal that may be noticeable in the classroom.

Cannabis

The DSM-5 refers to all marijuana products as cannabis. Cannabis has been steadily increasing in potency in recent years. It is generally smoked, producing a rapid high, but can be taken orally. Oral use has a slow onset and may cause a greater or less intense feeling of intoxication, depending on the amount consumed. The 12-month prevalence of cannabis use disorder is approximately 3.4% among 12–17-year-olds and 1.5% among adults 18 years or older. The rates are higher in males than in females. The disorder is more prevalent among teens who engage in conduct-disordered behaviors. Use prior to the age of 15 is a predictor of both substance use disorders and mental health disorders in late adolescence and adulthood.

Cannabis intoxication has two or more symptoms manifesting within 2 hours of cannabis use: increased appetite, dry mouth, rapid heart-beat, and conjunctival injection (red eyes). The individual also has significant psychological or behavioral changes such as euphoria, impaired coordina-tion, impairments in judgment, a sensation of slowed time, or social with-drawal. Symptoms of withdrawal are generally noted after stopping heavy and prolonged use. They include decreased appetite or weight loss, depressed mood, restlessness, sleep difficulties, nervousness, anxiety, irritability, anger or aggression, abdominal pain, shakiness or tremors, headache, fever, chills, and sweating. Withdrawal symptoms tend to begin within one to three days after discontinuing use and last for 1–2 weeks. Sleep disturbance may last for more than a month.

Diagnosis of cannabis use disorder is made based on a variety of fac-tors including direct observation (e.g., the odor of cannabis on clothing, dry mouth, red eyes) and by interviewing the individual and corroborative sources. It is often the case that adolescents do not see their use as a problem and do not consider cannabis to be a major drug like cocaine or heroin. Motivational interviewing, a technique that is focused on the individual's goals and motiva-tions, is more likely to elicit an accurate history than judgmental, confronta-tional, or adversarial interviewing methods.

Alcohol

As noted above, alcohol is used by many adolescents, and binge drinking is a common activity of high school seniors. The 12-month prevalence of alcohol use disorder is approximately 5% among 12–17-year-olds, and almost 9% among adults ages 18 years and older. Adult males outnumber females by more than 2:1. Most individuals who develop this disorder have their first episode of alcohol intoxication in their mid-teens and meet the criteria for the disorder by their late teens to mid-20s. Most individuals who develop the disorder do so by their late 30s. Onset of the disorder in school-age individuals tends to occur in those who have conduct problems and who have an earlier onset of intoxication. It is not unusual in clinical populations to see individuals who experienced intoxication at the age of 9 or 10 years. Many individuals who have this disorder attempt to discontinue their use and are able to do so for a period of time. However, when relapse occurs, the associated problems of alcohol use disorder tend to recur quickly. The disorder has a significant genetic component, and children of individuals who have the disorder are at a three-to-fourfold increased risk of developing the disorder even if they were adopted at birth.

Alcohol intoxication is present when there are significant problematic psychological or behavioral changes such as mood swings, poor judgment, or aggressive or inappropriate sexual behavior shortly after alcohol ingestion. Additionally, the individual will have slurred speech, incoordination, unsteady gait, nystagmus (rapid back-and-forth involuntary eye movements), impaired attention and memory, or stupor and coma. Alcohol withdrawal tends to follow years of having an alcohol use disorder and is relatively rare prior to the age of 30 years. It presents following cessation or reduction of prolonged heavy use and has features such as anxiety, agitation, brief hallucinations, autonomic hyperactivity (sweating or pulse over 100 beats per minute), hand tremors, insomnia, nausea and vomiting, or generalized seizures. Two of these symptoms are required for the diagnosis of alcohol withdrawal. For adults with alcohol use disorder, withdrawal has been noted in 50% of functional, middle-class adults and 80% or more of hospitalized or homeless adults.

The consequences of alcohol use in adolescents include fatality. Nearly half (45.1%) of all traffic fatalities are alcohol related, and it is estimated that 18% of drivers 16 to 20 years old—a total of 2.5 million adolescents—drive under the influence of alcohol. According to the Centers for Disease Control, unintentional injuries, including motor vehicle accidents, are by far the leading cause of death in adolescents, causing 29% of all deaths. It is estimated that 50% of these deaths are related to the use of alcohol.

Phencyclidines

Phencyclidines include the drug phencyclidine (PCP, angel dust) as well as less potent drugs such as ketamine, cyclohexamine, and dizocilpine. These drugs were initially developed as "dissociative anesthetics" because they caused a feeling of separation between mind and body. The effect of these drugs lasts a few hours, but the drugs stay in the system for several days. In some individuals, the hallucinogenic effect may last for days and may have psychotic features resembling schizophrenia. Only 0.3% of 12–17-year-olds report ever using phencyclidine. Nearly 2% of high school seniors report having used it. The prevalence of phencyclidine use disorder is unknown. Phencyclidine intoxication results in significant adverse behavioral changes including poor judgment, agitation, impulsivity, belligerence, assaultiveness, and unpredictability. Physical symptoms include nystagmus, high blood pressure, rapid heartbeat, muscle rigidity, increased sensitivity to sounds, diminished response to pain, loss of control of body movements, unclear speech, and seizures or coma. Intoxication may produce violent behavior. In addition to physical injuries due to combativeness, chronic users may have memory, cognition, and speech problems that may last for months. No withdrawal syndrome is known for phencyclidine use disorder.

Other Hallucinogens

Hallucinogens include a variety of substances that produce similar effects on the user. They include natural substances such as psilocybin mushrooms, peyote cacti, salvia and morning glory seeds, and synthesized substances such as LSD and MDMA (Ecstasy). Hallucinogens such as peyote and psilocybin mushrooms have been used in religious ceremonies for millennia by indigenous cultures. In DSM-5, hallucinogens other than phencyclidine are described as "other hallucinogens." The 12-month prevalence of other hallucinogen intoxication is approximately 3% for 12–17-year-olds and approximately 7% for 18–25-year-olds. The percentage falls to under 1% for individuals over the age of 25 years. There is no significant gender difference in 12–17-year-olds, but males outnumber females among older individuals.

There is a relatively low prevalence of other hallucinogen disorder. The 12-month prevalence in 12–17-year-olds is 0.5%.

Whereas some individuals report positive emotional experiences from hallucinogen use, hallucinogen intoxication may also manifest in significantly negative psychological or behavioral changes including anxiety or depression, delusions, paranoia, poor judgment, and fears of losing one's mind. Perceptual changes include depersonalization (believing that one's self is not real), derealization (believing that one's surroundings are not real), hallucinations, illusions, and synesthesias (sensory mix-ups such as "hearing colors" or "seeing music"). Additionally, intoxication produces physical symptoms such as blurred vision, rapid heartbeat, sweating, dilated pupils, incoordination, tremors, and heart palpitations.

Significant dangers are associated with hallucinogen use, including perceptual distortions that can lead to major injuries or fatalities and the risk of triggering severe psychopathology such as psychotic disorders in susceptible individuals. MDMA, which has both stimulant and hallucinogenic qualities, has been found to have long-term neurotoxic effects including memory impairments, sleep disturbance, and neuroendocrine dysfunction. Unlike the other hallucinogens, it has been noted to have evidence of a withdrawal syndrome.

Inhalants

Inhalants are volatile hydrocarbons such as toxic gases from substances such as paints, glues, and fuels (e.g., gasoline). Physical signs of inhalant use, if present, include odors on the user's clothing and a rash around the mouth or nose ("glue-sniffer's rash"). Intoxication is manifested in psychological or behavioral abnormalities including poor judgment, belligerence, assaultiveness, and apathy. Observable signs of intoxication include depressed reflexes, blurred or double vision, dizziness, nystagmus, euphoria, muscle weakness, incoordination, unsteady gait, slurred speech, lethargy, slowing of physical movements, tremors, and stupor or coma. Approximately 10% of teenagers report having used inhalants at least once. The prevalence of inhalant use in 12–17-year-olds is nearly 4%, and inhalant use disorder is estimated to have the same prevalence. In this age group, females slightly outnumber males. Inhalant use can be fatal, both due to the use of a plastic bag that can asphyxiate the user, and due to cardiac arrest that can result from inhaling these compounds. Inhalant use can lead to pulmonary, neurological, cardiovascular, and gastrointestinal disorders.

Opioids

The use of the opium poppy for its painkilling effect dates back thousands of years. Opioids are still used in their natural plant-based state or may be partially or wholly synthesized. Their analgesic effect is due to decreased reaction to pain, increased pain tolerance, and decreased perception of pain. Opioids bind to opioid receptors in the nervous system and in the gastrointestinal tract. Interestingly, humans produce opioid-like compounds called endorphins that can produce analgesic effects and a feeling of well-being. The runner's high experienced during long races has been attributed to the effect of these endorphins.

Opioids, when used legitimately for pain control, can produce tolerance with the need for higher doses to obtain the same effect. Therapeutic use can also lead to withdrawal symptoms if the medication is discontinued. Neither the tolerance nor the withdrawal are considered to be symptoms of opioid use disorder if they result from appropriate medical use of these medications. Opioids can produce symptoms of euphoria, which can lead to problematic usage of these substances. The 12-month prevalence of opioid use disorder in individuals ages 12–17 years is approximately 1%. Although the male:female ratio of opioid use disorder is 1.5:1 in adults, female adolescents may have a higher likelihood of developing this disorder. Problems associated with opioid use generally begin in the late teens and early 20s. Symptoms of intoxication include problematic behavioral or psychological changes including poor judgment, physical slowing or agitation, apathy, and dysphoria (the opposite of euphoria, including a sense of uneasiness). Physical signs include constricted pupils, drowsiness, slurred speech, and impairments in attention or memory.

Symptoms of withdrawal occurring after prolonged use include dysphoria, pupillary dilation, sweating, piloerection (goose bumps), nausea, vomiting, aching muscles, runny nose, lacrimation (excessive production of tears), insomnia, fever, diarrhea, and yawning.

In October 2017, President Trump declared the opioid crisis a public health emergency. In 2016, over 42,000 people were killed by opioids. Opioid overdoses increased by 30% from July 2016 through September 2017.

An estimated 5 million people in the United States have tried opioids as recreational drugs. There are now more deaths each year from prescription opioids than from heroin and cocaine combined. In 2016, 3.6% of adolescents ages 12–17 years reported misusing opioids over the previous year, and the percentage of misuse was twice as high among older adolescents and young adults ages 18–25 years. The vast majority of misuse was due to prescription opioids, not heroin.

Fortunately, opioid misuse by adolescents is decreasing. In 2017, the rate of heroin use by high school students was at a 25-year low, whereas the rate of past-year Vicodin use plummeted from 10.5% in 2003 to an all-time low of 2%. Oxycontin misuse decreased from a peak rate of 5.5% in 2005 to 2.7% in 2017.

However, overdose death rates continue to rise because adolescents who develop opioid use disorders are misusing increasingly more dangerous drugs, including contaminated fentanyl. In 2015, a total of 4235 youth ages 15–24 years died from a drug-related overdose. Over half of these were attributable to opioids.

The Centers for Disease Control estimated that for every young adult overdose death, there are 119 emergency room visits and 22 treatment admissions. Adolescents who are at increased risk of opioid misuse include those with acute and chronic pain, physical health problems, or a history of mental health disorders such as depression or a history of use of other substances. (U.S. Department of Health and Human Services, 2019)

Stimulants

Naturally occurring stimulants found in coca leaves, coffee beans, and khat have been used since ancient times. The extraction of psychoactive chemicals from plants (e.g., cocaine from the coca plant) or the synthesis of stimulants such as amphetamines produces much more potent stimulating compounds.

Therapeutic uses of stimulants include the treatment of ADHD and narcolepsy. Nonmedical uses of stimulants include attempts to increase alertness and decrease the need for sleep (e.g., college all-night cramming for tests, long-haul truck drivers). Stimulants can have appetite-suppression effects and may be used in attempts to lose weight. Stimulants also can produce a feeling of euphoria, which can lead to misuse of these substances.

Interestingly, it is unusual for children or adolescents who are being treated with stimulant medication for ADHD to experience euphoric effects. The opposite is noted in many instances, where the patient will complain of symptoms of dysphoria caused by the medication. Research indicates that medical use of stimulants for the treatment of ADHD does not increase the risk of substance use disorder.

Nonmedical use of stimulants is problematic in the adolescent and adult populations. Individuals who use amphetamine-type drugs or cocaine can develop stimulant use disorder in as little as one week. Most individuals who have this disorder develop tolerance and withdrawal. The 12-month prevalence of this disorder is 0.2% among 12–17-year-olds for both amphetamine-type stimulants and for cocaine. Stimulant intoxication has symptoms of significant psychological or behavioral problems including euphoria, hypervigilance (enhanced sensory sensitivity with scanning the environment for threats), changes in sociability, interpersonal sensitivity, tension, anxiety, anger, stereotyped behaviors (distinctive repetitive movements), and poor judgment. Physical symptoms include dilated pupils, blood pressure changes, rapid or slowed heartbeat, nausea or vomiting, confusion, seizures, muscle weakness, chest pain, abnormal heartbeats, physical agitation or slowing, perspiration, chills and evidence of weight loss. Stimulant withdrawal symptoms include physical agitation or slowing, increased appetite, fatigue, vivid nightmares, and insomnia or excess sleeping.

Tobacco

The tobacco plant is native to the tropical Americas and has been cultivated by Native Americans for over 3000 years. It was used in sacred ceremonies, to seal a transaction, and at major life events. Tobacco was believed to be a gift from the Creator, and the exhaled smoke carried one's thoughts and prayers to heaven. European settlers introduced tobacco use to their home countries, and it became a highly popular commodity. Today, tobacco use is declining in developed countries but increasing in developing ones. Worldwide, nearly 7 million tons are grown each year, and there are over a billion users of tobacco. Use in the United States had fallen significantly since the mid-1960s, from approximately 42% of adults to approximately 20% today. However, use has begun to increase since the introduction of e-cigarettes.

The most common methods of using tobacco include smoking, chewing tobacco, and inhaling snuff. Cigarette use represents over 90% of tobacco use in the United States, and 80% of smokers use tobacco on a daily basis. The 12-month prevalence of tobacco use disorder is 13% among adults. Sixty percent of smokers start when they are younger than age 13 years, and 90% start before the age of 20 years. By the age of 18 years, about 20% of teens smoke at least monthly, and most smokers become daily tobacco users. Initiation of smoking after the age of 21 years is rare. More than 80% of individuals who have tobacco use disorder attempt to quit, but 60% will experience a relapse within one week.

Although adolescent tobacco use had been in decline, the use of e-cigarettes (vaping) dramatically reversed that trend. E-cigarettes are devices that heat a liquid containing nicotine and flavorings into an aerosol that the user inhales. Ironically, they were initially seen as providing a health benefit to adult cigarette smokers who were trying to quit their use, who otherwise would be inhaling tobacco smoke. Instead, e-cigarettes have become a major public health hazard for adolescents. E-cigarettes entered the U.S. marketplace in 2007 and by 2014, they were the most commonly used tobacco product among U.S. youths. The use of e-cigarettes is higher among high school students than among adults.

In 2018, use of any tobacco product among high school students was 27.1% (4.04 million students) and among middle school students was 7.2% (840,000 students). Also in 2018, 3.6 million middle and high school students were vaping regularly. Increases in use have been dramatic. Between 2017 and 2018, e-cigarette use by middle school students increased by 48%, and use by high school students increased by 78%.

Given the public health hazard of adolescent nicotine use, and the growing popularity of e-cigarettes among teens, there is considerable public debate regarding whether e-cigarettes should be banned.

Tobacco intoxication is not a disorder in DSM-5, but tobacco withdrawal is. Symptoms of withdrawal include irritability, frustration, anger, insomnia, restlessness, depressed mood, anxiety, increased appetite, and difficulty concentrating. Withdrawal symptoms are a major contributor to individuals' difficulty in quitting smoking. Withdrawal symptoms usually begin within 24 hours of decreasing or stopping use, and can last two to three weeks.

Caffeine

Caffeine use is pervasive in U.S. society. More than 85% of children and adults use caffeine on a regular basis. In addition to coffee and caffeinated drinks, caffeine is added to food products, pain medications, vitamins, weight loss aids, and cold remedies. Not enough research data are available to determine the clinical significance of caffeine use disorder. It is clear, however, that caffeine intoxication and withdrawal are common features associated with caffeine use.

Symptoms of caffeine intoxication include nervousness, restlessness, physical agitation, excitement, periods of inexhaustibility, insomnia, flushed face, rapid or irregular heartbeat, frequent urination, rambling flow of thought or speech, gastrointestinal disturbance, and muscle twitching. Symptoms of withdrawal following cessation or reduction of caffeine use occur within 24 hours and include headache (which may be severe), flu-like symptoms, fatigue or drowsiness, difficulty concentrating, and dysphoric, depressed, or irritable mood. More than 70% of individuals who stop caffeine use develop withdrawal symptoms, and headaches are experienced by nearly half of them. Caffeine withdrawal symptoms can be disabling to the extent that an individual would have significant difficulty functioning in school or work environments.

MANIFESTATIONS OF SUBSTANCE USE

This chapter outlines the most typical substances used by adolescents and, in some cases, by children as well. Most users of these substances will not demonstrate signs of intoxication while at school, but those who do are at the highest risk of substance use disorder. It is helpful for teachers to be familiar with the signs of intoxication in order to identify these high-risk individuals. While the signs of intoxication of various substances are described in this chapter, it is more likely that teachers will notice the aftereffects of use and signs of substance withdrawal. Students may be hung over on Monday mornings as a result of extensive alcohol use over the weekend. Those who use during the week may show residual effects the next day. Cannabis is fat soluble and thus stays in the body for several days. Lingering effects of intoxication with cannabis may include cognitive difficulties and low motivation.

For students who smoke cigarettes, tobacco withdrawal may be problematic in the school environment. Students, unlike teachers, have no legal ability to use tobacco during the school day, and few students use tobacco substitutes such as gum containing nicotine. Restlessness, irritability, and difficulty concentrating may stem directly from tobacco withdrawal.

Caffeine is so commonly used by children and adolescents that teachers may not recognize that some students who are displaying abnormal behaviors may be experiencing caffeine intoxication or withdrawal. In schools where soda dispensing machines provide caffeinated beverages during the day, students often partake of significant amounts of caffeine while at school.

TREATMENT OF SUBSTANCE USE DISORDER

Successful treatment of substance use disorder requires the recognition that it affects an individual's brain function and that this can contribute to a significant risk of relapse weeks, months, or even years after successful initial treatment. Treatment needs to be of sufficient duration to be effective, and long-term relapse-prevention activities including programs such as Alcoholics Anonymous can significantly improve the odds for success. Multiple treatments may be necessary due to the significant risk of relapse for many individuals. Treatment needs to be individualized and needs to address multiple issues beyond the substance use problems, including associated family, vocational, social, medical, psychological, and legal problems.

Behavioral therapies, family therapy, group therapy, and peer support programs tend to be the most commonly provided interventions. They address the need to improve interpersonal relationships, skill-building techniques for resisting substance use, identifying replacement alternatives to substance use, and providing incentives for abstinence. Medication can be a useful adjunctive treatment, including the use of methadone or buprenorphine for opioids, disulfiram (Antabuse) for alcohol, and nicotine replacement (e.g., nicotine gum) or oral medication such as bupropion (Wellbutrin, Zyban) for tobacco. Given the comorbidity of substance use disorder and other mental health disorders such as ADHD and bipolar mood disorder, it is essential to treat coexisting mental health disorders in the process of treating the substance use disorder. Ideally, this would be provided within an integrated, dual-diagnosis treatment program.

Substance use problems are common in students, with cannabis, alcohol, tobacco, and caffeine being the most commonly used substances. Often, students who have substance use problems also have mental health disorders. If this is the case, both issues need to be addressed by clinicians, or problems are likely to continue. Educators play an important role in educating students about substance use, in watching for the signs of problem use, and in communicating their concerns to parents, school staff, and clinicians in the community.

INTERVENTIONS

The use of substances is so pervasive that students who are at high risk for substance use disorder often do not recognize the potential dangers of their use. They may think, "Everybody's doing it—it's no big deal." However, for those who are susceptible to developing severe substance use problems, it clearly is a big deal.

Unfortunately, many school programs have not been successful in prevention of drug and alcohol use. The "Just say no" approach has not resulted in significant reductions in teen drug and alcohol use. Research indicates that approaches that focus on the dissemination of information about the dangers of substance use tend to be ineffective. It is more effective to teach students how to resist peer influences, to provide opportunities to become involved in positive, nondrug experiences with others in the school and the community, to involve families, and to improve life skills. Adolescents benefit from interventions that build communication skills, assertiveness, self-efficacy, and drug resistance skills. In the elementary setting, addressing issues such as emotional awareness, communication skills, self-control, and social problem-solving skills are effective preventive measures. It is important for programs to be long term, with booster sessions that prevent the loss of program impact. Schools can partner with community prevention programs that focus on reducing risk factors such as the availability of drugs and alcohol and that promote non-using behaviors.

Some schools have chemical abuse counselors who meet with at-risk or using students to address their substance use. Students may feel comfortable revealing their use, believing that their statements are confidential. These counselors need to be aware of statutory mandates that require communication to parents about statements made by their children indicating behaviors that are seriously endangering their health (e.g., driving while intoxicated). The need to be trusted on the one hand needs to be balanced with the need not to keep secret a high risk of danger on the other. It is important for school administrators to understand this issue and to provide appropriate supervision of these counselors if they are working in schools.

Substance use disorders are not recognized as disabilities under the Individuals With Disabilities Education Act (IDEA). As a result, the mere fact that a student abuses substances or has been diagnosed as substance dependent does not make the student a "child with a disability" under IDEA. Similarly, the mere fact that a student uses substances does not trigger an obligation to evaluate the student under IDEA.

The illegal use of drugs can mimic mental health disorders, including mood disorders (such as major depression and bipolar disorder), anxiety disorders, and even psychotic disorders. As a result, substance use can lead educators to conclude that a student meets the eligibility criteria for special education under the categories of Emotional Disturbance (ED) or Other Health Impairment (OHI). Some states' rules mandate that a student whose emotional or behavioral problems are primarily due to substance use would not qualify for the ED category. Placing a student whose problems are primarily due to substances in ED services can have serious consequences for the student. Neither the adverse emotional effects of intoxication nor the effects of withdrawal will improve with special education and related services. Indeed, the introduction of special education and related services in response to a student's substance use will compound the problem and may even be harmful, because such services ignore the real problem and may enable the student to hide the substance use for a longer period of time.

FOR DISCUSSION

VIGNETTE: **Tom**

A sixth grade teacher overheard Tom, one of her students, boasting to friends that he had smoked marijuana for the first time. Later that day, she spoke with him privately about her concerns. He said, "It's no big deal; everybody does it. I'll bet that you smoked it when you were in college, didn't you?"

REFLECTION QUESTIONS

What would be the best response to Tom at this point? Should the teacher involve other school staff? Should the parents be contacted? Does the teacher have a legitimate concern that Tom has a significant risk of developing a significant substance use problem?

CHAPTER 7

Oppositional Defiant Disorder and Conduct Disorder

OPPOSITIONAL DEFIANT DISORDER

FROM TIME IMMEMORIAL, THERE HAVE BEEN CHILDREN AND adolescents who have opposed and defied authority figures, and who have broken societal rules and laws. They have been referred to by a variety of terms, including "juvenile delinquents," "social maladaptives," and "youth offenders." The DSM has assigned psychiatric disorders to many of these individuals, relying in particular on diagnoses of oppositional defiant disorder and conduct disorder. I do not believe that these behaviors indicate that these children and adolescents suffer from a psychiatric disorder in the same way that major depression and schizophrenia are disorders. But these youths also often display significantly challenging behaviors in the classroom environment and this chapter will therefore attempt to place their behaviors on the Clinical-Behavioral Spectrum described in Chapter 2 and describe the types of interventions that are most effective at different points along the spectrum.

In order to qualify for the diagnosis of oppositional defiant disorder (ODD), an individual must have a pattern of angry or irritable mood, argumentative or defiant behavior, or vindictiveness lasting for at least 6 months, with at least four symptoms from these categories. Criteria under angry or irritable mood include frequently losing one's temper, being touchy or easily annoyed, and being angry and resentful. Criteria under argumentative or defiant behavior include frequent arguments with authority figures or, for children and adolescents, arguing with adults, actively defying or refusing to comply with requests from authority figures or with rules, often deliberately annoying others, and often blaming others for one's mistakes or misbehaviors. The criterion under vindictiveness is being spiteful or vindictive at least twice during the previous 6 months.

Behaviors need to exceed the scope of behaviors normally seen at the child or adolescent's developmental age. Behaviors cannot be present exclusively during the course of a psychotic, substance use, depressive, or bipolar episode and cannot be diagnosed if the youth has disruptive mood dysregulation disorder.

ODD is estimated to have a prevalence ranging from 1% to 11%, the average being 3.3% of the population. Behaviors tend to appear within the preschool period. It may occur prior to the development of conduct disorder, but many youths with ODD do not develop conduct-disordered behaviors. Children and adolescents who have ODD are at increased risk of adult antisocial behaviors, impulse control problems, substance abuse, anxiety, and depression. As noted elsewhere in this book, the DSM-III listed a precursor to ODD called oppositional disorder of childhood. Subsequent research indicated that the oppositional disorder criteria were present in such a high percentage of children and adolescents as to make the diagnosis meaningless. Thus, oppositional disorder was beefed up with more stringent criteria, and became ODD.

ODD is essentially a pattern of behaviors in which the child or adolescent continually tests limits. The limit testing may result from not having received clear and consistent behavioral limits from parents or other authority figures. Often, the oppositional behavior is a symptom of a child or adolescent's maladaptive response to life stressors or another mental health disability, or it can be due to other factors. It may result from a sense of powerlessness and demoralization, leading to power struggles and oppositional behaviors. It is important to recognize that there are generally underlying reasons for the behavior and to focus on them, rather than engaging in power struggles with the child or adolescent.

Manifestations of ODD in the Classroom

Students diagnosed with ODD tend to have problems with authority figures, including teachers, and will display features of this disorder in the classroom. They may defy the teacher's, principal's, or other administrator's authority and may refuse to comply with rules and requests. They may be very argumentative with teachers as well. The diagnosis of ODD does not require problems with authority, as other criteria may meet the threshold for diagnosis. Students who do not demonstrate conflicts with authorities may be easily annoyed, angry, annoying, blaming, spiteful, or vindictive.

Some students who have been diagnosed with ODD do not display these problems in the school environment, and may show them only within the home environment. The opposite may also be the case. It is helpful to clarify whether the manifestation of these behaviors is related to environmental influences, such as lack of consistency, structure, and stability, or to excessively rigid rules and regulations.

Treatment of ODD

Parent management training can be a useful intervention for ODD and for conduct disorder. It is based on the principles of social learning theory and uses the techniques of behavioral interventions. Parents learn effective discipline strategies and learn to focus on positive reinforcement and to avoid engaging in power struggles. Psychotherapeutic interventions work best when they focus on strengths rather than on negative behaviors. Cognitive-behavioral techniques can help oppositional youths learn to identify self-defeating aspects of their oppositionality, to disengage from power struggles, and to learn appropriate methods of handling interpersonal conflict.

If the ODD symptoms are caused by another mental health disorder, then treatment of that disorder is indicated. To the degree that the oppositional behaviors are due to that disorder, they should improve as the disorder improves. Medication is not the first treatment of choice for ODD and generally would be used only to treat coexisting conditions such as ADHD. Some children and adolescents, however, may be treated with antipsychotic medications or mood-stabilizing medications if their behavior is significantly agitated or disruptive and potentially endangers themselves or others.

CONDUCT DISORDER

The diagnosis of conduct disorder is made based on the child's or adolescent's display of enough items on a list of misbehaviors for a long enough period of time. The DSM doesn't address the underlying reasons for the behavioral problems, and doesn't necessarily exclude the diagnosis if the child or adolescent displays these problems in the context of a psychiatric disorder.

If conduct-disordered symptoms are noted to be exclusively present along with another mental health disorder, and if they reflect the symptoms of the disorder (e.g., irritability in bipolar disorder), then conduct disorder should not be diagnosed as a separate mental health diagnosis. However, many mental health disorders are chronic, and it is often difficult to distinguish whether symptoms are due to another disorder. As a result, the diagnosis reflects a laundry list of behavioral problems that may not reflect clarity in regard to the environmental, medical, social, family, or psychiatric contributors to the problems. An adolescent who has a severe psychotic disorder such as schizophrenia, or a severe mood disorder such as bipolar mood disorder, and whose behavioral difficulties might at least partially stem from the psychiatric disorder, might receive the same conduct disorder diagnosis as an adolescent who had no underlying mental health disorder and whose misbehaviors and crimes were volitional and planned.

The basic problem with trying to determine whether a behavior problem is due to another mental health disorder is that it is rare for a behavior to be solely due to clinical issues or solely due to behavioral issues that have clear antecedents and functions. For most children and adolescents who have behavior problems and mental health disorders, a combination of these factors influences their behaviors. This issue is discussed in detail in Chapter 2.

To be diagnosed with conduct disorder, a child or adolescent would need to display a persistent and repetitive pattern of behavior that violates societal norms or the basic rights of others. Behaviors are categorized as aggressive, destructive of property, deceitfulness or theft, and serious violation of rules. Aggressive behaviors include bullying or threatening, initiating fights, using weapons, physical cruelty to people, physical cruelty to animals, stealing while confronting a victim, and forced sexual activity. Destruction of property includes fire setting with the intent to cause serious damage and deliberately destroying property. Deceitfulness or theft includes breaking and entering, lying to obtain goods or to avoid responsibility, and stealing (e.g., shoplifting) without confronting a victim. Serious violation of rules includes staying out at night against parents' wishes, beginning before the age of 13 years, running away overnight, and frequent truancy beginning before the age of 13 years. To qualify for the diagnosis of conduct disorder, an individual would need to have at least 3 of the above 15 criteria in the previous 12 months, with at least one in the past 6 months. The behaviors need to produce significant impairment in social, academic, or occupational functioning.

The DSM-5 added the potential specifier, "with limited prosocial emotions" to identify individuals who continually displayed at least two of the following characteristics for at least the past 12 months: lack of remorse or guilt, callousness or lack of empathy, unconcern about performance at school, work, or other important activities, and having shallow or deficient affect. The one-year prevalence of conduct disorder is estimated to be from 2% to more than 10%, with a median of 4%. Rates are higher for males. Behaviors usually begin in middle childhood through middle adolescence, but can begin as early as the preschool years. In most individuals, the disorder remits by adulthood. Individuals who had an early onset of the disorder (i.e., prior to the age of 10 years) have a higher lifetime risk of criminal behavior and substance abuse problems. In general, individuals who have conduct disorder are at higher risk for developing anxiety disorders, mood disorders, impulse control disorders, PTSD, somatic symptom disorders, substance-related disorders, and psychotic disorders as adults.

I do not agree that conduct disorder, in itself, is a clinical diagnosis in the way that schizophrenia or major depression are. The ultimate absurdity of this concept was clear before the Social Security Administration changed its rules for disability payments, when families were able to collect monthly sums of money because their child, who engaged in stealing, lying, aggression toward others, fire setting, and so on, and thus had a diagnosis of conduct disorder. I believe that, if a child or adolescent has conduct-disordered behaviors, a closer look for mental health disorders is in order. The presence of a mental health disorder does not necessarily mean that the disorder is causing the behavioral difficulties. An assessment of the nature of the disorder and its contribution to the conduct problems can clarify the issue. The label of conduct disorder is significantly stigmatizing and often leads to the perception that the child or adolescent who has this diagnosis is inherently antisocial. In fact, at least half of children and adolescents who are diagnosed with conduct disorder do not go on to have the diagnosis of antisocial personality disorder in adulthood.

Manifestations of Conduct Disorder in the Classroom

The diagnosis of conduct disorder is based on a repetitive and persistent pattern of behavioral problems, and children and adolescents who are diagnosed with it generally display their behaviors in multiple settings, including school. They may be aggressive and may bully and intimidate peers. They may cheat on homework or on tests and may lie about missed schoolwork. They may destroy property at school and may steal from peers and even from the teacher. They may be absent from class due to truancy.

There are some students who are very delinquent in the community, but who do not display behavioral problems in the school environment. In fact, some conduct-disordered adolescents who are incarcerated in juvenile justice facilities that provide a high degree of structure and natural consequences do well in school for the first time in their lives. Many students who are conduct disordered have other mental health diagnoses. If the other mental health problems (e.g., ADHD, bipolar mood disorder) are major causal factors leading to delinquent behaviors, then these disorders may be very recognizable in the classroom. For example, a student who has conduct problems may also be extremely impulsive, very distractible, and hyperactive. Or, significant mood swings may be apparent.

For students whose behavioral problems are predominantly due to clinical disorders, it is all the more important for school personnel to communicate their concerns about symptoms of these disorders so that, it is hoped, effective treatment will occur. Often, with effective treatment, the behavior problems seen at school will decrease or even disappear.

Treatment of Conduct Disorder

To the degree that conduct-disordered behavior is not due to another mental health disorder, interventions need to be specific, clearly defined, and focused on providing natural consequences for behavioral problems. Some children and adolescents simply have not learned appropriate life skills of social-ization and sustaining positive interactions with others. There is no research to support sending youth to boot camps, behavior modification schools, or wilderness programs that purport to treat conduct disorder. Parent manage-ment training can be effective for less severely conduct-disordered youth. The most effective intervention for intervening with children and adolescents who have significant, ongoing severe conduct-disordered behaviors is multisystemic therapy, which involves the whole family system (see Chapter 13 for details).

Cognitive-behavioral therapy can be useful in helping youths iden-tify and adopt more socially appropriate behaviors. Many conduct-disordered youths lack essential social skills, and social skills training can help them to learn more appropriate socialized behaviors. Anger management skills training and mindfulness techniques can also be of help. To the degree that conduct-disordered behavior stems at least in part from other mental health disorders such as ADHD, treatment of those disorders stands a good chance of reducing the behavioral problems.

Various medications may be prescribed to youths who have conduct disorder. For highly aggressive youth, mood stabilizers or atypical antipsy-chotic medication may be used. A thorough diagnostic assessment is essential to clarify whether the child or adolescent has an underlying mental health disorder such as a severe mood disorder that is triggering the aggression, so that medication interventions can be appropriately targeted toward the underlying problem.

The Relationship Between Youth Violence, Conduct Disorder, and Mental Health Disorders

The mass media tend to focus on dramatic, very rare events of youth violence such as mass murder school shootings. In fact, most adolescent homi-cides are committed in inner cities and outside of school. They most frequently involve an interpersonal dispute and a single victim. On average, six or seven youths are murdered in this country every day. Most of them are inner-city minority youths.

Multiple factors contribute to and shape antisocial behavior over the course of development. Many of them are within the social environment. Peers, family, school, community, and neighborhood contexts shape, enable, and maintain antisocial behavior, aggression, and related behavior problems.

Risk factors in the home environment include weak bonding with parents, ineffective parenting (poor monitoring, inconsistent discipline, inadequate supervision), exposure to violence in the home, and an environment that supports aggression and violence. Risk factors in the child or adolescent include early conduct problems, ADHD and associated impulsivity and poor judgment, depression, anxiety disorders, and lower cognitive and verbal abilities. External risk factors include peer rejection, competition for status and attention, association with antisocial peers who are experiencing academic failure, and peers who engage in violent activities.

The earlier the age of onset of antisocial behaviors, the more severe they tend to be and the more likely that they will persist into adulthood. Life course–persistent behaviors are correlated with neurological deficits, language deficits, and cognitive deficits and are exacerbated by stressful home situations. Youths with conduct problems plus a mental health disorder such as ADHD, depression, or anxiety disorders are more likely to engage in aggression than youths who only have conduct problems. Research indicates that placing violent youths together in self-contained special education programs (e.g., Setting 4 sites for emotionally disturbed delinquent students) increases the risk of violent behavior. Although students with the characteristics outlined above tend to be at a higher risk of violence, there are also those who are not conduct disordered but who suffer from mental health problems.

Some of these students have been victims of significant bullying. Their fragile mental health status and severe mental health symptoms may push them over the edge into committing violent acts. Highly adaptive parenting, good verbal ability, and success in school are protective factors against antisocial behavior.

It is clear that violence in the school setting is a real risk, and that there are major problems with accurately predicting violent behavior. Mental health disorders are generally not predictors of violence, but when they occur in the context of other behavior problems and significant stressors, they can lead to violent behaviors. Proactively addressing students' mental health problems through collaborative efforts can improve behaviors, reduce the risk of violence, and cut costs.

FOR DISCUSSION

VIGNETTE: Troy

Troy is a 16-year-old student who has engaged in delinquent behaviors since early childhood. He has been caught bullying vulnerable students, including one who used a wheelchair, on several occasions. He minimizes his behavior, saying that he was "just kidding," and shows no remorse for his actions. He has been in juvenile detention on a number of occasions, for auto theft, breaking and entering, and assault. He has been diagnosed with conduct disorder. He has no evidence of any other mental health diagnoses. He qualified for the Emotional Disturbance category of special education because he had impaired educational performance and inappropriate types of behavior under normal circumstances. Inappropriate behaviors included attacking a teacher, punching him in the mouth because he was angry about the grade that he had received. He has been receiving special education services for 2 years. Recently, he became angry with his math teacher and punched her in the face. The school district wanted to expel him, and a manifestation determination meeting was held. (At specific times, and for certain violations of the student code of conduct, IDEA's discipline procedures require school systems to conduct what is known as a "manifestation determination review" *in order to determine whether or not the child's behavior that led to the disciplinary infraction is linked to his or her disability.*)

Since his disability was in the Emotional Disturbance category, and since he qualified for that category partly because he had attacked a teacher, the parents' attorney argued that the assault was due to his disability, and therefore he could not be expelled.

REFLECTION QUESTIONS

Do you think that Troy has a mental health disability? Does he have an educational disability? Should he be protected from natural consequences because of his disability status? What does it mean to have an emotional disturbance when one's only problem is delinquency?

CHAPTER 8

Autism Spectrum Disorder

THE DSM-5 HAS COMBINED THE DIFFERENT DIAGNOSTIC CATegories of developmental disorders into one disorder, autism spectrum disorder (ASD). In DSM-IV-TR, the different disorders were autistic disorder (autism), pervasive developmental disorder not otherwise specified, Asperger's disorder, childhood disintegrative disorder, and Rett's disorder. In DSM-IV-TR, Asperger's disorder referred to high-functioning autism with intact verbal skills. Pervasive developmental disorder "not otherwise specified" referred to individuals who did not meet the full requirements of autistic disorder. The changes in criteria in DSM-5 now subsume all of these diagnoses into ASD.

The term "autism" was first used in its modern clinical sense in 1938 by Hans Asperger, who described high-functioning individuals who had autism spectrum symptoms. In 1943, Leo Kanner described 11 children who had striking behavioral similarities of autistic "aloneness" and insistence on sameness, and named their disorder "early infantile autism" (Kanner, 1943). Mental health diagnostic terms regarding development can be somewhat confusing. A developmental *delay* refers to a situation in which a developmental skill (e.g., walking or talking) develops late, but once it develops the activity's qualities are within the normal range. Developmental *disability* is a term that has been used to describe cognitive limitations, previously termed "mental retardation." (DSM-5 confuses the issue by referring to these as both "intellectual disability" and "intellectual developmental disorder"). Developmental *disorders* refer to stages of development that are abnormal, such as deficits in nonverbal communication, inflexible adherence to routines, and abnormal reactivity to sensory stimuli. ASDs are developmental disorders, and individuals who have them may also have developmental delays or developmental disabilities. The diagnosis is listed in DSM-5 in a newly created category, "neurodevelopmental disorders."

The types and severity of symptoms of ASD vary widely, from mild and not obvious to severe. (A person cannot be "a little bit pregnant" but can be "a little bit autistic.") Some of the most challenging students are those who have ASD in the more moderate range of severity, but who also have multiple other psychiatric disorders such as depression, bipolar mood disorder, ADHD, obsessive-compulsive disorder, panic disorder, and so on. If these students are in categorical special education programs, they may be placed in the Emotional Disturbance rather than the Autism Spectrum category. Given the dramatic symptoms of these other problems, their ASD may not be obvious. However, it is important to recognize that this disorder has unique characteristics that can interfere with a student's educational progress and social-emotional functioning in ways that other mental health disorders do not.

Individuals diagnosed with ASD have persistent deficits in social communication and social interaction. They have deficits in social-emotional reciprocity, with problems such as difficulty maintaining conversations, lack of emotional sharing, and a failure to initiate or respond to social interactions. They have nonverbal communication deficits, with problems such as poor eye contact, difficulty reading nonverbal communications, and lack of gestures. They have significant problems in developing, maintaining, and understanding relationships, problems such as a lack of sharing imaginative play, an absence of interest in peers, and difficulty adjusting their behavior to the social situation.

In addition, they have restricted, repetitive patterns of behavior, interests, or activities, with at least two characteristics in that category. The first group of characteristics includes stereotyped or repetitive motor movements, use of objects, or speech. The second group includes the insistence on sameness with inflexible adherence to routines. Next are highly restricted, fixated interests that are abnormal in intensity and focus. The last item is hyper- or hyperoactivity to sensory inputs (sights, sounds, smells, touches) or unusual interest in sensory aspects of the environment. Symptoms must have been present in the early developmental period and cause significant impairment in functioning.

The prevalence of ASD is estimated to be 1% in both children and adults. This is a significant increase from previous estimates, and may reflect improved diagnostic sensitivity and/or an increase in frequency in the population. This is a highly heritable disorder, with twin concordance rates ranging from 37% to over 90% in different studies. It is diagnosed four times as often in males as in females.

MANIFESTATIONS OF ASD IN THE CLASSROOM

Symptoms of severe ASD are easily recognizable in the classroom setting, as students who have this level of disability tend to have severe difficulties with language use, interpersonal relationships, unusual behaviors (e.g., repetitive rocking), and, often, significant cognitive difficulties. As this disorder occurs along a spectrum, there are many students who have milder forms that are not always obvious, and, in fact, are often not diagnosed at all by medical or mental health professionals. These students tend to have difficulty with social skills and have difficulty making and keeping friends. If they have poor eye contact and restricted gestures, they may be seen by peers as being different, strange, or weird. They tend to not fit into social groups and may prefer solitary activities, leading them to be teased, bullied, or shunned by their peers. They may have difficulty reading nonverbal communication such as gestures or facial expressions, and may not understand or may misinterpret others' emotions.

Often, students who have ASD have significant difficulty dealing with changes in routine. This could manifest in the classroom in the form of anxiety, and the student could respond to alterations in a previously fixed daily schedule with near panic. These students need to be prepared for major changes, often days or even weeks in advance, and they respond best to gradual rather than sudden routine changes.

Unusual movements or mannerisms are common, and may take the form of tiptoe walking, hand flapping, or rocking back and forth. Students who have ASD may have significant oversensitivity to touch, sound, or light. Touch sensitivity, known as tactile defensiveness, can be observed if a student cringes or becomes agitated when someone attempts to shake hands, pat him or her on the back, and so on. Sounds that are barely perceptible to other students (e.g., the background hum of machinery in the school building) may be very distracting to these students. Loud noises may trigger severe anxiety.

Many students who have ASD are very sensitive to fluorescent lighting, especially the type with the wider bulbs that have magnetic rather than electronic ballasts. Magnetic ballast fluorescent lighting has a flicker that is generally imperceptible to nondisabled individuals, but that can be very disturbing to students with ASD. Changing lighting to incandescent or, even better, daylight can result in significant reduction in anxiety levels and a reduction in behavioral difficulties as well.

These students may be very concrete in their thinking and may have difficulty with abstract concepts. Their speech may appear stilted, and their significant difficulties in initiating and maintaining a conversation may keep them from engaging in classroom discussions. Younger children, in classrooms where storytelling and make-believe play is encouraged, may have significant difficulty engaging in imaginative activities. A common feature of ASD that tends to manifest in the classroom is the excessive preoccupation with a topic of interest. The student will continue to refer to that topic and have great difficulty transitioning to another subject. The topic may be anything that may interest the student, such as a video game, cartoon character, weather patterns, airplanes, and so on. The student may have amassed a huge amount of information on the topic, and may want to talk about it with the teacher or classmates without recognizing others' lack of interest. This tends to alienate others and can lead to ostracism. Many high-functioning autism spectrum individuals have followed career paths along the lines of their excessive interests (e.g., computer science) and have been quite successful as a result. The challenge for the classroom teacher is to encourage topic exploration on the one hand while also encouraging a broader focus of study for a student who may be resistant to getting off the hyperfocused topic.

TREATMENT OF ASD

Psychotherapy

The choice of psychotherapeutic interventions for ASD depends on the severity of the disorder and the level of intellectual and verbal functioning of the child or adolescent. For individuals who are high functioning, cognitive-behavioral treatments that are based on assisting them to understand the nature of their disorder and to achieve clearly defined goals can be helpful. Social-skills groups can be very beneficial for learning and practicing appropriate social interactions.

Behavior interventions are very specific. For example, applied behavior analysis focuses on developing skills in attending, imitation, receptive and expressive language, preacademics, and self-help. It uses the ABC approach (antecedent, which is a directive to the child; behavior, which is the child's response; and consequence, which is the therapist's response). This approach requires intensive one-on-one behavioral interventions. Another example is the TEACCH Autism Program, which uses parents as co-therapists. Its curriculum is tailored to individual needs. It focuses on improved adaptation and increasing functional skills and encourages generalization of skills to other environments. It emphasizes visual learning modalities and uses functional contexts for teaching concepts.

Skills training within the school environment can assist the child or adolescent in social, academic, communicative, and appropriate behavioral skills. Behavioral modification techniques that focus on eliminating inappropriate behaviors and improving appropriate ones can be helpful for individuals at all levels of functioning; the techniques need to be tailored in frequency and intensity to match the needs of the child or adolescent. Early intervention is very important, and services often need to be intensive and continuous throughout the school year. It is important for parents to be involved in all aspects of the therapeutic process. Because of the high degree of stress that family members often experience, family therapy can be of considerable help.

Medication

Numerous medication interventions have been used in the treatment of ASD. Unfortunately, the core symptoms of the disorder, such as deficits in social and emotional reciprocity, do not tend to respond to medication interventions. Medication treatment generally focuses on the psychiatric symptoms that are often associated with ASD, especially when other disorders (e.g., bipolar mood disorder, major depression, ADHD, obsessive-compulsive disorder) are also present. For example, antidepressants such as the SSRI medications, the dual serotonin and norepinephrine reuptake inhibitor venlafaxine (Effexor), and the serotinergic and noradrenergic medication mirtazapine (Remeron) have shown promise in the treatment of symptoms such as irritability, hyperactivity, depression, insomnia, obsessive-compulsive symptoms, and repetitive behaviors. Buspirone (Buspar) may be prescribed for anxiety, and clonidine, guanfacine, atomoxetine, and stimulant medications may be used for ADHD symptoms. Mood stabilizers and atypical antipsychotics are also frequently prescribed.

As children and adolescents who have ASD often have multiple psychiatric symptoms, it is essential to monitor for the side effects of medications (e.g., stimulants for ADHD) that may exacerbate coexisting symptoms (e.g., obsessive-compulsive symptoms). Many students who have ASD are on multiple psychiatric medications, and educators can be very helpful in providing feedback about the effects and side effects of these medications.

FOR DISCUSSION

VIGNETTE: Susan

Susan is a 6-year-old student who has been demonstrating socialization difficulties since kindergarten. She avoids eye contact, has difficulty maintaining conversations with others, and has problems interpreting her peers' nonverbal communication (e.g., gestures, facial expressions). She has some hypersensitivity to noises, lighting (especially fluorescent lighting), and the texture of her clothing. She has some unusual movements including flapping her hands when excited and tiptoe walking on occasion. Her grades are good, but her teacher is concerned about Susan's social difficulties, as she is at risk for teasing and ridicule by peers. A special education evaluation was done to see if she qualified for the Autism Spectrum Disorder (ASD) category, but her problems were not severe enough.

REFLECTION QUESTIONS

What do you think the next steps should be to address her at-risk status? Who should be involved in the discussions? What interventions would assist her in overcoming her difficulties? What would be her teacher's role in this process?

CHAPTER 9

Psychotic Disorders

PSYCHOSIS IS A TERM THAT DESCRIBES STATES OF MIND IN which an individual's thoughts and emotions are not in touch with reality. Psychotic symptoms include hallucinations and delusions.

SYMPTOMS OF PSYCHOSIS

Hallucinations are generally visual or auditory. Tactile (felt on the skin), olfactory, and gustatory (taste) hallucinations may occur, but are more often related to underlying medical or neurological problems or are the effects of drugs. Hallucinations are perceived as actual sights, sounds, smells, tastes, or touches. For example, if someone has an auditory hallucination, it is as if someone were in the room talking to him. It should be noted that some children and adolescents experience brief hallucinations, generally under stress, that do not lead to a psychotic disorder. They may manifest, for example, as hearing one's name being called.

Delusions are beliefs that are firmly held despite rational evidence to the contrary. They may be delusions of reference, in which the individual interprets cues from the environment (e.g., television commercials) as having specific personal significance. Paranoid delusions are fixed beliefs that one is being followed, monitored, plotted against, and so on. Grandiose delusions are beliefs that one has special powers, has godlike qualities, and so on. Other types of delusions are beliefs that one's mind is being read, that one can read other people's minds, that one's thoughts are being controlled, that one's body has been severely altered, and such. Individuals who suffer from delusions cannot be talked out of their beliefs with rational explanations that present evidence to the contrary.

The classic disorder in which psychotic symptoms are present is schizophrenia. This disorder generally begins in the late teens or early 20s and is uncommon in childhood. It affects approximately 1% of the general population. Only about 4% of the total number of cases of schizophrenia occur at the age of 15 years or under, and less than 1% of the total occur prior to the age of 10 years (Remschmidt, Schulz, Martin, Warnke, & Trott, 1994). When it does occur in childhood or adolescence, it tends to have a more severe course than schizophrenia that begins in adulthood. Prior to its onset, children who have schizophrenia tend to have disabilities in social, motor, and language functioning and a higher risk for learning disabilities and conduct-disordered behavior. Children and adolescents who have schizophrenia generally have difficulty carrying out routine activities of daily living.

Symptoms of schizophrenia may include delusions, hallucinations, disorganized speech, grossly disorganized behavior, and negative symptoms, which are lack of emotions, lack of normal speech production, and lack of motivation. Prior to the onset of psychotic symptoms, individuals who have schizophrenia generally have a history of problems with self-care, interpersonal relationships, and work or school.

Schizophrenia and the other disorders that have prominent psychotic symptoms are severely debilitating conditions that have a markedly adverse impact on all levels of functioning, including academic performance in the school environment.

MANIFESTATIONS OF PSYCHOTIC DISORDERS IN THE CLASSROOM

In general, psychotic symptoms are so disabling as to make it obvious to others that the person who is experiencing them clearly has some sort of mental health problem. Prior to the development of the full-fledged psychotic symptoms seen in schizophrenia, symptoms of disorganization, social withdrawal, poor hygiene, and possibly bizarre behaviors may be noticed in the classroom.

Once psychotic symptoms appear, even more deterioration of functioning takes place. A student who is actively hallucinating may appear to be listening to a voice. He or she may verbally respond to auditory hallucinations, appearing to be talking to himself or herself. Thought processes may be significantly altered, and the student may speak incoherently. He or she may stop speaking in the middle of a sentence due to thought blocking. A student who is experiencing delusions may talk about them and may describe paranoid fears of being plotted against, of being watched, of mind control, and so on.

Younger children who are experiencing psychotic symptoms may not have the verbal skills to describe their inner experiences, but may instead manifest symptoms through bizarre or inappropriate behaviors that are a significant change from their previous mental state. If the psychotic symptoms are due to the student experiencing the extremes of a mood disorder (e.g., psychotic mania or depression), then the psychotic symptoms would be observable in the context of the symptoms of the mood disorder. For example, a person experiencing mania can develop grandiose delusions, and severe depression might lead to a psychotic delusion that one is suffering from a terrible disease when none actually exists.

Psychotic symptoms due to drugs of abuse may include hallucinations, such as those caused by LSD. Drugs such as amphetamines and cannabis can lead to significant paranoia. Amphetamines and cocaine can cause tactile hallucinations called formication (the term is taken from the formic acid produced by ants) in which the individual feels as if bugs are crawling under his or her skin. Phencyclidine (PCP or angel dust) can cause hallucinations and paranoia as well as violent behavior. Psychotic symptoms caused by drug abuse may appear indistinguishable from symptoms stemming from psychiatric disorders such as schizophrenia.

TREATMENT OF PSYCHOTIC DISORDERS

Treatment of psychotic symptoms first requires a careful diagnostic assessment to clarify the underlying reason for the symptoms. If they are due to use of a drug such as cannabis, the focus of intervention needs to be on discontinuation of that drug. In many instances, the psychotic symptoms will remit if the drug use is stopped. In some situations, the abused drug triggers the manifestation of a chronic psychotic disorder that will require ongoing treatment. Similarly, if the culprit is a medication that is causing psychotic side effects, the medication should be switched to a different one whenever possible. If the psychotic symptoms are the result of a mood disorder, treatment of the mood disorder with antidepressants, mood stabilizers and possibly antipsychotic medication, depending on the type of mood disorder, should take place.

In the case of childhood or adolescent schizophrenia, antipsychotic medication is the treatment of choice. Supportive psychotherapeutic interventions for the patient and for family members are also helpful, but psychotherapy alone is not effective in stopping the severe psychotic symptoms of schizophrenia.

FOR DISCUSSION

VIGNETTE: Michael

Michael is a 17-year-old high school senior who has had deterioration in his grades for the past year. He has also begun to isolate himself from peers, has had difficulty maintaining his physical hygiene, and has been observed talking to himself in the school hallways. When he was seen by his school social worker, he told her that he believed that he was being followed, that someone was reading his mind and controlling his thoughts, and that there was a conspiracy to kill him. He said that he wasn't worried about his safety, because he had a gun that was given to him by his grandfather. He denied any immediate plan to harm himself or others. The school social worker reported this information to Michael's parents, but their response was that he was just a "weird kid" and would outgrow the problem. They were not interested in getting a mental health diagnostic evaluation. They also refused a special education evaluation for him.

REFLECTION QUESTIONS

What should the next step be? Should child protective services be called, and are they likely to open a case for medical neglect? Should the school suggest that he be on a homebound schedule? Should the school try again to communicate their concerns to the parents, this time possibly with the assistance of a psychiatric consultant? What options should be considered, and which school staff should be involved? What should his teachers do in the meantime, as Michael continues to be in school?

CHAPTER 10

Violent Behaviors across the Spectrum of Mental Health Disorders

VIOLENCE COMMITTED BY YOUTH IN SCHOOL AND COMMUNITY settings is a real but very rare risk. It is far more likely for youth to be victims of violence. One in five victims of serious violent crime are between the ages of 12 and 17. Youth aged 12–17 years are three times as likely as adults to be victims of simple assault and twice as likely to be victims of serious violent crimes. About 1 in 20 high-school seniors say they have been injured with a weapon in the past year. And almost one in seven say someone has injured them on purpose without a weapon.

Some youth do, however, engage in violence. About one in nine murders are committed by youth under 18 years old. On average, about five youths are arrested for murder in this country each day. Youth under 18 years old account for about one in six violent crime arrests. Between 30–40% of male teens and 16–32% of female teens say they have committed a serious violent offense by the age of 17 years. With respect to gun access, almost 1 in 20 high school students say they have carried a gun in the past month and almost 1 in 4 teens report having easy access to guns at home.

Despite dramatic mass media accounts of violence at school, it is not prevalent in most areas, though it does exist. Almost 1 in 14 students (and more than 1 in 10 male students) said they had carried a weapon to school in the past month. More than 1 in 13 students said they had been threatened or injured with a weapon such as a gun, knife, or club on school property in the past year. However, less than 1% of all violent deaths of school-aged children and teens occur in or around school grounds or on the way to and from school.

The earlier the age of onset of antisocial behaviors, the more severe they tend to be and the more likely that they will persist into adulthood. Interestingly, 45–69% of violent girls were violent in childhood. Teens who were engaged in serious violence before 13 years of age generally commit more crimes, and more serious crimes, than those teens who start later. They are also more likely to continue to engage in violence into adulthood. Still, only about 20% of all seriously violent teens continue to commit violent acts as adults.

Violence risk factors for youth under 13 years of age are: early involvement in serious criminal behavior, early substance use, being male, a history of physical aggression toward others, low parent education levels or poverty, and parent involvement in illegal activities. Risk factors for youth over age 13 years are friendships with antisocial or delinquent peers, membership in a gang, and involvement in other criminal activity. Overall, multiple factors contribute to and shape antisocial behavior over the course of development. Many of these are within the social environment. Peers, family, school, community, and neighborhood contexts shape, enable and maintain antisocial behavior, aggression, and related behavior problems.

THE RELATIONSHIP BETWEEN VIOLENT BEHAVIORS AND MENTAL HEALTH DISORDERS

In general, mental health disorders do not raise the risk of aggression. The vast majority of people who are violent do not have psychiatric disorders, and the vast majority of people who have psychiatric disorders are not violent.

Exceptions include individuals who have paranoid delusions and those who have agitated bipolar mood disorder. Highly impulsive conduct-disordered youth who have ADHD are at increased risk, as are youth who are abusing substances such as alcohol and PCP. Youth with conduct problems plus a mental health disorder such as ADHD, depression, or anxiety disorders are more likely to engage in aggression than youth who only have conduct problems.

TREATMENT OF VIOLENCE AND AGGRESSION

When aggression is a chronic component of a mental health disorder, treatment tends to be longer, more intensive and to have poorer outcomes. When clinical factors are at the root of the problem, (e.g., irritability and agitation stemming from bipolar mood disorder), then clinical interventions that may include medication management are the treatment of choice. Medication management ideally is specifically focused on the nature of the mental health disorder, and typically, it would utilize stimulants, antidepressants, mood stabilizers, antianxiety medications or antipsychotics in the treatment of underlying pathology.

Some clinical disorders (e.g., autism spectrum disorders, phobias) are also treated with behavioral interventions, and these interventions are generally more effective with violence stemming from behavioral factors.

Proactively addressing youth's mental health problems through collaborative efforts can improve behaviors, reduce the risk of violence and, reduce costs. Specifically, co-locating mental health services from a community mental health clinic at the school can enhance treatment effectiveness.

Many aggressive youth have simply not yet learned the skills of self-management and self-control, and have not learned prosocial alternatives to aggressive behavior. They can benefit from skills training, including learning mindfulness techniques such as those taught in curriculums such as the MindUP program (Dikel, 2015).

FOR DISCUSSION

VIGNETTE: Tony

Tony is a 17-year-old student who has a long history of unusual behavior at school. He sits by himself in the lunchroom and is never observed socializing with peers. Peers have called him a "weirdo," and tend to avoid contact with him. He rarely talks in class. He gets average grades. One day, his history teacher saw a picture of a handgun, a shotgun and an automatic weapon that Tony had drawn in class. Tony was then seen by the school social worker, and said, "sometimes I just feel like shooting someone.". He made no specific threat to harm any individual. The school's police liaison officer was called, and Tony became angry and agitated. He was brought to the local hospital's emergency room and was subsequently hospitalized for one week on the psychiatric unit. Prior to his discharge, his parents were contacted by the school social worker hoping to gain information about Tony's diagnosis, his treatment plan, and his potential needs for additional school services. Tony's parents refused to share any information with school staff and refused to sign a release of information that would allow communication between the school and the hospital staff. Several teachers and students expressed fears that Tony was potentially dangerous, and the principal received several phone calls requesting that Tony not be permitted to return to school.

REFLECTION QUESTIONS

Does the school have the right to refuse to allow Tony to return to school, given the lack of information about his mental status and potential danger to others? Should homebound services be offered as an alternative plan? What should school administrators do if Tony's parents demand that Tony return to school and continue to refuse to share mental health information including danger assessments with school staff?

PART III

The Diagnosis and Treatment of Child and Adolescent Psychiatric Disorders

CHAPTER 11

The Professionals Who Diagnose and Treat Mental Health Disorders

MANY DIFFERENT TYPES OF PROFESSIONALS TREAT CHILD and adolescent mental health disorders. It is important to understand the background, training, and expertise of these clinicians in order to be effective participants in the treatment process.

Sadly, since up to 80% of children and adolescents who have mental health disorders receive no treatment, "No one" is the correct answer to the question, "Who is treating most children and adolescents who have psychiatric disorders?" Thus, the odds that a psychiatrically disturbed child or adolescent in a classroom will be receiving no treatment are as high as four out of five. However, there are trained individuals in several professions who do work successfully with children with disorders.

THE ROLE OF PRIMARY CARE PROVIDERS

Of the children and adolescents who are receiving treatment, approximately 70% are never seen by a mental health professional trained in the diagnosis and treatment of mental health disorders. Instead, they are treated by primary care professionals, mostly primary care physicians, and other types of primary care professionals who provide direct treatment such as advance practice registered nurses (APRNs) and physician's assistants.

APRNs have postgraduate clinical training, expanding their expertise and scope of practice beyond that of a registered nurse. Nurse practitioners are APRNs who have postgraduate training (master's or doctoral degrees) in medical treatment, giving them the expertise to diagnose and treat physical and mental health disorders. Physician's assistants have 2 to 3 years of training in the diagnosis and treatment of medical disorders and provide medical and mental health treatment in coordination with a physician.

Although primary care professionals are providing the majority of mental health treatment, many of them have minimal training in mental health diagnosis and treatment. The problem is compounded by the fact that visits to primary care professionals tend to be brief and do not allow the amount of time necessary to address complex emotional and behavioral difficulties. As Table 12.1 describes further, time should be taken to cover all of the essential possibilities of diagnosis through interviews with parents and the child or adolescent and through collection of corroborative information from teachers.

As there are no laboratory tests that confirm the diagnosis of mental health disorders, it is all the more important to be thorough in assessing them in other ways. Brief diagnostic assessments and periodic brief medication management appointments by primary care physicians may be sufficient for straightforward, obvious, and uncomplicated problems such as moderate ADHD in a child who is in a well-functioning family and who has no other significant mental health issues. However, this model is insufficient for children or adolescents who have multiple problems, complex disorders, major life stresses, family dysfunction, social difficulties, academic concerns, or significant behavioral problems. Unfortunately, child mental health referral resources for primary care clinicians are scarce to nonexistent in many parts of the country. It takes more time to diagnose and treat a child or adolescent than an adult, as there is a need to gather information from parents as well as other professionals (e.g., teachers, county social workers, corrections officers). This extra time is not reflected in reimbursement rates, and many clinicians are at an economic disadvantage treating children and adolescents despite their additional training in working with this population. This issue is a major contributor to the dearth of child clinicians across the United States.

THE ROLE OF SCHOOL PROFESSIONALS

Educators can play a vital role in assisting the process of diagnosis and treatment of students in their classes. They can work with school staff to document observations of students' behaviors and, with parents' permission, communicate this information to a medical professional for use in the diagnostic process.

If a student is receiving treatment but is continuing to have symptoms of emotional and behavioral problems, educators can help communicate this information as well. Unfortunately, educators cannot assume that their students are always diagnosed accurately and provided the optimal mental health treatments. If care is being provided by primary care professionals, and if no treatment other than medication management is being provided, then there is an even greater need for educators to be vigilant regarding the possible need to communicate problems to parents and treating professionals.

Psychiatrists

Child and adolescent psychiatrists are physicians who have completed 4 years of medical school and at least 3 years of residency training in medicine, neurology, and general psychiatry and an additional 2 years of specialized training in working with children, adolescents, and their families. They receive comprehensive medical training in medical school and in their internships, followed by comprehensive training in the nature of child, adolescent, and adult mental health disorders and their treatment. They have an extensive working knowledge of all aspects of mental health, including biological, genetic, developmental, psychological, social, educational, and family components. They have intensive training in childhood mental health disorders including autism spectrum disorders, ADHD, developmental disabilities, learning disabilities, anxiety disorders, psychotic disorders, mood disorders, substance use disorders, and behavioral disorders. Their medical training assists them in accurately assessing medical contributions to mental health difficulties and in prescribing medications when appropriate. Child and adolescent psychiatrists often work in a variety of settings and may consult with schools, social service agencies, corrections departments, and medical and mental health professionals.

Child psychiatry services are scarce in the United States. Approximately 7000 child psychiatrists are practicing, with an overall ratio of approximately 9 per 100,000 youths. Their practices are not distributed evenly, and children and adolescents in rural areas and in areas of low socioeconomic status have even greater difficulty accessing services. General (adult) psychiatrists attend medical school for 4 years, followed by 4 years of psychiatric residency, which includes training in medicine, neurology, and general psychiatry. They receive some exposure to child psychiatry but do not have anywhere near the intensive training in child and adolescent issues that child and adolescent psychiatrists do.

Because of the shortage of child and adolescent psychiatrists, some general psychiatrists treat adolescents, and some even treat young children. They generally have a greater overall knowledge of child and adolescent mental health problems than do primary care physicians. Both general and child and adolescent psychiatrists are trained in a wide variety of interventions including medication management, as well as various types of individual and family therapy. However, many psychiatrists have become increasingly specialized in the practice of doing diagnostic evaluations for the purpose of determining whether medication is warranted and then primarily in providing psychiatric medication to patients who could benefit from this intervention.

Clinical Nurse Specialists

Clinical nurse specialists are APRNs who have master's- or doctorate-level training in a specific field. Psychiatric clinical nurse specialists have training focused on delivering care to patients who have psychiatric disorders. Their work is generally coordinated with a treating psychiatrist.

Psychologists

There are many different types of psychologists, each of which has its own training and practice components. Not all psychologists are mental health professionals who can diagnose and treat clients who have mental health disorders. Those who do diagnose and treat may have significant differences in the scope of their training, especially in regard to expertise with children and adolescents.

Doctoral-level clinical psychologists have training that includes a 4-

year undergraduate degree plus up to 7 years of training in a doctoral program. Doctoral programs tend to be either PhD programs, which often have a
strong focus on research, and PsyD programs, which tend to emphasize clinical treatment. Licensure requires training, clinical supervision, and passing
an examination. Clinical psychologist training includes an understanding of
development, behavior, cultural factors, personality, diagnosis, psychological
assessment, psychopathology, and psychotherapy.

Master's-level psychologists' training is generally 2 to 3 years following an undergraduate degree. Depending on state statutes, master's-level psychologists may be licensed to diagnose and treat patients. Some may practice
as licensed professional counselors, licensed psychological associates, or mar-
riage and family therapists. Clinical psychologists may provide a large variety of services including psychotherapy, administering psychological testing,
teaching, and consulting. They may specialize in specific disorders (e.g., mood
disorders, anxiety disorders) or age groups (e.g., children and adolescents, or
the geriatric population).

Counseling psychology is a field of psychology in which practitioners
facilitate personal and interpersonal functioning with a focus on emotional,
social, educational, vocational, health-related, and developmental concerns.
Counseling psychology activities overlap with those of clinical psychology. In
general, counseling psychologists work with clients who are not experiencing
the severe level of dysfunction of clients seen by clinical psychologists.

School psychologists are trained in both education and psychology
and complete a minimum of a specialist-level degree program of at least 60
graduate semester hours. Training focuses on issues such as mental health and
educational interventions, behavioral issues, child development, assessment,
learning theory, instruction and curriculum issues, consultation, and school
law. They require state certification or licensure. They have expertise in the
nature of the educational process, including the identification of learning disabilities, effectiveness of teaching methods, instructional design, classroom
management, and the design of educational interventions including classroom
accommodations and modifications. School psychologists play a wide variety
of roles, depending on their school district and even on the school in which
they work. In some districts, school psychologists spend the bulk of their time
conducting special education evaluations, whereas in others their work may

be varied, including the provision of counseling to students, assessing barriers to learning, consulting with educational teams, providing in-service presentations for teachers and other school staff, and working with parents to enhance coordination and collaboration with school staff activities. They may design behavioral and academic interventions, assist in monitoring student progress, design effective classroom interventions, design prevention programs, and coordinate with community services.

Some school psychologists have clinical training and licensure that would allow them to provide diagnostic and treatment services to children and adolescents. In general, school psychologists provide counseling, not therapy, to students who have mental health problems that are affecting their educational progress. Whereas school psychologists tend to provide direct services within schools, educational psychologists tend to be research based. They study issues such as instructional design, curriculum development, classroom management, educational technology, and organizational learning.

Neuropsychologists focus on analysis of brain functioning as it relates to specific behaviors and psychological processes. They work with patients who have sustained neurological damage (e.g., traumatic head injuries, strokes) and with individuals who have mental health disorders that have neurological underpinnings (e.g., ADHD). They can provide in-depth neuropsychological testing that assesses brain functioning with much more specificity than do the typical intelligence and achievement tests administered by school psychologists. Some neuropsychologists are also licensed to do clinical work as well.

Other types of psychologists work in academia, doing research in various fields or providing consultation to systems such as government or private industry. These include developmental, experimental, industrial or organizational, and social psychologists.

Social Workers

Just as there are several kinds of psychologists, the field of social work encompasses a wide variety of professionals who have different types of expertise and practice. A clinician with a bachelor's degree in social work (BA, BSc, BSSW, BSW) generally provides services under the supervision of a licensed social worker who has a master's degree (MSW). Social workers may provide case management services, counseling, psychotherapy, teaching, or administrative activities.

Training for a master's degree generally requires 2 years of graduate study combined with 2 years of a field practicum experience. Most social workers go into the clinical practice training track, focusing on direct practice with clients, but some go into a macro practice track that focuses on systems work such as policy analysis and human services management. Some programs have combined tracks. Clinical training focuses on issues of human development, diversity, diagnosis and assessment, psychotherapy and clinical practice, communication, the therapeutic relationship, professional ethics, consultation, and clinical practice.

There are different levels of licensure for social work practice. The types vary by state, but include terms such as licensed baccalaureate social worker, licensed social worker, certified master social worker, licensed advanced social worker, licensed graduate social worker, licensed independent social worker, and licensed independent clinical social worker. School social workers provide both direct services (e.g., assessments, counseling, community liaison, skills training) and indirect services (e.g., case management, consultation, care coordination, advocacy) for students. Most states require a master's degree for school social work licensure, but a small number also license bachelor's-level social workers.

Social workers who have adequate training and supervision based on state licensure rules are eligible to practice as mental health professionals, providing diagnostic and treatment services to their clients. Some school districts utilize them to provide these services and may also bill Medicaid for IEP-related mental health services for some special education students. Other districts do not sanction this, due to concerns about data privacy, malpractice coverage, crisis coverage, and role definitions. They define the school social worker's role as one of providing counseling rather than therapy services.

CHAPTER 12

Comprehensive Mental Health Evaluations

AS MENTAL HEALTH DISORDERS ARE COMMON IN CHILDREN and adolescents, chances are that every classroom in America's K–12 schools has at least one student who has a mental health disorder, either treated or, more likely, untreated. When students have been diagnosed and are receiving treatment, educator involvement may range from minimal (when the parents do not reveal their child's mental health issues) to extensive (including symptom monitoring, symptom documentation, communication with physicians and parents, and providing accommodations and modifications). Educators may have access to students' mental health diagnostic records, if there is a need to know this information, and if the parent has signed a release of information allowing school professionals to access it. The educator may also learn about the student's mental health history in discussions with the parents. For these reasons, it is helpful for educators to understand the nature of the diagnostic process.

The components of a mental health evaluation address the child or adolescent's history as well as documenting symptoms experienced at the time of the assessment. The majority of mental health services in the United States are provided by primary care clinicians, many of whom have limited training in making diagnoses, as noted in the previous chapter. Their evaluations may not be comprehensive, and some children and adolescents may not receive the correct diagnosis. Teachers and other school staff can be helpful to clinicians by providing crucial information, both during the diagnostic process and after treatment has been initiated.

If school staff are concerned that a child has not been diagnosed correctly, they can communicate to the clinician, with a signed parental information release, outlining the behaviors noted in the classroom that do not reflect the behaviors that would be expected to be present if the diagnosis were correct. For example, if a teacher had never observed a student to have a history of distractibility, short attention span, or impulsivity, and if the teacher had not been contacted as part of the diagnostic process, communication about the lack of symptoms would provide valuable information to a physician who had recently diagnosed the student as having ADHD. Teachers can provide information about the student's educational history that is very helpful in clarifying diagnostic issues. Also, feedback from teachers to treating clinicians can provide crucial information about the effectiveness of treatment, once it has begun.

The field of mental health is hampered by the lack of medical tests that could diagnose psychiatric disorders. Although there is compelling research evidence of a biological basis of many psychiatric disorders, the research tools are not refined to the point that they can be used as diagnostic tools. The National Institute of Mental Health Research Domain Criteria project is exploring the underlying common roots between depression and other mental health disorders, in an attempt to identify how and where in the brain illnesses start before symptoms develop. This research will ideally lead to biological markers of mental health disorders similar to those used in the rest of medicine. However, as there are no laboratory tests at this time that can confirm psychiatric diagnoses, it is essential that mental health diagnostic evaluations be thorough and comprehensive, in order to ensure that the diagnoses that are made are accurate. Otherwise, treatment will not be effective.

Thus, the process of making a correct psychiatric diagnosis requires a comprehensive evaluation. A mental health diagnostic evaluation can be performed by a professional such as a clinical social worker, psychologist, or psychiatrist. Medical professionals (physicians, physician's assistants, nurse practitioners, and clinical nurse specialists) also do diagnostic assessments and have the potential to do comprehensive assessments as well. The same basic format is recommended for all of these professions in their textbooks and training. Unfortunately, this is not always practiced in the field.

A psychological evaluation may include psychological testing, but the testing should be used in addition to the evaluation protocol described in this chapter and should never be used by itself as a basis for mental health diagnosis. Psychological testing may include cognitive assessments that determine academic abilities or achievement levels, using tests such as the Wechsler Intelligence Scale for Children (WISC) and the Woodcock-Johnson Tests of Achievement. Neuropsychological testing can assess more specific aspects of brain functioning such as memory, language, visuospatial abilities, and executive functioning abilities. Other psychological tests (e.g., MMPI, TAT, Rorschach) can assess personality and can identify evidence of mental health disorders. Test results may be useful in generating hypotheses for diagnosis but do not result in diagnoses in themselves. A number of disorders have no valid or reliable tests that can diagnose them (e.g., ADHD). Computerized performance tests have such a high degree of false positives and false negatives that their use in the clinical evaluation process is not recommended. Tests such as the MMPI generally have both false negatives and false positives that can inappropriately suggest either normalcy when a diagnosis is present, or suggest a diagnosis when none is present. Some projective personality tests (e.g., the Rorschach "ink blot" test) can be very subjective in their interpretation and may have poor reliability and validity. Psychological testing alone cannot be used to make a comprehensive mental health diagnosis. Unfortunately, it is not a rare occurrence for psychological testing to be the sole report in a psychological evaluation.

A psychiatric evaluation is an evaluation conducted by a psychiatrist. A psychiatrist has medical training, and has specialized skills in addressing medical, neurological, and medication issues. The psychiatric evaluation also needs to address all of the areas within the outline below, and it may address medical contributors to the individual's psychiatric symptoms and may focus on medications presently prescribed. It may also outline a medication intervention plan for the patient.

Given the comorbidity (commonly seen multiple diagnoses when a diagnosis such as depression or ADHD is present) of mental health disorders, it is inappropriate to conduct "an ADHD assessment" or a "depression assessment." If there is a focus on ruling in or ruling out only one disorder, then other disorders may be missed and treatment will be ineffective. All assessments should be comprehensive. It is not uncommon for children and adolescents to have multiple diagnoses, and if only one is identified, treatment may be not only inadequate but actually harmful. For example, a child who has ADHD and obsessive-compulsive disorder who is given a stimulant medication for ADHD might experience significant worsening of obsessions and compulsions as a medication side effect. The cornerstone of effective mental health treatment is a comprehensive and thorough diagnostic evaluation. When this is not done, the diagnostic process can result in misdiagnosis, underdiagnosis, and over-diagnosis, which can lead to lack of treatment or expensive and inappropriate treatments and failed outcomes.

The only way that a valid and reliable mental health diagnosis can be made is through clearly established diagnostic criteria, both to rule in the diagnosis that the individual has and to rule out diagnoses that are not present. If a diagnostic evaluation report does not clarify that the individual has these criteria and has no evidence of the presence or absence of criteria that would suggest other diagnoses, then the report should be suspect. Criteria in children and adolescents are best identified through both a clinical interview with them and through collection of corroborative information from teachers, parents, and other caregivers. Abundant research indicates that an evaluation involving only the child or adolescent is likely to miss a significant amount of data and may result in an inaccurate or incomplete diagnosis (e.g., oppositional defiant disorder) when other disorders (e.g., learning disabilities, ADHD, depression, PTSD) that may have contributed to or caused the behavior problems are missed. Many youths do not have the self-monitoring ability to recognize symptoms of disorders such as the inattentiveness and disorganization of ADHD, and corroborative information from other sources is essential.

COMPONENTS OF A COMPREHENSIVE MENTAL HEALTH EVALUATION

The format for a mental health diagnostic evaluation includes the following elements:

Social History

A social history reviews the types of stressors that an individual may have experienced over the years. These stressors, if present, may contribute to or even cause the mental health symptoms that the patient is experiencing. For example, an individual who has no history of mental health symptoms, who experienced a rapid onset of symptoms of anxiety shortly after being molested, would most likely be experiencing PTSD. Another individual who is experiencing significant anxiety attacks with no history of major stressors would likely be experiencing panic disorder, which has a strong endogenous (internal) biological component.

Items to review on the social history begin at the child or adolescent's conception. For example, if the mother's pregnancy was unplanned or even unwanted, this fact may have created ongoing stress in the family over the years. A history of domestic violence has major negative repercussions for the child and other family members. Domestic violence is harmful when a child is the victim of child abuse, as well as when a child witnesses domestic abuse perpetrated on others (e.g., witnessing one parent attacking the other). Sexual abuse and physical abuse can have lifelong negative impacts and can contribute to symptoms of anxiety, depression, attachment difficulties, inappropriate sexual behaviors, and difficulty with anger management. It is important to clarify whether the child or adolescent has a history of involvement with the child protection system and whether social services is involved at the time of the assessment. It is important to clarify, if possible, if either parent has a history of mental health or substance use difficulties that may have adversely impacted the child. A history of out-of-home placement in foster care or residential placement is an important factor to identify. Financial problems and bankruptcy add to family stress and can trigger anxiety. Other life stressors include a history of multiple moves, major health problems experienced by family members, and loss of major attachment figures (e.g., death of a parent or grandparent). If a social history is not gathered as part of the assessment, valuable diagnostic information may be missed.

Medical History

Medical issues can play a major role in contributing to or causing mental health symptoms, and a review of a child or adolescent's medical history is crucial in making a correct diagnosis. The medical history begins in the prenatal period and should include questions about the mother's medical problems (e.g., gestational diabetes, preeclampsia, poor weight gain) and their treatment during pregnancy. It is important to clarify whether the mother used drugs, alcohol, or tobacco during the pregnancy, as these substances can have significant effects on the developing fetus and can contribute to cognitive and emotional difficulties during childhood and adolescence. Problems with labor and delivery can contribute to oxygen deprivation and subsequent neurological development. A developmental history should be obtained to clarify whether the child or adolescent has had delays in speech and language or in fine or gross motor development. A history of head injuries, loss of consciousness, or seizures can contribute to mental health symptoms. It is essential to clarify whether there is a history of major medical disorders or surgeries and to ask about ongoing medical or neurological disorders and about whether the child or adolescent is taking medication on an ongoing basis. Both the disorders and the medications may have a contributory role in the mental health symptoms that are being evaluated.

Educational History

As mental health disorders can contribute to educational difficulties, and as learning disabilities can lead to mental health symptomatology, it is essential to review a child or adolescent's educational history in the process of conducting a diagnostic evaluation. It is important to ask about academic performance, both at the present time and in the past, and to clarify whether problems are chronic or whether they had their onset later in childhood. Chronic problems are more suggestive of learning disabilities, whereas the sudden onset of educational difficulties in the context of a recent life stressor or the development of a mental health disorder such as depression suggests a primary mental health causal factor. It is important to ask whether the child or adolescent is receiving special education services and, if so, the type of services (e.g., for learning disabilities, speech and language, emotional disorders) and the intensity of services, ranked as follows:

TABLE 12.1 Settings for Special Education Services

SETTING 1	special education outside regular class less than 21% of day
SETTING 2	special education outside regular class at least 21% of day and no more than 60% of day
SETTING 3	special education outside the regular classroom more than 60% of the day
SETTING 4	special education services at separate school facilities for more than 50% of the day
SETTING 5	special education services at a private, separate day school for more than 50% of the day
SETTING 6	public residential treatment facility
SETTING 7	private residential treatment facility
SETTING 8	homebound or hospital setting

Mental Health History

It is of course necessary to review the child or adolescent's history of involvement with mental health services in order to clarify the nature and types of diagnoses made, when the diagnoses were made, and by whom. It is important to ask about the types of treatment provided in the past, including individual psychotherapy, family therapy, medication management, and so on. If medications have been used, it is important to clarify their types and dosages, their effectiveness, and whether any major side effects may have caused the medications to be discontinued. The intensity of previous mental health services (e.g., outpatient, day treatment, residential treatment, psychiatric hospitalization) and the effectiveness of various treatments should be documented. If parents do not recall the details of these interventions, it is important to request a release of information so that treatment records can be obtained to clarify these issues.

Family History

There are two reasons why it is important for a diagnostician to ask about a history of mental health disorders in family members (parents, grandparents, uncles, aunts, and siblings). First, since there is a strong genetic component in many mental health disorders (e.g., autism spectrum disorder, ADHD, bipolar mood disorder, schizophrenia), a strong family history of one of these disorders would add to the likelihood that the child or adolescent has the disorder if symptoms were also present that suggested the diagnosis. Second, the child or adolescent may have developed adjustment-related mental health symptoms as a result of experiencing the relative's symptoms. For example, a child whose parent has severe obsessive-compulsive disorder and a germ phobia might be required to wash his or her hands multiple times per day. This behavior would not necessarily indicate that the child has obsessive-compulsive disorder but rather may result from the parent's demands. A child whose mother had a severe postpartum depression may have experienced a lack of nurturance, leading to attachment difficulties. A child whose sibling experiences severe mood swings and violent outbursts may have been traumatized by the sibling's behavior, possibly to the point of developing PTSD. Thus, both the genetic and the environmental influences of a family mental health history can contribute to child and adolescent mental health disorders.

Substance Use History

For adolescents and older children, screening for substance use problems should also be a part of a mental health diagnostic evaluation. Although it may sound shocking, adolescents who have substance use disorders frequently report that their use began at 9 or 10 years of age. The use of drugs or alcohol can produce symptoms suggestive of psychiatric disorders, during both the intoxication and withdrawal phases. If drug abuse is not identified, then there is a high risk of misdiagnosis and the initiation of treatments that not only will be ineffective but may be harmful as well. When there is evidence of mental health problems in an individual who is using drugs or alcohol, the diagnostician needs to recognize the various potential causes of the problem. The first possibility is that the individual has a significant mental health disorder and is self-medicating to try to relieve the mental health symptoms. For example, a person who has severe social phobia may drink alcohol in order to be able to go to a social gathering. The core problem is the anxiety, which, if treated effectively, will no longer prevent the person from socializing without alcohol. The second possibility is that the individual does not have an underlying mental health problem, and that the core problem is a substance use disorder. Drugs and alcohol can produce many mental health symptoms. For example, alcohol is a depressant, and chronic users may appear to be suffering from depression when in fact they would not be depressed if they were to stop drinking. Amphetamines can cause agitation and paranoia. Cannabis can cause significant cognitive problems, paranoia, and a pervasive lack of motivation (amotivational syndrome). Individuals whose core problem is due to substance use need treatment for that problem and will generally experience a clearing of psychiatric symptoms over time as a result. The third possibility is that the individual has a dual diagnosis. In other words, both a mental health disorder and a substance use disorder are present simultaneously. In this situation, treating only one problem or the other will not be effective. Both disorders need to be treated simultaneously, and with a unified, integrated approach.

It is often easier to clarify these distinctions in adults than in children and adolescents. For example, if an adult has a history of untreated depression that lasted several years, followed by self-medication with alcohol, it would be clear that the depressive symptoms did not arise solely from alcohol use. It may be difficult to determine whether a child or adolescent had a preexisting mental health disorder due to the early age of onset of the substance use issues. An adolescent may have a genetic predisposition to a mental health disorder that is triggered by drug use (e.g., the abuse of marijuana triggering a psychotic disorder that does not clear when the drug use is discontinued). It is better to err on the side of dual diagnosis than to initiate treatment for only a part of a complex problem that requires dual diagnosis–integrated treatment. Children and adolescents who use drugs or alcohol often do not tend to be forthcoming about their use. They may deny use or significantly minimize it. It is important that the diagnostician be able to establish rapport and trust in order to maximize self-disclosure.

Children and adolescents may be more willing to answer a question about whether their friends use. If the response is in the affirmative, this is a significant red flag suggesting that they use as well. Various screening tools (e.g., PESQ, CRAFFT, POSIT) can help identify evidence of a problem and provide a foundation of information for a more in-depth substance use assessment. Questions about whether individuals have ridden in a car with someone who had been using, whether they have used alone, whether they previously felt better about themselves, whether they have gotten into trouble as a result of their use, or whether they have been told that they should cut down on their use will shed light on the nature and extent of the problem. The substance use section of a mental health diagnostic evaluation report should indicate that screening questions were asked (with corroborative information obtained by parents and possibly teachers) and, if there was evidence of a problem, that a more in-depth inquiry took place. The report needs to indicate the severity of a substance use disorder, if present.

If mental health symptoms are also noted, the report, if possible, should clarify whether the symptoms stem from the drug or alcohol use, whether they led to the use, or whether they coexist with the use. The treatment plan needs to indicate whether substance use treatment is indicated, and whether it needs to be provided in an integrated manner with dual diagnosis interventions for the mental health disorders that coexist with the drug or alcohol problem.

Mental Status Exam

Just as medical evaluations include a physical examination, mental health evaluations need to include a mental status examination. By reviewing various emotional and cognitive functions, it is possible to identify signs and symptoms that lead to a mental health diagnosis. A mental status examination begins with a description of the patient's appearance and behavior. This would include the patient's grooming (well-groomed versus poor personal hygiene), activity level (hyperactive, normal, slowed down), and whether unusual mannerisms or nervous tics are observed. Patients who suffer from anxiety disorders or ADHD might have psychomotor hyperactivity, whereas depressed patients would be more likely to have psychomotor retardation. Psychotic patients may have unusual mannerisms, called stereotypic behaviors. Side effects of some medications such as antipsychotics can cause movement disorders. Speech and language are assessed, with a focus on the clarity, coherence, and fluency of the speech and the rate, rhythm, and tone of the speech. Unclear speech, or speech that is not fluent or that is incoherent, can suggest neurological problems or intoxication. Rapid speech suggests anxiety, mania, or intoxication, and slow speech may be seen in depressive states. Abnormal speech rhythms may have a neurological basis, and abnormal tone (monotonous, strident, agitated) can indicate underlying psychiatric or neurological problems.

Mood and affect are assessed during the diagnostic process. Mood is the person's underlying emotional state, which can range from severe depression, to a normal, "euthymic" mood, to states of highly agitated mania. A patient may also have an anxious mood or may have a lack of emotional symptoms that would reflect normal processes (e.g., feeling no emotion following a traumatic event). Affect refers to the physical expression of one's mood. A flat affect refers to unresponsive facial expressions, suggesting no emotion being experienced. Mood and affect can be congruent (e.g., a patient who is crying while feeling depressed) or incongruent (a patient who is smiling while describing clearly painful emotional experiences). Mood and affect can be stable, or can be very labile (rapidly changing).

Thought processes are the ways that one's cognitive processes manifest themselves. Examples of abnormal thought processes include loose associations in which thoughts are barely connected or are unconnected from each other, flight of ideas, in which there are rapid switches from topic to topic, and thought blocking, in which the patient cannot complete a thought and will stop talking in the middle of a sentence as a result. Loose associations are commonly seen in psychotic disorders and mania, flight of ideas is frequently seen in mania, and thought blocking may be seen in depression.

Abnormal thought content could include delusions, manifested in psychotic disorders, in which the patient has a fixed belief that is unchanging despite evidence to the contrary. Delusions can include paranoid delusions, in which the patient believes he or she is in danger of attack, or delusions of reference, in which the patient believes that he or she is receiving special messages through television, billboards, and such. They include delusions of thoughts being inserted into or removed from the patient's brain, thought control by others, delusions of grandeur in which the person believes that he or she has special powers or is much better than the rest of humanity, somatic delusions (such as not having a heart), and so on. Hallucinations can be listed under abnormalities of thought content and refer to sensory experiences (i.e., auditory, visual, olfactory, tactile, gustatory) that are not associated with any external source of stimulation. Hallucinations that stem from mental health psychotic disorders tend to be auditory or visual, whereas the other types of hallucinations suggest an organic origin. Tactile hallucinations can suggest medical disorders (e.g., diabetes) and evidence of drug abuse (e.g., the sensation of bugs crawling under the skin experienced by some amphetamine or cocaine addicts). Brain tumors can lead to olfactory hallucinations. It is important to identify evidence of suicidal or homicidal thoughts, which are clearly evidence of abnormal thought content.

Cognition is addressed in the mental status examination either informally or by the use of standardized questions. It is important to clarify whether the patient is alert or is displaying evidence of a lack of alertness. Orientation to person, place, and time (e.g., whether the person knows who and where he is, the day and date), need to be assessed. Level of general knowledge, ability to use abstract thinking, judgment ability, and insight are also assessed. Short-term memory can be assessed by having the patient repeat three words, and then be asked 5 minutes later to repeat them again. Depending on his or her age, the patient may be asked to name objects, to repeat phrases, to read words on a page, to copy a drawing of a simple object, to spell a word backward, or to follow a multiple-step command.

Thus, a normal mental status exam would be reported as follows: "The patient was well groomed and had a normal level of psychomotor activity. No unusual mannerisms or tics were noted. Speech was clear, coherent, and fluent, and of normal rate, rhythm, and tone. Mood was euthymic, and affect was congruent with mood. Thought processes were goal directed, and there was no evidence of loose associations, flight of ideas, or blocking. Thought content revealed no evidence of hallucinations, delusions, or thoughts of harming self or others. Cognition showed the patient to be alert and oriented to person, place, and time, with good general knowledge, good use of abstractions, good judgment, and good insight."

DIAGNOSTIC CRITERIA

Mental health diagnoses are made based on diagnostic criteria. These criteria include the symptoms of the disorders, the length of time that symptoms have been present, and exclusionary factors that would indicate that another disorder is more likely. For example, the diagnosis of a major depressive episode requires the presence of five of nine symptoms: depressed mood (or irritable mood for children or adolescents), loss of interest or pleasure, decreased or increased appetite, insomnia or hypersomnia, being physically agitated or slowed down, loss of energy, feelings of worthlessness or guilt, difficulty concentrating, and recurrent thoughts of death. The symptoms need to have been present during at least a 2-week period and need to represent a change from previous functioning. The symptoms cannot be due to a medical condition or due to the effects of medications or intoxicants.

Criteria are chosen to have maximum statistical sensitivity (i.e., to identify the maximum number of individuals who have the disorder) and specificity (i.e., to not identify individuals who do not have the disorder). Some criteria of mental health disorders refer to the individual's experience of symptoms, whereas others refer to symptoms observed by others. A mental health evaluation needs to include the criteria that are used to make a diagnosis. Thus, major depression cannot be diagnosed based solely on psychological testing or on the judgment of the diagnostician who believes that the patient is depressed. The criteria are crucial to making the diagnosis, and treatment success can be measured based on the resolution of these symptoms.

Further, a diagnostic evaluation report should indicate that criteria of other disorders were reviewed and the symptoms were found not to be present. For example, the report may note, "There was no evidence of symptoms of mania, psychosis, anxiety disorders, or conduct disorder." This documents that potentially comorbid conditions were considered but found not to be present.

THE DIAGNOSTIC EVALUATION REPORT

The report has several components based on the evaluation of the student, described above.

Presentation of the Evaluation Results

The diagnostic assessment thus far has included medical, social, educational, mental health, and family histories, review of criteria to rule in and rule out mental health disorders, and a thorough mental status examination. Information has ideally been gathered from the patient as well as from teachers and parents, and possibly others (e.g., county social worker, probation officer, if applicable). The report should also outline information obtained from other reports that were reviewed in the process of conducting the evaluation, including educational records, mental health diagnostic and treatment records, child protection reports, corrections records, and so on. At this point, there may be ample information to make a diagnosis. Otherwise, further testing may be indicated. Psychological testing may be helpful in clarifying issues such as cognitive deficits, presence of learning disabilities, evidence of personality disorders, and so forth. A neurological evaluation may be necessary in order to rule out neurological disorders that manifest as psychiatric symptoms (e.g., absence seizures that appear to be attention deficits).

Treatment Plan and Recommendations

Finally, a diagnostic evaluation report should include a plan of treatment, based on the patient's diagnosis, the frequency, severity, and chronicity of symptoms, and the context in which symptoms manifest. A plan includes mental health treatments (e.g., medication management; individual, group, or family therapy; skills training) as well as services that are needed from other systems (e.g., social services, corrections, education). The education component of the treatment plan may include recommendations for a special education evaluation or, if the child or adolescent is already receiving special education services, recommendations for additional accommodations and modifications may be included in the report.

A mental health professional cannot dictate special education eligibility or mandate accommodations and modifications. Recommendations need to be reviewed by the educational team, at the parents' request. Mental health professionals may or may not be familiar with school issues such as special education eligibility or appropriate accommodations and modifications for students who have mental health disorders. They may mistakenly believe that they can dictate educational interventions for students based on their diagnostic assessment. It is important for clinicians to recognize that service decisions are based on team activities and that clinicians' input is useful but is not the final word regarding necessary interventions. The treatment plan may also include information regarding the timelines of interventions and their expected results. For example, if an antidepressant medication is prescribed, the plan may indicate that weeks may pass before a clinical response is noted. This information can be very helpful to parents, teachers, and other professionals who are working with the child or adolescent.

Thus, a comprehensive mental health evaluation is similar to other health care evaluations, as it reviews all pertinent historical information, evaluates the mental health status of the patient, reviews corroborative information from a variety of sources, reaches diagnostic conclusions, and outlines a treatment plan. This then creates the foundation upon which effective treatment can take place.

CHAPTER 13

Overview of Psychotherapy for Children and Adolescents

MANY TYPES OF PSYCHOTHERAPY ARE USED WITH CHILDREN and adolescents. They may be used alone, in combination with other types of psychotherapy, or in combination with psychiatric medication treatment. Research has indicated a significant positive effect of psychotherapy for a wide variety of child and adolescent mental health disorders.

Mental health services can broadly be defined as being either counseling or therapy. Counseling is the process of providing information, improving skills, and assisting a student in succeeding within the school environment. Counseling is routinely done by school social workers, psychologists, nurses, and counselors. Therapy is a clinical service that constitutes treatment of a disorder; for example, the treatment of clinical depression (Dikel, 2013). This chapter describes the most commonly used therapy types and illustrates how they relate to school interventions.

Therapies can be subdivided into behavioral and nonbehavioral interventions. Behavioral treatments include cognitive-behavioral therapy (CBT), an intervention that assists individuals in self-monitoring their thoughts and emotions. Another type of behavioral intervention involves teaching parents how to manage their child's behavioral outbursts. Nonbehavioral approaches include talk therapies that focus on psychodynamic methods (addressing conscious and unconscious thoughts and emotions), group therapies, and client-centered groups. Behavioral interventions have been studied to a much greater degree than nonbehavioral ones and may have greater efficacy overall.

It should be noted that there is considerable overlap between behavioral and nonbehavioral interventions. In addition to treatments that focus on the child or adolescent, some treatments focus on the family (family therapy) or on larger systems (multisystemic therapy).

COGNITIVE-BEHAVIORAL THERAPY

Cognitive-Behavioral Therapy (CBT) focuses on identifying and changing a person's thoughts (cognitions) as a method of ultimately changing emotions, coping mechanisms, and behaviors. It addresses dysfunctional thought patterns such as overgeneralizing (making broad assumptions about one's specific circumstances), catastrophizing (viewing one's situation as much worse than it actually is), and magnifying the negatives while minimizing the positives in one's life. CBT helps an individual to learn and practice more adaptive methods of dealing with his or her thoughts, emotions, and behaviors.

CBT merges aspects of behavioral therapies such as exposure therapy (as in gradually exposing a phobic patient to the feared circumstance until the phobia is tolerable) and cognitive therapies that focus on altering dysfunctional cognitions (thought processes). CBT requires the therapist and client to set specific, measurable goals and to be able to measure outcomes accurately. This is a problem-focused treatment that addresses specific problems in an action-oriented manner. It is a here-and-now approach that does not dwell on or revisit past experiences. The approach also analyzes and addresses the function of maladaptive behaviors, in order to make positive changes.

Families are often involved in CBT interventions with their children. The process of therapy starts with the identification and assessment of the presenting problem. This is followed by psychoeducational information about the problem (its symptoms and the treatment plan that will be used to address the symptoms). The next phase involves learning and utilizing the treatment strategies that provide symptom relief. Finally, techniques are taught that maintain positive goals and prevent relapses. Various studies have noted efficacy in treating children and adolescents who have problems ranging from depression to eating disorders and anxiety disorders.

CBT can be adapted for younger children through the use of puppet scenarios and play therapy. CBT can address maladaptive behaviors within the classroom and therapists can work with teachers and other school staff to identify problem areas noted within the school environment. For example, if a student struggles with anxiety in social situations to the point that he or she is unwilling to speak in class, CBT can be used to assist the student in overcoming this difficulty.

DIALECTICAL BEHAVIOR THERAPY

Dialectical behavior therapy (DBT) is similar to CBT and can be useful in treating adolescents who engage in self-injurious behaviors or who have chronic suicidal thoughts. This therapy helps patients find better methods of dealing with interpersonal conflicts and with their own negative emotional experiences. This therapy is focused on enhancing coping skills and in identifying healthy methods of dealing with life stresses.

INTERPERSONAL PSYCHOTHERAPY

Interpersonal psychotherapy (IPT) is a brief, time-limited therapeutic technique that was initially developed to treat adult depression, but that has been adapted to treat adolescents as well. IPT focuses on the quality of interpersonal relationships, as these relationships can suffer as a result of an individual's depression. This can create a vicious cycle, as deteriorating relationships can then worsen one's mood even more. The goal of IPT is to decrease depressive symptoms by focusing on current interpersonal difficulties and helping the individual improve his or her relationships and interpersonal interactions. IPT teaches individuals how to improve their interpersonal skills and to effectively resolve relationship problems. IPT has well-established evidence of treatment efficacy. Techniques used in IPT include identifying specific problem areas, practicing interpersonal problem-solving strategies in the therapeutic session, and then using these strategies in real life. IPT addresses conflicts in relationships, problems dealing with changes in relationships and life circumstances, social isolation, and grief following the loss of a loved one. IPT can have positive effects in the classroom when the therapy focuses on relationship difficulties with a teacher or classmates.

FAMILY THERAPY

Family therapy, like interpersonal psychotherapy, focuses on human behavior and psychiatric disturbances in the context of interpersonal relationships. Therapy focuses on relationships within the family system, rather than on individuals, and is based on observations that mental health symptoms appear in individuals involved in dysfunctional family relationships and that healthy functioning can stem from positive family interactions. Family therapy explores the family's interactions and dynamics, seeks to mobilize the family's strengths, restructures maladaptive interaction patterns, and strengthens the family's ability to solve problems. Family therapy emphasizes that family relationships are an important factor in one's emotional functioning and that improving family dynamics can result in improvements in a family member's mental health symptoms. For example, family therapy can be helpful in treating a child or adolescent who has ADHD, by reducing the family conflicts and stresses triggered by the condition, helping build the youth's self-esteem, and teaching the parents how to enhance their child's social skills, improve behaviors, and improve the ability to remain on task. This ultimately helps the child or adolescent within the classroom environment.

MULTISYSTEMIC THERAPY

Multisystemic therapy (MST) was developed to treat adolescents who have conduct disorder by addressing multiple systems (e.g., family, individual, peer, school, community) to teach effective parenting skills and to improve the adolescent's coping skills. It focuses on emotional strength-building in order to enhance protective factors. This is an intensive community-based and family-focused intervention that can be an alternative to residential placement. Treatment may take place in the home, in school, and in the community.

MST is focused on accentuating individual and family strengths, holding youths and family members responsible for their behaviors, identifying and targeting the sequences of behaviors that maintain behavior problems, addressing present situations rather than dwelling on past events, maintaining continuous effort toward reaching goals, addressing problems in the context of the youth's developmental level, providing ongoing outcome evaluation, and building strengths to maintain and generalize the skills that are learned. Although this treatment is intensive (multiple therapists, 24-7 availability), it is ultimately significantly less expensive and more successful than the out-of-home residential placement that would be the alternative intervention.

PSYCHODYNAMIC PSYCHOTHERAPY

Psychodynamic psychotherapy is an offshoot of traditional psychoanalytic therapy and is based on the theory that conflicts that are not consciously recognized by an individual can lead to significant mental health symptoms. The goal of treatment is symptom improvement resulting from addressing these unconscious conflicts. Psychodynamic psychotherapy with adults emphasizes the need to address unconscious intrapsychic conflicts and a patient's defense mechanisms. Insight is important for successful therapy. Therapy may focus on childhood traumas and their resulting impact on the patient's emotional functioning. Therapy with children and adolescents also addresses underlying issues that influence thoughts, feelings, and behaviors, and identifies and addresses the responses to these inner struggles. The therapy is geared to the child or adolescent's developmental level.

PLAY THERAPY

Play therapy is especially useful with younger children who have difficulty verbalizing their emotions. It may involve toys, games, dolls, puppets, drawings, or other play interventions that help a child recognize and deal with emotional conflicts.

GROUP THERAPY

Group therapy refers to any type of therapy (e.g., social skills, substance abuse, psychodynamic) that is provided by one or more therapists to multiple patients simultaneously. The group dynamic can be a very powerful therapeutic device, as the children or adolescents in the group tend to have similar problems and are able to support each other within the therapeutic process.

OPTIMAL DELIVERY OF SERVICES

It is increasingly apparent that traditional mental health approaches are clearly inadequate for a large segment of the population of seriously emotionally disturbed children and adolescents. Thus, innovative collaborative programs between community mental health programs and school districts and schools are slowly being developed to increase the delivery of mental health services to youth who need them, as well as provide supports to their families.

The collaboration model integrates services from providers inside and outside of the school system. In some states, schools can bill Medicaid for IEP services such as skills training and skills practicing. These activities are generally considered consistent with schools' mandates. Schools can partner with community providers, splitting the therapy and skills-training roles between them (Dikel, 2012).

One example of such a program is the Child and Adolescent Service System Program (CASSP) model of services described by Schlenger, Etheridge, Hansen, and Fairbank (1992; cited in Dikel, Bailey, & Sanders, 1994). It emphasizes coordination of services among all professionals (special education, mental health, social services, corrections, etc.) that deal with these children and adolescents. This model also emphasizes intermediate and adjunctive services such as day treatment, respite care, family support, and community support.

Anderson (1976; cited in Dikel et al., 1994) described another comprehensive model of community mental health–school collaboration that moves in the direction of systems change, with a strong focus on prevention. Lastly, see Dikel et al., 1994, for a description of an effective comprehensive collaborative program in a Minnesota county.

Unfortunately, despite these and other advances in the area of community mental health–school collaboration, the vast majority of public schools are not involved in these types of collaborative programs and are required to educate disturbed students without having adequate funds and backup from community social services and mental health agencies.

CHAPTER 14

Rational Use of Psychiatric Medications

PSYCHIATRIC SYMPTOMS (E.G., ANXIETY, DEPRESSION, INAT-tention) can stem from a variety of factors and medication, possibly along with other types of treatment, can be useful in ameliorating them. Some symptoms, however, are caused by factors that make medication ineffective, or even harmful, and thus a comprehensive evaluation of an individual is necessary to determine the efficacy of medication.

SYMPTOMS THAT DO NOT REQUIRE MEDICATION

Adjustment-related symptoms comprise a symptom category that is not based on medical problems, but is due to a natural reaction to toxic emotional events in the environment. For example, a child or adolescent living in an abusive environment, experiencing poverty, homelessness, domestic abuse, or other severe stresses, would be very likely to experience negative emotions of fear or anxiety. Resolving these symptoms involves effectively addressing the underlying causes of stress, and medicating such a problem without attention to its causes can perpetuate it. It is therefore important for mental health professionals to obtain a good social history as part of the diagnostic process in order to identify stressors that are causing an individual's difficulties. Otherwise, medication may be inappropriately prescribed when other interventions are indicated. Except for specialized circumstances in which a brief course of medication may help an individual cope in a crisis, it is not appropriate to treat adjustment-related stress reactions with medication, in my opinion.

Under situations of severe stress, medication may be used temporarily (e.g., to assist sleep) but would not be considered the primary treatment of choice.

Another category of symptoms that do not warrant a medicinal response results from underlying medical disorders (e.g., depressive symptoms due to postviral syndromes), from medication side effects (e.g., hyperactivity secondary to asthma medication) or from drugs or environmental toxins (e.g., anxiety from caffeine use, depression from alcohol use, or cognitive problems stemming from lead in the environment). In addition, low thyroid functioning can cause symptoms of depression, whereas hyperthyroidism can cause significant anxiety. Absence seizures can be mistaken for the inattention seen in ADHD. Sleep apnea, not uncommon in overweight children, can cause daytime sleepiness and inattention. Poor nutrition and vitamin deficiency states can also result in mental health abnormalities. Individuals who have psychiatric symptoms should therefore have comprehensive physical examinations and laboratory testing to rule out these possibilities. The treatment of these symptoms is directed at the underlying medical issue, and psychiatric medication would not be the treatment of choice and might actually add to the problem.

Psychiatric side effects are common for a wide variety of medications, including medications used to treat psychiatric disorders. For example, steroids, commonly used to treat asthma, can produce depression or mood swings. Asthma medications such as terbutaline can cause agitation that could be mistaken for the hyperactivity of ADHD. Stimulants used to treat ADHD can cause symptoms of anxiety, compulsive behaviors, and even severe depression. Antipsychotics can cause agitation, lethargy, and significant cognitive difficulties.

Toxins and intoxicants can also produce psychiatric symptoms. Lead poisoning can cause significant cognitive problems including inattention. New research indicates that some children are sensitive to artificial colorings, which can trigger ADHD symptoms. Caffeine can cause agitation and anxiety, and caffeine withdrawal can lead to lethargy, inattention, and headaches. Alcohol, cannabis, and other drugs can cause psychiatric symptoms in both the intoxication and withdrawal stages.

A careful medical history should be part of every mental health diagnostic evaluation in order to identify potential medical causes of psychiatric symptoms. Clearly, the treatment of choice is to treat the underlying medical

disorder, to switch medications causing side effects if possible, and to eliminate toxins rather than to add psychiatric medications to the problem. The use
of psychiatric medications to treat adjustment disorders, or to treat symptoms
arising from undiagnosed medical disorders, medication side effects, or the
effects of toxins can lead to significant worsening of a patient's condition. This
is known as an iatrogenic effect, namely the worsening of a patient's condition
resulting from medical interventions.

SYMPTOMS THAT CAN IMPROVE WITH MEDICATION

Another category of disorders that can cause psychiatric symptoms is
also medical, but at this time we do not have laboratory tests or other objective
medical procedures to diagnose them. Psychiatric medications are intended
to treat biologically based disorders that produce psychiatric symptomatology. Research indicates that the major psychiatric disorders experienced by
children, adolescents, and adults (e.g., schizophrenia, bipolar disorder, major
depression, autism spectrum disorder, ADHD, obsessive-compulsive disorder, panic disorder) have a biological basis. All of these disorders have ample
evidence of an underlying medical basis, with research indicating abnormalities in areas such as brain functioning, neurotransmitter activity, and hor-
mone metabolism. To date, the research findings are not sensitive or specific
enough to translate into medical diagnostic tests, but it is only a matter of
time until this occurs. It is clear, however, that the term "mental illness" is
a misnomer for the major psychiatric disorders, as these disorders are just as
medical as diabetes, coronary heart disease, or arthritis. As no cures have yet
been identified for these disorders, medication is used, ideally in conjunction
with psychotherapeutic interventions and parent education, to treat the target symptoms of the disorders. Target symptoms are the manifestation of the
patient's underlying psychopathology. They are similar to the criteria used to
diagnose the psychiatric disorder. They are targeted for treatment, with the
goal of eliminating or reducing them. The use of target symptoms in the evaluation of the effectiveness of treatment assists medical and school professionals in the process of symptom monitoring, adjustment of medication dosage,
monitoring for medication side effects, and outcome analysis.

Typical target symptoms include the frequency and severity of off-task behaviors and hyperactivity (for ADHD), repetitive compulsive behaviors (for obsessive-compulsive disorder), the presence of hallucinations or delusions (for schizophrenia), and symptoms of sleep, appetite, concentration, energy, and mood abnormalities (in major depression). Unfortunately, some psychiatric medications are prescribed without any focus on specific symptoms. This results in difficulty monitoring for medication effects and the possibility of inappropriate use of medication. The rational use of psychiatric medications is based on using medication to treat medical disorders. It is unfortunate that some of the major psychiatric disorders share the same language as normal states of emotional experience.

For example, feeling depressed as a result of unfortunate life circumstances is a normal emotion. It is far removed from the experience of major depression, in which an individual may have severe disruption in sleep, appetite, energy level, ability to concentrate, and so on. Many people experience normal everyday anxiety, and some anxiety can actually be helpful in spurring us on to finish tasks, to avoid dangerous situations, and such. Everyday anxiety is in no way similar to the anxiety experienced by individuals who have panic disorder, when panic attacks bring on overwhelming anxiety and leave the individual shaken and feeling frightened about a recurrence of the attacks. This can lead to agoraphobia, with avoidance of public places to the point that many people with this disorder become housebound. It is important for individuals who have these types of psychiatric disorders to recognize that they are experiencing medical disorders and that treatment of the disorders with medication can relieve symptoms and significantly improve functioning.

Some of these disorders, especially in their milder forms, can effectively be treated with psychotherapy alone. However, if problems are severe enough and not responding to therapy, then medication is a reasonable intervention. Many individuals who have mental health disorders, or parents of children who do, are reluctant to consider medication because they believe it to be a crutch. It is important for them to understand that they would not have the same opinion about antihypertensive medications, epilepsy medications, or insulin.

Medication for this category of disorders works to varying degrees, depending on the type of disorder being treated. In some disorders, such as major depression or panic disorder, symptoms can completely clear up and return the individual to a completely normal level of functioning. Other disorders tend not to respond to medication with a complete clearing of symptoms. For example, most patients being treated for severe obsessive-compulsive disorder have a reduction in symptoms, but generally do not have complete remission of their disorder. Continuing to raise the dose of medications beyond the optimal dose has the potential for creating significant medication side effects. In other disorders such as autism, there are no medications that can effectively treat the core symptoms such as poor social skills or lack of empathy, but medication can still be helpful in treating associated symptoms of mood, anxiety, or attention.

When multiple medications are used, or when patients have complex assortments of multiple disorders, medication interventions need to be done with great care. For example, a child with autism spectrum disorder may have a positive response of attentional symptoms to a stimulant medication used for ADHD, but the medication may worsen the child's obsessive-compulsive symptoms. Treating depressive symptoms with an antidepressant in an individual who has bipolar mood disorder may trigger a manic episode.

The rational use of medication dictates great caution in initiating medications, raising dosages, adding other medications, and switching from one medication to another. It is important to have reasonable expectations of medication response and to use the lowest effective dose of medication. It is also important to have objective measurements of baseline symptoms and of improvement as a function of treatment response. Educators can be a vital link in the process of diagnosis and treatment monitoring.

Psychiatric medication management ideally involves feedback from the patient, his or her parents, and school staff. School feedback is very useful if the student's disorder significantly impacts educational issues, if medication side effects are observed by school staff, if the disorder manifests differently at home or at school, or if parents have difficulty being objective about medication response.

School staff can be very helpful in the process of medication initiation and dosage adjustment by monitoring the nature and extent of target symptoms that manifest in the school environment. If information releases are obtained, school staff can communicate with physicians on an ongoing basis as necessary in order to assist the rational use of medications. If school staff are not involved in this process, inappropriate medication use can result. At times, psychiatric symptoms are more prominent at school than at home (e.g., ADHD). Parents may not be able to adequately detect the ongoing residual symptoms manifested in the school environment after a low dose of medication is initiated, and the student may remain on a subtherapeutic dose as a result. In other circumstances, a parent may not have an objective view of the child's problem and may overreport pathology. This is not unusual, for example, if a parent has significant untreated depression. School feedback is essential to avoid overmedication or other inappropriate medication interventions.

Even when information releases are sent to physicians, school staff do not always receive diagnostic or treatment information or requests for symptom monitoring. School staff can take the lead in symptom monitoring and communication with physicians. This requires clear role definitions, monitoring of paperwork, use of appropriate rating forms, and staff accountability. When this is done effectively, medication treatment tends to be significantly more effective, resulting in improved academic performance and decreased behavioral difficulties.

Teachers and parents can provide valuable information to the child's clinician regarding the nature and degree of symptoms noted prior to treatment and as a result of medication interventions. Unfortunately, in some circumstances feedback is not objective but is adversely influenced by bias or other factors. This can result in the overreporting or underreporting of symptoms. For example, research indicates that depressed parents, whose depression makes coping very difficult for them, have the tendency to overreport behavioral problems in their children. In some situations, a child with normal behavior may be brought to a physician and started on medication based on the parent's report of out-of-control behavior. The diagnostic process should include information obtained from teachers as well as parents, in order to obtain an accurate picture of the nature, extent, and severity of symptoms.

Unfortunately, this is not always the case. If parents are willing to sign a release of information allowing communication with the child's prescriber, it would be appropriate for the teacher or other school staff (e. g., counselor, social worker, psychologist) to communicate with the prescriber and to document the presence or lack of symptoms noted prior to the initiation of medication. A small percentage of teachers are very biased against the use of psychiatric medication in children and adolescents and may fill out questionnaires in a way that minimizes the child's problems. Also, a small percentage of teachers may overemphasize a child's problems, when the real problem may be a chaotic, overcrowded classroom filled with numerous disruptive students. Only by gathering information from a variety of sources can an objective assessment of a child or adolescent's mental health be made.

Even when reports about a child or adolescent's behavior are accurate, they may vary based on the type of diagnosis and the context in which the child was observed. Some disorders manifest differently in different settings. For example, a child who has ADHD may demonstrate severe problems with on-task behavior, hyperactivity, and impulsivity in the school environment, where there are demands to sit still and focus, and numerous distractions are present. The same child may have significantly less severe difficulties at home, where there are fewer demands for on-task behavior and may be low activity levels. Unless parents and teachers appreciate that the disparity in reports is due to the nature of the disorder, the disagreement in symptom ratings can lead to mistrust and negative judgments. For example, the parents may feel that the teacher is not competent and is thus reporting problems that are absent in the home environment. Meanwhile, the teacher may believe that the parents are underreporting serious behavior problems in the home environment. It is essential to avoid these misunderstandings in order for parents and teachers to work effectively with each other. Education about the nature of these disorders and their manifestations in different environments is the key to understanding.

The rational use of psychiatric medication also requires the awareness that, even though many psychiatric disorders are biologically based, nonmedication interventions may be effective. Research indicates that psychotherapeutic interventions not only can relieve symptoms of many disorders but also may improve the biological abnormalities in brain functioning associated with psychiatric disorders. For less severe psychiatric symptoms, different types of psychotherapy may be quite effective. Psychotherapeutic interventions take more time to initiate and sustain but may have longer lasting effectiveness in some clinical situations.

In summary, if psychiatric medications are to be used, clinicians should ensure that they have made a correct diagnosis, that feedback from teachers and parents is valid and accurate, and that information about potential medication side effects is communicated to the parents. It is essential to communicate to parents about reasonable expectations of medication response and to obtain feedback about medication response from the patient, the parents, and teachers. The lowest effective dose of medication should be used, and polypharmacy approaches (the use of multiple medications) should be used only when it is clear that a single medication does not work effectively. It is important not to change more than one variable at a time (e.g., don't change two medications simultaneously, or don't start a new medication at the same time that a student has a new school placement) in order to assess the reasons for problems, should they arise. Dosage changes should be based on the mechanism of action of medication. For example, a stimulant medication for ADHD tends to demonstrate immediate effects, whereas an antidepressant may take up to 8 weeks to be effective.

When psychiatric medications are used judiciously to treat disabling symptoms of psychiatric disorders, they can produce significant improvements resulting in reduced suffering, improved family functioning, improved academic achievement, and a reduction in behavioral difficulties in the educational environment. Educators can play a vital role in assisting in this process.

GUIDING PRINCIPLES OF CHILD AND ADOLESCENT PSYCHOPHARMACOLOGY

Melvin Lewis, in *Lewis's Child and Adolescent Psychiatry: A Comprehensive Textbook* (Martin, Volkmar, & Lewis, 2007) describes seven guiding principles for the use of psychiatric medication in children and adolescents, as follows:

• Development has a major impact on the metabolism of medications, and responses to medications may be significantly different between child and adult patients. Children may metabolize medication more quickly than adults and may need a higher weight-adjusted dose as a result.
• Child and adolescent disorders do not fit neatly into the categories devised in the DSM framework, and there is a high degree of co-occurrence

of multiple disorders in many patients. For example, tic disorders often coexist with obsessive-compulsive disorder and ADHD often coexists with autism spectrum disorders, and these co-occurring disorders do not necessarily respond to medication as well as they do when they occur separately.

• It is important to obtain information from multiple informants (the patient, parents, and teachers) and to define specific symptoms that are being targeted for treatment.

• It is essential to provide ongoing monitoring for potential medication side effects, especially given the expanded role of new medications such as atypical antipsychotics.

• Prescribers' questions about medication response and potential side effects can be a mixture of open-ended and specific questions regarding the medication that is being prescribed.

• Family members need to be well informed about medications and need to be active partners in the treatment process.

• It is important to recognize that psychotherapeutic interventions can be significantly helpful as adjuncts to medication treatments.

• Whenever possible, medication choices should be made based on evidence-based clinical decision making.

Although there are numerous psychiatric medications, few have been approved by the Food and Drug Administration for use in children. For example, two medications are FDA approved for the treatment of depression in children and adolescents. Fluoxetine (Prozac) is approved for children age 8 years or older, and escitalopram (Lexapro) is approved for children age 12 years and older. Fluoxetine is also FDA-approved to treat obsessive-compulsive disorder in children, as are the antidepressants sertraline (Zoloft), fluvoxamine (Luvox), and clomipramine (Anafranil).

The use of medications for purposes other than those for which they are FDA approved is common, and is called off-label use. For example, a physician may prescribe citalopram (Celexa), a medication approved for a child or adolescent suffering from depression. As a result, teachers may find that their students may be treated with a wide variety of non-FDA-approved medications.

The use of psychiatric medication in children is controversial. Whereas some medications such as stimulants for ADHD have been prescribed for decades, others such as the new atypical antipsychotics are recent pharmacological additions. Thus, no data on possible long-term negative effects of newer medications are available.

The potential risks of medication need to be compared to the potential benefits and to the potential risks of not providing the medication. Some disorders are so severe (e.g., schizophrenia, bipolar mood disorder) and have such disabling symptoms that do not respond to psychotherapy that parents generally feel that medication benefits outweigh their risks. Other disorders may be effectively treated or accommodated without medication. I have been asked numerous times by parents, "Does my child need stimulant medication for ADHD?" The answer is that no child needs the medication as a diabetic child would need insulin. The challenge for physicians and parents is to maintain clear communication about the potential risks and benefits of medication. This ensures that informed consent can take place if medication is to be used.

Psychiatric medications may be used for a variety of treatment interventions. For example, a benzodiazepine medication such as Valium may be effective for reducing anxiety, for insomnia, for treatment of seizure disorders, or for muscle spasms. Antidepressants may treat depression, panic disorder, and obsessive-compulsive disorder, and may even be helpful in pain syndromes. Antipsychotic medications are effective in treating psychotic symptoms of delusions and hallucinations but also can be helpful as mood stabilizers in patients who have bipolar mood disorder. Antiseizure medications treat epilepsy but also can be effective mood stabilizers.

NEUROTRANSMITTERS AND PSYCHIATRIC MEDICATIONS

Psychiatric medications generally have their effect at the level of the neural synapse, which is a structure that permits the passage of chemical or electrical signals from one neuron (the presynaptic neuron) to the other (the postsynaptic neuron). Neurotransmitters are chemicals that pass through the synapse and bind to the postsynaptic neuron, and have either an excitatory or inhibitory action at that site. For example, dopamine is a neurotransmitter that is affected by psychiatric medications. It affects motor behavior (and is deficient in Parkinson's disease), as well as emotional arousal, motivation, the reward system, and pleasure. Serotonin regulates many functions including mood, behavior, cardiovascular and endocrine functioning, sleep, and appetite. Norepinephrine, also known as noradrenaline, affects functions including attention, mood, heart rate, and blood pressure. Areas that produce or that are affected by norepinephrine are called noradrenergic. Agonists bind to cell receptors and trigger the response by the cell, whereas antagonists block the action of the agonists.

Psychiatric medications may have generalized or selective effects on neurotransmitters. They may increase the amount of release of a neurotransmitter at the presynaptic neuron. They may increase the amount of a neurotransmitter in the synapse by inhibiting its reuptake in the synapse. Thus, some antidepressant medications are called selective serotonin reuptake inhibitors because they selectively inhibit the reuptake of the neurotransmitter serotonin in the synapse.

It is beyond the scope of this book to provide a detailed account of the molecular pharmacological details of the mechanisms of action of different psychiatric medications. Interested readers are encouraged to explore this topic in more detail. The mood stabilizers, antidepressants, antipsychotics, and ADHD and antianxiety medications are described in the chapters in Part II on the mental health disorders affecting children and adolescents.

PART IV

School District

and School Policies

and Procedures

CHAPTER 15

The Roles of School Districts, Schools, and Staff

SCHOOL DISTRICTS GENERALLY HAVE CLEARLY DEFINED medical plans for addressing a variety of health disorders. For example, they may have a protocol for working with students who have asthma or diabetes. Unfortunately, it is uncommon for school districts to have a mental health plan that clarifies policies, procedures, and guidelines for working with students who have mental health disorders. For example, staff roles may not be accurately defined, and there may be significant overlaps in some areas and major gaps in others.

Although schools are educational and not clinical settings, staff members are addressing students' mental health problems on a daily basis. The ways in which they address these problems substantially affect students' success in the educational environment. In my work with school districts across the United States, I am impressed by the skills and dedication of teachers, administrators, social workers, psychologists, counselors, nurses, and support staff as they respond to students' mental health needs. I am also disheartened, however, by the lack of an overall mental health plan in most school districts but convinced of the likelihood that there will be improved educational outcomes when a plan is created and implemented. When there is no overall plan that outlines the necessary action steps and that provides accountability to ensure that they will be completed, major gaps in service result. One reason that school districts are often reluctant to address mental health issues is because the Individuals with Disabilities Education Act (IDEA) makes the schools be the payer of last resort for special education–related services including mental health–related services and, in fact, districts have been forced to pay hundreds of thousands of dollars for services such as residential treatment because a hearing officer concluded that the student's mental health needs were "inextricably intertwined" with educational needs.

Nevertheless, districts do need a plan to address students' mental health needs, but there is no single plan suitable for adoption for all of them. Because of the huge variability of school district resources, staff skill sets, community services, student population, and so on, mental health plans need to be tailored to each district and sometimes to each school.

That said, a school district's mental health plan should include the components listed in Box 15.1.

BOX 15.1 Necessary Components for a School or District Mental Health Plan

- A description of the roles and responsibilities of teachers, social workers, psychologists, counselors, nurses, administrators, and other school staff in their work with students who have mental health disorders
- Establishment of methods of supervising, coordinating, and documenting staff activities to ensure accountability and to measure outcomes
- Participation in teams, such as teacher assistance teams and IEP teams
- Provision of skills training for school professionals and in-service presentations about mental health issues
- Serve as a resource about identification and report of child abuse and neglect
- Establishment of protocols for working with families and medical and mental health professionals, with a focus on optimal communication
- Development of methods of gathering and analyzing mental health information (e.g., presence of mental health disorders, types of disorders, whether treatment is being provided, contact information for treatment providers, outcome analysis of educational interventions). Data analysis to include data on both individual

students and groups of students (e.g., what percentage of students who are receiving Emotional Disturbance special education services have been diagnosed with ADHD, depression)

- Development of methods of conducting special education evaluations with students who have mental health disorders, including the use and interpretation of screening tools and of functional behavioral assessments
- Effective use of the clinical-behavioral spectrum concepts (see Chapter 2 above)
- Provision of appropriate accommodations and modifications for students who have mental health disorders
- Identification of evidence of substance use problems
- Establishment of protocols for working with students who have substance use disorders
- Assistance in the development of Individual Education Programs for students with disabilities
- Establishment of protocols for handling and keeping confidential mental health records in school files
- Establishment of procedures for emergency crisis interventions
- Development of seclusion and restraint measures (ideally, methods to eliminate the need for these interventions)
- Establishment of protocols for utilizing psychiatric consultation when there are unanswered questions about diagnosis and medical or medication issues
- Guidelines for establishing co-located, on-site mental health diagnostic and treatment services
- Provision of individual and group counseling
- Administration of medication
- Facilitation of due process procedures
- Maximization of financial reimbursement for mental health services
- Establishment of successful methods of collaboration with external systems (e.g., corrections, social services, public health)
- Regular communication with parents to inform them of their child's problems and successes and to elicit relevant information from them

A mental health plan that is tailored to a school district's needs can be very beneficial to the students, parents, and school staff. I encourage educators to work with administrators and school mental health colleagues to establish policies, procedures, and guidelines in their work with students who have mental health problems. If the district needs help in this process, consultation can be very useful in creating and implementing a school mental health plan.

THE COLLECTION, MAINTENANCE, AND PRIVACY PROTECTION OF RECORDS

The Family Educational Rights and Privacy Act (FERPA) protects most education records by classifying them as confidential and limiting their disclosure. FERPA applies to educational agencies and institutions that receive funds under programs administered by the U.S. Department of Education. The disclosure of students' educational records and the personal identification of information derived from these records cannot be released without the written consent of parents, or of the student if the student is at least 18 years old. Mental health data obtained in school records that was received from a medical or mental health provider would be considered educational records under FERPA, which also applies to mental health data generated by school staff. This includes mental health diagnostic and treatment records generated by school mental health staff in the process of providing IEP mental health–related services.

An exception is desk drawer records, which are kept in the teacher's sole possession and used as a personal memory aid and are not accessed by or revealed to others unless they are a temporary substitute for the maker of the record. These records are strictly defined, with different parameters in different states, and may include such criteria as the requirement that they be destroyed at the end of the school year. Desk drawer records are not protected from disclosure in litigation against school districts. Crucial information about students' mental health status should not go into desk drawer records that are subsequently destroyed.

The Health Insurance Portability and Accountability Act (HIPAA) protects the privacy of health records generated by health plans, health care clearinghouses, and health care providers. HIPAA does not generally apply to mental health data maintained by public school districts. An exception would be a situation in which a school employed a health care provider that electronically billed Medicaid for special education–related services under IDEA.

Some states have additional requirements beyond FERPA regarding the gathering of private information, including mental health information, by school districts. For example, a state may require that the school staff clarify the purpose and intended use of requested data, potential consequences for providing or not providing the data, and the identity of the individuals who will have access to the information. It is important for teachers and other school staff to be aware of federal and state statutes, because they may be required to outline specific issues with parents and document this in writing, in the process of obtaining their child's mental health information. Given the sensitive nature of students' mental health information, it would be best for a student's mental health data to be separated from the rest of the educational record and placed in a sealed envelope within the student's educational file. The envelope should be labeled with a statement indicating that it contains mental health data, and that it should be reviewed only by instructional personnel who have a need to review it as part of their employment duties. Individuals who review the record should document their name, date, and legitimate educational interest for reviewing the information.

In cases of emergency, school staff may need to share a student's mental health information with a third party. For example, if a student is demonstrating an imminent threat of suicide, or of harming others, school staff may have a legal obligation to share this information with third parties such as emergency room personnel, even if the school staff was not able to reach the parents in order to obtain a release of information to do so. If a student transfers to another district, under FERPA the district may be able to forward the student's mental health data in the educational record as long as the mental health data are related to the student's educational needs. It is important for the district staff to be aware of state law, especially in regard to the forwarding of mental health information that was sent to the school by outside medical or mental health providers.

USE OF A CONTRACTUAL RELATIONSHIP FOR MENTAL HEALTH SERVICES

As noted throughout this book, a variety of types of professionals in the employ of school districts and schools provide students with mental health services. There are serious problems, however, with school staff delivery of these services. Among them is the fact that school districts are not likely to be able to obtain malpractice insurance, and their general liability and errors and omissions insurance may not protect them in situations such as a student's suicide, where the clinician is sued for providing inadequate care and the district is sued for providing inadequate clinical supervision. Insurers write policies for school districts based on their understanding of the risks associated with providing traditional programs of education. Insurers may not contemplate a risk based on the negligent provision of mental health treatment services. Further, the records of treatment provided by a school employee do not have the degree of confidentiality as those of mental health professionals in the community; in fact, these treatment records become part of the student's educational record.

Procurement and Use of an On-Site Clinic Contractor

Thus, the ideal method of providing on-site mental health services in a school setting resolves the problems indicated above by the district's leasing of space to a community mental health clinic. The clinic would be the employer of the clinicians and responsible for malpractice insurance, backup crisis coverage, record-keeping, billing, and so on. This keeps the school district "out of the mental health business" of diagnosis and treatment.

The ideal clinic would be one that is overseen by a county or nonprofit agency that has a multidisciplinary team of psychologists, social workers, and psychiatrists, and that can provide services to students and their families during non-school hours when appropriate (e.g., evening appointments for family therapy, summer follow-up appointments for students on vacation).

A "joint powers agreement" between the clinic and the district should be clearly defined from the district's perspective. It should clarify the financial responsibility, accounting, and payment procedures and standards of the participating parties. Further the agreement should serve as a lease of space by indicating a location in a school building convenient to school students (a "colocation" agreement) where the services can be provided.

When the relationship is with a county that has the responsibility to assure accessible mental health services, the agreement should also obtain a guarantee of access to county-funded mental health treatment facilities for IDEA students who require such treatment as a related service. It should also provide for convenient and perhaps guaranteed access to day treatment services for IDEA students who are determined by the county to be eligible to receive them but who do not require them as a related service. Similarly, it should provide for convenient access for non-IDEA students determined by the county to be eligible to receive such services. Other important issues for the district to resolve through the contract include provision by the contractor of criminal background checks for its staff, security and access issues related to the school where services will be delivered, and procedures for ensuring the privacy of data (Dikel & Ratwik, 2009).

FOR DISCUSSION

VIGNETTE: **Mary**

Mary, age 7, is a very hyperactive, impulsive, and distractible student. She is having problems in the classroom as a result. A meeting was held with her parents, who said that they would bring her to a psychologist for an evaluation. The school received the psychologist's report 2 weeks later. The report was essentially a list of tests, and no school feedback had been requested by the psychologist. The psychologist concluded, "Testing does not indicate ADHD. Mary passed the computerized performance test, and thus does not have this disorder."

REFLECTION QUESTIONS

What, if anything, do you think that the district should do at this point?

CHAPTER 16

The Roles of District and School Professionals

WHEN A STUDENT IS EXPERIENCING MENTAL HEALTH PROB-
lems, and when these problems manifest within the school setting, professionals from several disciplines can assist the student in being successful in school.
School psychologists, social workers, counselors, and nurses are the mental
health staff within schools who work with students, their parents, teaching
and administrative staff, and community professionals to design and implement successful interventions. There is a great deal of variability in the roles of
these professionals from district to district and even within a district from
school to school. It is important for educators to understand the specific roles
that these professionals have within their schools. If these roles are not clearly
defined, then educators can bring this concern to school administration in
order to initiate a mental health plan for the school or the district that will
clarify these roles and ensure a seamless system of intervention for
students in need.

There are significant variations in mental health staffing in schools,
with some schools having no social workers, some having minimal nursing
availability, some having no counselors, some having only part-time psychologists, some having deans, and so on. Even when schools are fully staffed, there
are significant variations in the activities of these professionals. A review of
national organization criteria (e.g., National Association of School Psychologists) and of various school districts across the United States provides information about job descriptions of school psychologists, social workers, counselors,
and nurses. There is a large degree of overlap between the professions.

SCHOOL PSYCHOLOGISTS

School psychologists are trained in both psychology and education, with a focus on child development, behavior, learning, curriculum and instruction, psychological assessment, consultation, and collaboration. School psychologists work with parents and educators to assist students in succeeding in the school environment. Their activities include the provision of counseling, instruction, and mentoring for students who have social, emotional, or behavioral problems. They can assist teachers in identifying the best teaching strategies for students who have academic difficulties. They may provide skills training to assist students who have difficulty with issues such as social skills, anger management, problem solving, and self-regulation. School psychologists can identify and describe specific learning difficulties that interfere with school success, assist their multidisciplinary team in determining eligibility for special education services, work with students' parents in coordinating educational activities between the home and school environments, and work collaboratively with community agencies that are serving the students. School psychologists can identify academic barriers to learning and can design interventions that assist students in overcoming these barriers. They can design and implement student progress–monitoring systems and can assist teachers in creating positive classroom environments and in implementing school-wide prevention programs. They can assist schools with creating policies regarding school violence, bullying, and harassment. They can work with community agencies to coordinate services to students and their families and can assist students who are transitioning out of mental health and correctional residential placements.

Despite this full range of potential activities, it is unfortunate that in many school districts, school psychologists spend most of their time conducting educational assessments for special education evaluations. It is ironic that some of these evaluations would not have been necessary had the school psychologist been able to assist the process of helping the student receive mental health treatment. Often, the referral for a special education evaluation is due to untreated or inappropriately treated symptoms of mental health disorders.

SCHOOL SOCIAL WORKERS

The job description of school social workers may include the provision of counseling to students and parents, including individual and group counseling and individual and group skills training activities. Social workers can assist in the provision of psychosocial assessments and in the evaluation of students' behavioral difficulties; can make recommendations for environmental manipulations in the school, the home, or the community; and can be involved in case conferences with school and community agencies. They may serve as a liaison between the school, the family, and community agencies. They maintain appropriate records, provide written reports and communications, and can assist with in-service presentation planning activities. They participate in the multidisciplinary special education team, assisting the Individualized Education Program (IEP) process and assisting the team in determining eligibility for special education and in designing appropriate accommodations and modifications. They may facilitate due process procedures to ensure that parents and guardians have full access to procedural safeguards and are involved in the educational planning process. The social worker may work one-on-one within the classroom or in school-wide sessions to address such problem areas as school attendance, illegal drug or alcohol use, teen pregnancy, and difficulties coping with school. Social workers may serve as a resource to students and families experiencing crisis and as a resource to staff regarding the identification and reporting of child abuse and neglect. School social workers provide professional social work assessments and evaluations as outlined by IDEA. They can monitor and facilitate the transition of students with disabilities between schools and from mental health and correctional placements.

SCHOOL COUNSELORS

School counselors play a variety of roles in school districts. They work with junior and senior high school students to assist them in choosing courses that will help them with their future careers. They assist students, individually and in groups, in developing academic, career, personal and social skills, goals, and plans. For students who plan to go on to college, they can provide guidance about academic and extracurricular activities and provide information about scholarships and specific colleges. They may provide individual and group counseling to at-risk students and to students with identified mental health disabilities, to meet the students' developmental, preventive, and remedial needs. Through the use of appropriate educational assessment strategies, counselors can assist teachers with the educational placement of students. Counselors may conduct classroom guidance lessons on topics such as character education. Counselors may collaborate and consult with parents or guardians, teachers, administrators, and other educational and community resources regarding students' identified concerns and needs.

SCHOOL NURSES

School nurses play a significant role in providing mental health services, as many students take psychiatric medication at school. Also, a significant percentage of students who have mental health problems also have medical disorders, such as asthma, and interact with school nurses in that regard.

Besides distributing medication, or providing oversight to other staff who do so, school nurses are involved in a number of other activities that positively impact students who have mental health disorders. They may communicate directly with physicians and other prescribers of psychiatric medication, in order to communicate concerns such as possible side effects, lack of efficacy, and so on. Nurses may take a lead role in addressing school safety issues including bullying and school violence. School nurses may be involved in screening activities for issues such as vision, hearing, body mass index, and mental health problems. They may develop an individualized health care plan and an emergency care plan for students who have mental health disorders.

SCHOOL ADMINISTRATORS

School principals, assistant principals, deans, and other administrative staff also respond to students who have mental health disorders. For example, a student who has poor impulse control as a result of ADHD may engage in inappropriate behaviors that result in being sent to the principal's office. A student with autism spectrum disorder may become agitated and may act out physically toward people or property if there is an alteration in his or her daily routine, resulting in a referral to the principal. A student who has a mood disorder may be experiencing significant irritability, which may lead to aggressive or noncompliant behaviors and a trip to the principal's office. If the principal understands the underlying disability that leads the student to have difficulties in the classroom, then interventions following these behavioral incidents are more likely to be effective than are generic behavioral responses.

TEACHERS

Although teachers are not mental health professionals, they have a pivotal role in addressing the mental health needs of their students. They are with them for several hours a day, helping them to master skills of social interaction, impulse control, anger management, organization, and self-regulation as well as mastering the academic subjects taught in class.

They may meet with students in one-on-one or group settings to address problems in the classroom, settle disputes, and so on. Every time a teacher responds to a student's misbehavior, the response has the potential to replace the behavior with a more prosocial interaction, or to exacerbate the problem with a negative interaction with the student. Teachers have the primary roles of behavior management, skills training, monitoring of symptoms of mental health disorders, and coordinating educational services with parents. They often communicate with parents about students' difficulties in the classroom, and many of these difficulties stem from underlying mental health disorders. Teachers may also communicate with health and mental health providers in the community. Special education teachers, especially those serving students in the Emotionally Disturbed, Other Health Impaired, and Autism Spectrum categories, spend a significant amount of their time addressing students' mental health problems, both through counseling activities and through the provision of accommodations and modifications in the classroom. Teachers can carry out these roles best when the roles of school social workers, counselors, psychologists, and nurses are clearly defined, so as to avoid duplications of efforts and gaps in services. Because this lack of definition is common in many schools across the country, teachers can be very helpful in the process of clarifying roles. They can work with the school's mental health professionals and administrators to ensure that students in general and in special education receive integrated, coordinated services from all school professionals.

THE FLUIDITY OF THE ROLES OF PROFESSIONALS

Depending on the specific district or school, the psychologists, social workers, counselors, and nurses may carry out the job descriptions outlined above to varying degrees. For example, in some school districts, school psychologists spend most of their time conducting psychological testing for the purpose of special education evaluations and reevaluations. In other districts, psychologists play a major role in assisting educators to understand students' disabilities, such as language processing difficulties, mathematics learning disabilities, and various mental health disabilities. They may provide counseling, consultation to school staff, liaison with professionals in the community, and so on. In some schools, the majority of individual and group counseling activities are provided by social workers, and in other schools it is provided by school counselors or psychologists.

The activities of school mental health professionals are partly related to their funding. School social workers might be funded through special education funding streams, which could result in all of their services going to students in special education. There is also variability in the training of school counselors, social workers, psychologists, and nurses. Some school social workers are licensed mental health professionals who are qualified to diagnose and treat children and adolescents, while others are not. Some school nurses are licensed RNs, whereas others are not. Some school nurses are public health nurses as well. Some school psychologists and school counselors have had extensive mental health training, while others have not.

Even within a single school, the activities of these professionals may vary significantly. For example, some psychologists feel more comfortable spending the majority of their time conducting testing for educational evaluations, whereas others prefer to provide counseling and consultation. Some social workers may spend the bulk of their time in direct service to students, whereas others may spend a great deal of time addressing due process and other Individual Education Plan issues.

As many students receive mental health treatment (e.g., medication management, psychotherapy) in the community, it is important for school staff to have an understanding, with parental consent, of the nature of students' mental health difficulties, the type of treatment that is provided, the target symptoms being treated, and the expectations of treatment. Although parents may not want school staff to have access to highly personal and family information in mental health reports, they are generally willing to share diagnostic and treatment information that is relevant to the students' education to school staff who have a need to know the information. It is therefore important to ensure that school professionals are available for the role of interfacing with mental health treatment professionals in the community.

Some school districts have staff provide direct services to students that go beyond counseling; they have licensed school psychologists or licensed social workers provide mental health diagnostic and treatment services. Other school districts may have relationships with community health or mental health clinics that co-locate their services on-site within the school building.

It is not surprising that many teachers are confused about the roles and responsibilities of various school professionals regarding students in general and in special education who have mental health problems. When there is lack of clarity of roles, it is likely that there will be an overlap of services in some areas and gaps in others. It is not necessary for school districts to have rigid role definitions of all staff; flexibility is important given the individual differences of each school and its student population. It is important, however, to ensure that staff are assigned to carry out all of the crucial activities that must be done to ensure success for students who have mental health disorders. Teachers can work with school administrators to ensure that these tasks are clearly defined and assigned appropriately. A list of school district and school tasks that involve a variety of types of education professionals is presented in Box 16.1.

STAFF COLLABORATION AND COMMUNICATION WITH PROFESSIONALS IN THE COMMUNITY

It is important for school professionals to dovetail their activities with medical and mental health professionals who are evaluating or providing treatment for students who have mental health disorders. They should also establish direct lines of communication instead of expecting parents to comprehensively describe signs and symptoms of mental health disorders in the school environment. Providing information to community professionals can facilitate the diagnostic and treatment process and assist them in monitoring the effectiveness of treatment. Diagnostic and treatment information from community professionals can help school staff ensure that educational interventions are sensitive to the mental health needs of the student in the educational environment. These activities, listed in Box 16.1, are especially useful when mental health diagnostic and treatment services are co-located in the school.

BOX 16.1 Essential Communications between School Staff and Other Professionals

- Gathering mental health information, with parental permission, from treating professionals in the community
- Reviewing the information obtained and translating it into educational terms for educational staff
- Monitoring and assisting educational staff in monitoring target symptoms of students' mental health disorders
- Documenting the nature, frequency, and severity of the target behaviors
- Communicating with community professionals about students' symptoms at the time of their evaluations, and subsequently during treatment
- Coordinating activities with county and community agencies
- Developing a case management system (e.g., coordinating services with community mental health professionals, and assisting families to obtain services)
- Consulting with educational staff
- Making referrals to community resources for students and families
- Coordinating on-site, co-located mental health services provided by community mental health staff

---

An effective way to assign these various activities to school staff is to clarify which activities can only be carried out by staff who have specific licensure (e.g., psychometric testing conducted by school psychologists, disbursal of medication by school nurses), and which activities can be done by several different professionals (e.g., social skills can be taught by teachers, counselors, social workers, and psychologists). It is essential that supervisors ensure that these roles are assigned to someone and that the activities are carried out and documented on an ongoing basis.

COLLABORATION AND COMMUNICATION WITH PARENTS

Teachers, social workers, counselors, nurses, psychologists, and principals all have different roles in working with parents of students who have mental health disorders. It is crucial that they all work together when problems arise in teaming with parents concerning their children's difficulties in the school environment. It is also important for school professionals to respect the contributions of parents and to recognize the multiple difficulties in parenting a child with a mental health disorder.

The Parent-Staff Relationship

Working with students who have mental health disorders can be very challenging for educators. The students may be uncooperative or even defiant, may be depressed and emotionally shut down, may have mood swings, may be disruptive in the classroom, may have significant difficulty following directions, and may not respond to the typical behavioral interventions that are generally successful with other students.

Unfortunately, for many educators, it may also be challenging to work with some of the parents as well. They may perceive the parents as being part of the problem or, in fact, the cause of a student's problems. However, just as it may be difficult to teach a student who manifests mental health symptoms, it may also be difficult to parent that student. Parents may be frustrated or even burned out by the stresses that are experienced on a daily basis as they attempt to be good parents to their challenging children and adolescents. They may not want to be called by educators and told about their child's latest behavior problem at school and may feel that it is the school's problem to deal with the issue.

Parents may have had their own negative experiences with school systems, either in their own educational backgrounds or in their children's previous grades. It is not uncommon for parents to feel frustrated every year when the same problems that their child had in the past manifest in September or October. They may feel that the school staff are ineffective in teaching or managing the child's behavior. Just as some teachers may blame parents for the student's problems, some parents may blame the teachers.

Another factor that may lead to difficulties in parents' interactions with schools is the situation in which a student's parents are undocumented aliens. They may have the perception that they are at risk of being reported by school staff to the authorities and to be subsequently deported. School staff need to be sensitive to this possibility.

Due to the significant heritability of many mental health disorders (e.g., ADHD, ASD, bipolar mood disorder) it is possible that parents may have the same mental health disorders that are being experienced by their children. A parent of a student who has ADHD who also has the same disorder may have difficulty overseeing homework assignments due to his or her own disorganization and distractibility. A parent who suffers from the mood swings of bipolar mood disorder whose child also has that disorder may be irritable with teachers and may be perceived by teachers as being emotionally abusive with them. A parent of a child who has ASD may also have characteristics of the disorder and may be perceived as being difficult to work with due to difficulties with social awareness, compulsivity, and rigidity. Of course, teachers may not be told whether a parent has a mental health disorder, and many of the parents may not be aware that they have one, but it is helpful to keep that possibility in mind. When teachers understand the nature of mental health disorders, whether they are manifested in the students or the parents, they can be more effective.

Another potential source of conflict between teachers and parents arises when parents and teachers have markedly different perceptions of students' behaviors. For example, a teacher might be very concerned about a student's off-task behavior, distractibility, and hyperactivity, while a parent might acknowledge these symptoms but not perceive them as being significantly problematic at home. This can lead the teacher to believe that the parents are not seeing an obvious problem and that they therefore may not be providing good parenting. The parents, on the other hand, might perceive the teacher as lacking competence because the problems described as being so significant at school are not highly problematic at home. In fact, a student who has ADHD might behave very differently at school than at home, and both the teacher's and parents' perceptions might be very accurate. In the school environment, where the student is expected to be quiet, to sit at a desk for extended periods of time, to ignore distractions, and to remain on task, ADHD symptoms may be very prominent. At home, the same child might have fewer cognitive demands and more options to engage in spirited play, and therefore might not be perceived as having a significant problem.

The opposite scenario also occurs. A parent may request a special education evaluation or, if the student is already receiving special education services, may request additional accommodations and modifications, based on the parents' perception that their child has unmet needs. Educators, on the other hand, may not see major emotional, behavioral, or academic problems in the school environment. In this scenario, the parents may view the school staff as being insensitive, while the teachers may view the parents as exaggerating the problem. In fact, when experiencing anxiety or depression, some children and adolescents may be compliant and unexpressive at school and then display excessive anger, anxiety, or sadness in the home environment where they feel safe doing so.

It is essential for educators to be able to understand the multiple factors that can contribute to difficulties in working with parents. They need to be able to work effectively with parents even under challenging conditions that have the potential to produce defensiveness on the educator's part and a less than optimal alliance with the parents. Since educators are often involved in obtaining, reviewing, documenting, and sharing students' mental health information, it is helpful for them to have a basic understanding about data practices, as described in Chapter 15.

Input from Parents

Parents may choose to reveal their child's mental health diagnosis and treatment to teachers and other school staff. They may want to let teachers know about their child's mental health needs in order to provide a tailored educational program for the child that takes into account the mental health disability and provides appropriate services in response to the child's needs. They may want the teacher to monitor their child's response to medication or psychotherapeutic treatment by documenting behavioral symptoms on an ongoing basis that are shared with the parents and the mental health and medical clinicians. They may want to have the teacher and other school staff watch closely for medication side effects and report these effects to them and possibly to the prescriber as well. They may want to ensure that the teacher is familiar with the mental health disorder that their child has and, if this is not the case, they may provide information to the teacher to help him or her become knowledgeable about the nature of their child's mental health disorder and its impact on the educational process. They may want to become an active member of the educational team if their child is going to be receiving special education services, and thus be able to influence decision making about educational interventions, accommodations, modifications, and disciplinary decisions. They may want to have the school's mental health staff work with their child in conjunction with community services in order to provide a seamless system of mental health supports throughout the week. If on-site, co-located mental health services are available at the school, parents may want to take advantage of these services, have their child be seen at school, and have the clinician communicate issues of educational needs to the teacher and other school staff.

Other parents, conversely, believe that it is best not to share their child's mental health information with teachers and other school staff, for a variety of reasons. They may feel that mental health information about their child is very personal and confidential and feel uncomfortable sharing the information with anyone outside of the family who is not a medical or mental health professional. They may be concerned that private information about other family members might be revealed if diagnostic evaluation reports are sent to the school. They may feel that individuals who do not have a need to know the mental health information may gain access to it and may be concerned that the information may be leaked in the community. This concern is often noted in small rural communities but is also problematic in urban communities. Parents have every right not to share information with the school.

Some parents would feel more comfortable doing so if they understood that the information is private, cannot be shared with individuals outside of the school system without a parental release of information, and is only available to school staff who have a need to know the information.

Another valid reason why parents may not want to share their child's mental health information with school staff is that they may be concerned about teacher bias regarding their child if the child's diagnosis and treatment is revealed. Bias can be either positive or negative. For example, if a teacher is told that a medication trial is about to begin, it is possible that the teacher would pay more attention to the student, may relate to him or her differently, and may have a perception that the medication had a greater positive effect than it actually did. On the other hand, parents may be concerned that teachers have a negative bias toward mental health issues, may have lower educational expectations of the student, may relate to the student in a negative manner, or may even reveal the fact that the student is receiving treatment, stigmatizing the student in front of peers.

Parents may seek a mental health diagnosis and may initiate treatment without sharing this information with school staff. Then, after they receive feedback from school staff about their child's subsequent emotional and behavioral status, they may then disclose the mental health information. If parents take this approach, it is important for school staff to appreciate the reasoning behind this decision.

Staff Input to Parents

As noted, most students who have mental health disorders have never been diagnosed or treated. It is common for teachers to notice behaviors that suggest the presence of a mental health disorder. Once teachers have a basic understanding of the warning signs indicating that a student might have a mental health disorder, they require clarity regarding the process of communicating their concerns to the student's parents. There is a remarkable degree of variation across the United States regarding school district policies, procedures, and guidelines on this issue. In many school districts, there are no specified guidelines for teachers to follow. It is important for teachers to understand how their school approaches this issue. If they have concerns about these approaches, they need to be able to address them with fellow staff and administrators. There are also wide variations in parents' attitudes about being informed that their child may have a mental health disorder.

Here are some useful guidelines for school professionals to follow:

- First of all, they should seek clarity regarding the existence of a school protocol for communicating this information. Protocols could, for example, clarify that teachers should observe their students for signs of a possible mental health disorder, and then communicate their findings to a school psychologist, social worker, counselor, or nurse who would then meet with the parents to communicate concerns. Or protocols might direct the teacher to communicate concerns directly to the parents.

- It is clearly reasonable for teachers to describe student behaviors that are interfering with a student's ability to benefit from the educational program. Describing these behaviors to parents is part of an overall process of teacher-parent communication. It is also helpful for teachers to clarify whether these behaviors are common among the student's classmates or whether they are significant and only seen in a small percentage of students.

- It is important for teachers to clarify whether the student's behavior is affecting only his or her own education, or whether it is disrupting the classroom and affecting other students' educational progress as well.

- If the behaviors are known by the teacher to be criteria of a mental health disorder, the teacher may communicate this fact to the parent. The teacher is not reaching any diagnostic conclusions and is not telling the parents that their child has a mental health disorder.

- In the next step of the communication process, the teacher or other school staff might recommend that the parents consider seeking a diagnostic evaluation to clarify whether their child has a mental health disorder, and to find out about treatment options if a disorder is present. Or the teacher could avoid making a specific recommendation but might say to the parents that they may choose to seek a follow-up medical or mental health consultation to clarify these issues. Many school districts are much more comfortable with the latter approach, believing that since it does not involve specific recommendations, the district would not be financially liable.

Sample Parent Notification By Teacher

"Johnny appears tired and listless in class. He tells me that he doesn't sleep well at night. He rarely eats lunch, saying that he isn't hungry. He often starts crying when receiving feedback about his schoolwork. He says that he can't concentrate on his schoolwork. He says that he thinks that he is stupid. I'm not a mental health professional, but I am aware that these could be symptoms of depression. I felt that it was important for you to know how he has been doing at school."

Some parents are very appreciative of this information and respond by seeking a diagnostic evaluation and follow-up treatment. However, some parents respond very negatively and believe that schools should stick to educational concerns and should have nothing to do with mental health. Some parents have strong negative attitudes about the concept of mental health disorders and treatment, especially in children and adolescents. These parents may believe that children are being overdiagnosed and overmedicated, that normal childhood behavior is being pathologized, and that schools are partners in this process "because drugging children makes classroom management easier."

These parents tend to be strongly against mental health screening in schools and against school staff—including teachers—communicating mental health concerns to parents. The issue of psychiatric medication use is very controversial, and some state statutes have attempted to address the issue of psychotropic medication use by school children. For example, Connecticut and Minnesota passed statutes that clearly define the decision for children to take stimulant medication to treat ADHD as being up to parents and not schools. Thus, if parents choose to not have their child take these medications, this decision would not constitute medical neglect.

Some school districts are concerned about the potential financial repercussions of communicating mental health concerns to parents, as, if the student is receiving special education services, schools have the potential of being the payer of last resort for interventions that they recommend. Thus, teachers may be justifiably concerned about the repercussions of communicating mental health concerns to parents.

FOR DISCUSSION

VIGNETTE: Richard

Richard is an 8-year-old student who was recently diagnosed with ADHD and started on Ritalin by his family physician. His teacher had filled out a checklist of ADHD symptoms from the doctor, and she had endorsed most of the symptoms. She has noted Richard to have a somewhat improved attention span, but also has been observing him engaging in repetitious behaviors such as continually rearranging his desk, washing his hands repeatedly, and blinking frequently.

VIGNETTE: Sara

Sara is a 16-year-old student who has a 2-year history of significant mood swings. Her mother and maternal uncle have been successfully treated for bipolar mood disorder. Sara was recently seen by her pediatrician, who diagnosed her with ADHD and started her on a stimulant medication. In the past 4 weeks, Sara has demonstrated increasing behavioral problems in the classroom, hallways, and lunchroom. She has been verbally and physically assaultive. A special education evaluation is being considered.

REFLECTION QUESTIONS

What do you think that the best course would be for the school to take for Richard and Sara? What would be the best approach for teachers to identify and document concerns and have them communicated to the students' parents and to the physicians? How is this done in the district where you work? Could different approaches be considered in your school that would improve the communication process?

CHAPTER 17

The Relationship Between the School and Mental Health Professionals

A GOOD RELATIONSHIP BETWEEN SCHOOL STAFF AND THE mental health professionals providing mental health services is important to the success of the work of both entities and helps promote a student's well-being For example, only a few years ago, the majority of medications used by schoolchildren were the stimulant medications used to treat ADHD. Since these medications were generally short acting, students would need to go to the nurse's office at lunchtime to take their noon dose. Now students who take these medications generally take long-acting forms, and often take them only at home before leaving for school. Despite this reduction in medications administered at school, school nurses are now finding that psychiatric medications have become among the most common, or are even the most common, medications prescribed for children and adolescents that are taken at school. Antidepressants, mood-stabilizing medications, antianxiety medications, and even antipsychotic medications are prescribed to an increasing number of students.

Clearly, it is essential for prescribers to make accurate diagnoses and to initiate medication only when it is clearly indicated. Medications can be very helpful when prescribed appropriately, but can also have significant side effects and need to be monitored closely. Educators can play a vital role in ensuring that professionals who prescribe psychiatric medications (physicians, nurse practitioners, certified nurse specialists, physician assistants) have accurate information about students' mental health symptoms prior to diagnosis and during the course of medication treatment.

For students who are receiving psychotherapeutic services, it is helpful for their therapist to have school information about the student at the time of the diagnostic evaluation, and periodic updates informing the therapist about the effectiveness of the psychotherapy.

PARENTAL PERMISSION TO SHARE INFORMATION

Communicating with medical and mental health professionals who are providing diagnostic or treatment services requires a release of information signed by a parent or guardian. Without the release, school professionals cannot share educational information with clinicians, and clinicians cannot share diagnostic and treatment information with school staff. Some parents are reluctant to have their children's full mental health records sent to the school, as they contain sensitive information about the child or other family members that is not pertinent to the child's educational needs. It is acceptable for clinicians to send a summary of their diagnosis and treatment plans to the school without revealing this sensitive information. Some parents are not willing to sign a release that allows two-way communication between school professionals and clinicians, but are willing to allow a one-way release (e.g., the teacher's information can be shared with the physician, but not vice versa). This is not ideal, but is better than no communication.

Some parents will not agree to allow any communication between the school and clinicians, and, of course, some parents won't even reveal to school staff that their child has been diagnosed and is receiving mental health treatment.

ELEMENTS OF COMMUNICATION

This chapter applies to situations in which parents inform school professionals that their child has a mental health diagnosis or is in the process of being seen for a diagnostic assessment, and are willing to have school professionals and clinicians communicate with each other. In many school districts, educational staff communicate with prescribers in response to forms sent to them for the purpose of diagnosis but have limited or no contact after that. For example, a physician who is doing a diagnostic evaluation of a student who is displaying symptoms suggestive of ADHD may send a form that lists the diagnostic criteria of this disorder and requests that the teacher rate the symptoms on a scale from "absent" to "severe." If a diagnosis is made and if medication is initiated, it is essential for the physician to have a clear understanding of the effectiveness of the medication (or of evidence of medication side effects). However, this accurate communication does not always occur.

In many districts, school professionals communicate to prescribers indirectly, by telling students' parents about how their child is doing in school, and expecting parents to then communicate this information to prescribers. This can work well, but there is a risk of miscommunication, as parents may have difficulty accurately describing in detail the emotional and behavioral problems that their child manifests within the school setting. Parents may have difficulty fully and accurately describing school-based behaviors, and their information may be incomplete or even inaccurate. If the school staff communicate symptoms directly to the clinician and send a copy of the symptom checklists to the parents, optimal accuracy is obtained.

Reviews of special education evaluations that result in placement in the Emotional Disturbance category indicate that a substantial percentage of students are referred for evaluation who are taking medication for a mental health disorder (most often ADHD), but who continue to have all of the symptoms of that disorder. They are then referred for a special education evaluation because of the behavioral manifestations (e.g., hyperactivity, impulsivity, short attention span, disorganization, distractibility) of that disorder. In this situation, communication with the prescriber is essential, if parents are willing to give permission, in order to clarify why these symptoms remain highly problematic. Potential reasons why medication is not effective include the following:

- The diagnosis may not be correct.
- The medication dosage may be too low.

- The student may not be taking the medication as prescribed.
- A different medication needs to be considered.
- The medication's effectiveness is limited due to other factors such as severe social stressors including poverty, homelessness, child abuse, and so on.
- The student is experiencing psychiatric side effects such as somnolence, agitation, irritability, and so on.

Sending a symptom checklist to treatment providers indicating that a medication lacks efficacy can be a pre-referral intervention prior to initiating a special education evaluation. It may lead to changes in medication treatment that result in significantly improved symptoms, no longer necessitating a special education evaluation. This is far superior to doing an assessment and placing the student who is having ongoing, potentially treatable psychopathology into a special education program that will have a poor likelihood of success due to ongoing symptoms. Prescribers generally appreciate feedback from school staff regarding a student's mental health symptoms within the school environment. Written documentation informs the prescriber and also creates a document in the educational file that can be useful in designing modifications and accommodations to assist the student and in monitoring the student's educational progress. For this process to be successful, it is necessary for the school to have procedures and guidelines that outline the importance of requesting releases of information from parents, of communicating with physicians, and of integrating the clinical information with the educational issues involved.

Since the symptoms of a mental health disorder that has been diagnosed are often identical to the problems identified in a special education student's IEP, it is important to recognize the connection between clinical and educational issues. This is because the mental health symptoms that are contributing to or causing problems in the classroom can improve in many situations as a result of ongoing communication with medical and mental health professionals. This results in improved educational performance, a reduction in behavioral incidents, and, often, cost savings that result from the reduction of the intensity of special education services that are no longer necessary.

BENEFITS OF COMMUNICATION

Communication Between Clinicians and School Staff

There are numerous reasons why communication between school staff and treating professionals is beneficial to students and their families. In the process of making a mental health diagnosis of a child or adolescent, clinicians need to ask about educational issues, as these are very pertinent clues to the nature of the mental health problems that are being assessed. For example, a student who has had ongoing problems with distractibility, impulsivity, and hyperactivity at school presents significant evidence of having ADHD. However, if teachers observe no evidence of these symptoms, then that diagnosis would be unlikely. Ideally, this educational information should be obtained directly from the school, as there are risks of miscommunication if parents act as a liaison of information between the school and the clinician.

In addition to communicating information about a student's baseline mental health status prior to diagnosis, school information is very valuable to clinicians once the diagnosis is made and treatment has commenced. If medication is initiated, school feedback is invaluable in the process of monitoring the medication to clarify whether the correct dosage has been reached, and whether there is evidence of side effects. If psychotherapy is the treatment of choice, school feedback is also very helpful to the clinician in order to clarify how and to what degree the therapy is effective.

As is noted above, symptom checklists are helpful to identify the presence or absence of symptoms of the disorder being treated and can gauge the severity of symptoms as well. They can identify students' baseline symptoms prior to initiation of medication or psychotherapy, assist in the process of diagnosis, improve communication with prescribers, clarify the efficacy of medication, assist the prescriber in the process of dosage adjustment, help monitor for side effects, identify undiagnosed conditions, and promote a public health versus strictly behavioral model in the school setting.

The optimal effective dose of many medications used to treat mental health disorders cannot simply be calculated based on the child or adolescent's weight, due to variations in medication metabolism in the general population. Therefore, it is not unusual for a prescriber, when treating disorders such as ADHD, depression, anxiety, and so on, to start with a dose that is generally too low and increase the dose over time depending on response. Teachers can play an invaluable role in identifying baseline and residual symptoms to ensure that the prescriber's decisions are based on accurate information about the student's emotional and behavioral symptoms in the school environment. Teachers and other school staff can monitor for symptoms and communicate their findings to parents and prescribers.

School feedback is very helpful to clinicians in monitoring for side effects. Side effects of psychiatric medications can be physical (e.g., stomachache, dizziness, loss of appetite, sedation, lethargy, weight gain) as well as in the psychiatric realm (e.g., agitation, anxiety, depression, mood swings, increased compulsivity, confusion, and even psychosis). If students are taking medication for medical disorders, it is also important to monitor for psychiatric side effects. For example, steroids can cause mood changes, and some asthma medications can cause anxiety and hyperactivity. Providing this information to parents and prescribers can result in medication adjustments or changes that are beneficial to the student.

On occasion, school observations may not be consistent with diagnoses that are made. For example, without having obtained school feedback, a clinician may have diagnosed a student as having ADHD. If the student in fact did not have any observable symptoms of ADHD at school prior to the diagnosis, the clinician would want to know this. With a release of information, the school staff can provide this information. There are also situations where a student may be diagnosed with a disorder but may in fact be manifesting symptoms of other disorders that were not communicated to the professional who made the diagnosis. For example, a student might be diagnosed with ADHD but may be manifesting multiple symptoms of depression, one of which is difficulty concentrating. In addition, the student may have sleep disturbance, appetite disturbance, low self-worth, lack of enjoyment of activities, generalized sadness, irritability, and so on, suggesting the presence of a mood disorder.

Sending a symptom checklist to the prescriber that outlines the presence of these symptoms in the school environment is simply a way of adding information to the diagnostic picture. School staff are not making the diagnosis of clinical depression; they are simply communicating to the prescriber information that the prescriber may not have had when the diagnosis was first made. Feedback about evidence of depression, anxiety, or other symptoms that had not been diagnosed can be useful to the clinician in reconsidering diagnoses or in clarifying whether these symptoms might reflect medication side effects.

Communication Between Clinicians, School Staff, and Parents

As indicated in Chapter 1, children may exhibit signs of mental disorders that are really the result of other factors, about which their parents would be most knowledgeable. For example, clinicians and school staff can ask parents, in a nonjudgmental way, whether they know if their child was exposed to toxins such as pesticides, lead, and mercury. Further, parents can be asked about their children's usual diet, since food additives and excess amounts of sugar can induce behavior that mimics ADHD. Deficiencies in some vitamins and other nutrients can cause other types of mental health problems, such as depression and irritability. Parents who do acknowledge detrimental environmental and dietary factors can be provided with appropriate medical resources and information to help remediate their negative effects.

PROTOCOLS FOR COMMUNICATION WITH PRESCRIBERS

Schools can have protocols that outline the various steps that need to be taken to ensure that communication with medication prescribers is optimal. There are a number of steps in this process.

1. *The initial step is to clarify whether or not a student is taking medication,* at home or at school. Medications for nonpsychiatric disorders such as asthma, diabetes, and so on are also helpful to know about, as these medications can have both medical and psychiatric side effects. It is of course the parents' choice whether information about medication is shared with the school, but most parents realize that it is in their child's best interest for school staff to be aware of medication issues, to monitor for their effects and possible side effects, and to communicate, when appropriate, with prescribers. Many schools ask parents to fill out a medical history form when they enroll their

child in school and subsequently at the beginning of each school year. The form explains that the information that is given to the school is private and cannot be shared with outside systems or with school professionals who do not have a need to know the information. It is best to incorporate mental health medication questions into the overall health questionnaire, as mental health disorders that are treated with medication are essentially medical disorders. The form may ask questions such as, "Is your child being treated on an ongoing basis for a medical disorder? If 'yes,' which disorder?" and, "Does your child take medication on a regular basis, at home and/or at school? If 'yes,' what medication and dosage?" Parents can also be asked to notify the school nurse if a new medication is initiated during the school year.

2. *The next step in the process involves asking parents to sign a release of information* allowing school personnel (e.g., the school nurse) to communicate with the prescriber. When asking for the release of private information, it is important for school staff to communicate to parents what information is being requested from or communicated to prescribers, how the information will be used, who will have access to the information, and potential consequences of not allowing the information to be shared.

3. *It is also necessary to clarify the roles of the different school professionals* who are involved in observing, documenting, and monitoring symptoms, so that communicating the symptoms to the physician happens. Some schools may have the school nurse be the go-between with prescribers, whereas in other schools the teacher, the school psychologist, the school counselor, or the school social worker will do this. It is important to clarify who does what in order to have accountability to ensure that the steps in the communication process are accomplished.

4. *Roles also need to be clarified regarding which school professionals will review diagnostic and treatment records* sent to the school from the treating professionals in the community and who will interpret this information to those who have a need to know it. There is significant disagreement in the educational community regarding teachers' need to know students' mental health diagnosis. Some argue that teachers only need to observe behaviors, and that the underlying diagnosis that may be causing those behaviors is not relevant. I suggest that, if parents are comfortable having the teacher be

aware of the child's mental health diagnosis and medication treatment, it is clearly appropriate to communicate this information to the teacher if there is evidence that the mental health disorder is adversely impacting the student's academic or social-emotional functioning in the classroom. Awareness of the student's mental health status also helps prevent situations where the behaviors that directly stem from mental health disorders are viewed as being volitional, attention getting, willful, or oppositional. Having protocols for medication tracking moves the mindset of school district staff into a public health model. This is especially helpful if the school had been operating predominantly within a behavioral model of intervention.

As indicated in the steps above, the process of communication has several steps. A release of information needs to be obtained from the parent or guardian. The prescriber needs to be contacted, and the reason for the contact (communication of symptoms to the clinician, request for information from the clinician, or both) needs to be explained. Data about the nature, extent, severity, and periodicity of symptoms need to be gathered by an individual who has the expertise to make accurate and reliable assessments. Training may be necessary to ensure that data are gathered effectively. The decision needs to be made about which checklists need to be filled out. Someone needs to be the contact person for information sent from the clinician about changes in treatment, and this person needs to document this information and communicate it, on an as-needed basis, to other school staff. Someone also needs to analyze the data to clarify the outcome of clinical and educational interventions. Finally, there needs to be a process of oversight to ensure that all of these activities are completed.

Depending on the size of the school, the staff available for the communication process, and the general severity of problems noted in the student population, decisions can be made regarding the nature and extent of the communication process. For a small school that has adequate staffing, there may be a universal protocol that has a goal of communicating with all clinicians about students' symptoms. Other schools may take a targeted approach, focusing on students who are having significant problems. It can be argued that, if a student is diagnosed, is receiving treatment, and is displaying no significant emotional or behavioral problems in the school environment, then it is not necessary to have periodic communication with the treating clinician.

The students for whom communication of symptoms to the clinician are the highest priority are the following:

- Students who are in the process of having a diagnostic evaluation
- Students who have started taking medication, for whom feedback to the clinician assists the process of adjusting the dose
- Students who have had recent changes in type or dosage of medication
- Students who are taking medication but continue to demonstrate the symptoms that the medication is targeting
- Students who are demonstrating evidence of medication side effects
- Students who are demonstrating evidence of mental health disorders that are not being treated

Symptom checklists can be used even if medication is not being prescribed to a student. For example, some students who have been diagnosed with ADHD have parents who would prefer the use of behavioral interventions, accommodations, and modifications prior to considering medication treatment. The checklists can quantify whether and to what degree these interventions are having a positive effect on the student's progress in the educational environment. Also, the checklists can be used to describe the quality and quantity of difficulties that are being addressed in 504 plans, on IEPs, and so on.

Ideally, the symptoms being monitored are objective, observable, and measurable in frequency and severity. It would generally be inappropriate to put teachers in the position of having to make subjective judgments, such as, "I believe that this student is very depressed." Objective behavioral observations, however, are appropriate, such as, "The student sleeps in class every morning, cries when mistakes are corrected, does not socialize with peers, doesn't eat lunch, moves slowly," and so on.

Symptom documentation is relatively easy for students who are diagnosed with ADHD combined form, as this disorder tends to have observable behavioral symptoms that can be measured objectively. Items such as "interrupting others," "difficulty finishing tasks," and "difficulty remaining seated" are observable and quantifiable.

Other disorders are internalizing and have symptoms that are not easily observable. Internalizing disorders, by their very definition, have symptoms that are within the person experiencing them, such as many symptoms of depression or anxiety. These symptoms may or may not manifest themselves externally in an easily objective and observable manner. Identifying and rating symptoms such as low self-worth and excessive worrying requires individuals who are familiar with the student and familiar with the manifestations of mental health disorders to make subjective judgments. I recommend that checklists of subjective, internalized symptoms be filled out by school mental health staff who work with the student (counselors, school social workers, or school psychologists), in conjunction with input from the teacher.

Ideally, symptom checklists should mirror the criteria in DSM-5 for the disorders being monitored. Also, as assessment of the severity of the symptom, terms such as "absent to mild," "moderate," or "severe" are helpful in gauging the response or nonresponse to treatment. In addition, the Child Global Assessment of Functioning Scale is very helpful in clarifying the level of function or dysfunction of a student who is having mental health problems. This scale is based on objective observations and can be filled out with input from the student's parents.

School nurses typically have forms that document students' physical disabilities and their treatments; the same approach can be taken with mental health disabilities. Symptom rating forms can be a part of a larger packet of information about the student's mental health issues. It is also helpful to have an activities report that monitors the overall activities of school staff by month (e.g., contacts with physicians, discussions with the school team). An individual health plan can be created, which includes the student's diagnosis, medications being prescribed (type and dosage), target symptoms, and goals of treatment.

The frequency of sending checklists to the prescriber depends on the stage of treatment (has it just begun, or has the student received treatment for months or years with stable symptoms?), the process of medication adjustment (has the dose recently been changed, or has a different medication been initiated?), and the severity of symptoms (severe symptoms require closer monitoring and more frequent communication). A general rule of thumb is to send baseline information, if possible, prior to the initiation of medication, and follow-up information depending on the natural course of medication response. Stimulant medication tends to produce a rapid response, so that checklists within a week or two will generally reflect the medication's efficacy. Antidepressants may take up to 8 weeks to begin to work; monthly checklists until symptoms remit would be appropriate. If symptoms are severe, or if medication adjustments are being made, more frequent communication is appropriate. Prescribers should be asked how frequently they would like this information sent to them.

Sample Letters to Medication Prescribers

It is not unusual for school professionals to complain that they can't get through to physicians on the phone, that the doctors never return their phone calls, and that the process of communication is difficult and time-consuming. I recommend that communication take place in written form. When prescribers receive written information, they tend to pay attention to it. In fact, it would be considered negligent not to do so, as the information sent by the school is often crucial to diagnostic or treatment issues. When school staff are proactive in establishing a two-way channel of communication with medical and mental health professionals, they increase the likelihood of more accurate mental health diagnoses and more finely tuned medication management and psychotherapeutic interventions.

The following is an example of a sample letter that can be used to obtain information about a student:

Dear Dr. Jones,

Your patient, John Smith, is a student at _____ School. John's parents have signed a two-way release of information (copy enclosed), and are requesting that we communicate with each other so that John will have the best chance of educational success in our program. We understand that you are providing treatment to John. We are requesting diagnostic and treatment information. This will be used to help us identify issues that require accommodations and modifications in the educational setting.

We would appreciate receiving the following information:

- Diagnoses made
- Type of treatment provided
- What symptoms are being targeted?
- Is medication being used?
- What kind of medication? What dose?
- Is medication treatment successful?
- How long has John been in treatment?
- Frequency of appointments
- Is treatment successful at this time?
- Recommendations made for other services (e.g., psychotherapy). Have these recommendations been followed?

If you make changes in your treatment plan, or if there are treatment issues in the future that you believe are likely to impact John's school performance, we would appreciate updated information at that time. We recognize that you are very busy, but would appreciate a prompt response so that we can provide appropriate educational services in a timely manner.

Sincerely,

_____

This is an example of a sample letter that can be used to send information about a student to the treating provider:

Dear Dr. Jones,

Your patient, Jane Smith, is a student at _____ School. Jane's parents have signed a two-way release of information (copy enclosed), and are requesting that we communicate with each other so that Jane will have the best chance of educational success in our program. We understand that you are providing treatment to Jane. [Alternately, "We understand that you are in the process of conducting a diagnostic evaluation with Jane."] We are enclosing our behavioral observations of Jane, and hope that you will find them useful in your work with her.

Sincerely,

_____

A sample checklist for students who have ADHD and the severity of symptoms:

ADHD Symptom Checklist
Symptoms of inattention

	ABSENT	MILD	MODERATE	SEVERE
Carelessness				
Poor attention span				
Not listening				
Difficulty following instructions				
Disorganized				
Avoids mental effort				
Loses items				
Distractible				
Forgetful				

Hyperactive/impulsive symptoms

	ABSENT	MILD	MODERATE	SEVERE
Fidgety				
Difficulty remaining seated				
Runs/climbs excessively				
Trouble playing quietly				
Always on the go				
Talks excessively				
Blurts out answers				
Trouble waiting turn				
Interrupts				

Symptoms of internalizing disorders such as depression or anxiety disorders are more subjective and would ideally involve teachers collaborating with a school social worker, counselor, or psychologist.

Mood Disorder Symptom Checklist

	ABSENT	MILD	MODERATE	SEVERE
Depressed mood (can be irritable mood for children or adolescents)				
Decreased interest/pleasure				
Significant failure to meet expected weight, or excessive weight gain				
Sleep disturbance (insomnia or hypersomnia)				
Psychomotor retardation or agitation				
Fatigue, tiredness, loss of energy				
Feelings of worthlessness or guilt				
Difficulty concentrating				
Recurrent thoughts of death				
Persistently elevated, expansive, or irritable mood				
Inflated self-esteem or grandiosity				
Decreased need for sleep				
More talkative than usual or pressure to keep talking				
Flight of ideas, thoughts are racing				
Distractibility				

Increase in goal-directed activity				
Excessive involvement in pleasurable activities that have a high potential for painful consequences				

Anxiety Disorders, Obsessive-Compulsive Disorder, PTSD Checklist

	ABSENT	MILD	MODERATE	SEVERE
Panic attacks				
Obsessions (describe below)				
Compulsions (describe below)				
Phobias (describe below)				
PTSD symptoms:				
Intrusive recollections				
Avoidance/numbing				
Hyperarousal				

Generalized anxiety symptoms (e.g., significant difficulty in controlling anxiety and worry, feeling wound-up, tense, or restless, easily becoming fatigued or worn out, concentration problems, irritability, significant tension in muscles, difficulty with sleep)

Description of symptoms noted above (list type and nature)

_____

_____

_____

_____

_____

Psychotic Disorder Symptom Checklist

	ABSENT	PRESENT
Delusions		
Hallucinations		

The ultimate goal of communicating with treating clinicians in this collaborative activity is to significantly improve educational outcomes for these at-risk,
highly vulnerable students.

FOR DISCUSSION

VIGNETTE: **James and Jennifer**

Two students, James and Jennifer, were first graders. Both had been
diagnosed with ADHD by their pediatricians. Both had information
releases in their files, but there was no record of communication with
the physicians for either student.

1. James's mother had a severe personality disorder and
untreated chemical dependency. When James was placed on a reasonable dose of medication for ADHD, school staff noted an immediate response. However, one month later, during the physician
appointment, James's mother said that the medication wasn't doing
anything, and the dose was doubled. School staff were surprised at
the increase but did not attempt to contact the physician to communicate their own observations. One month later, at the doctor's office,
the same thing happened again and the dose was again doubled. One
week later, James became psychotic from the toxic dose of the stimulant and was hospitalized.

2. Jennifer's ADHD was more prominent in the school environment than in the home environment. During her first appointment with
her doctor, a low dose of stimulant medication was started. School
staff noted no effect from the medication. During the next appointment with the doctor, Jennifer's mother said that she thought that the
medication seemed to be helping, and the dose was thus kept at that

level for the entire school year. ADHD symptoms persisted at school, and Jennifer's academic performance continued to suffer.

REFLECTION QUESTIONS

What policy should the district have had that would have prevented these problems from occurring? How would the policy be carried out? What should the school have done if the physicians had not responded to the communication from the school staff in either situation with an appropriate medication change? What types of behavioral observations, symptom monitoring, and side effect monitoring should have taken place?

PART V

School Practices
to Promote Learning

Overview of the Ways Schools Are Meeting the Challenges of Students' Mental Health

SCHOOLS ACROSS THE COUNTRY ARE ADDRESSING STU-dents' mental health problems with a wide variety of interventions. Some are preventive, some involve direct service to students, and some involve collaboration with various community systems. By considering the various models of service, school team members can work together in order to select and institute the most effective mental health activities within their schools.

Howard Adelman and Linda Taylor, directors of UCLA's Center for Mental Health in Schools, emphasize that school mental health activities need to be integrated into a larger framework of learning supports for all students (Please refer to the website for the UCLA Center for Mental Health in Schools.) It provides a wealth of information about effective school mental health programming). The National Center for School Mental Health, based at the University of Maryland School of Medicine, also provides information about successful models of school mental health services (University of Maryland School of Medicine, 2019).

PREVENTION PROGRAMS

It is useful to apply a public health model to school mental health problem prevention activities. This model utilizes the concept of primary, secondary, and tertiary prevention activities.

Primary prevention refers to interventions that can prevent the occurrence of a problem. An example in physical medicine is the polio vaccine. There are environmental contributors to the major psychiatric disorders, such as bipolar mood disorder, schizophrenia, and panic disorder, that can be ameliorated, but to date no interventions have been as effective as are vaccines for infectious disease. Another example of primary prevention involves behaviors that can lead to the development of mental health difficulties. Antibullying efforts result in reduced stress and suffering for students who would otherwise be victimized. Preventing bullying prevents trauma, which in turn can prevent a child or adolescent from developing PTSD. Another disorder that can be prevented utilizing primary prevention intervention is fetal alcohol syndrome, which causes multiple mental health symptoms and neuropsychological problems of judgment and cognition. Prevention efforts are aimed at the use of alcohol during pregnancy.

Secondary prevention interventions focus on the early identification of a disorder and providing treatment early in the course of its manifestation. For example, if major depression is identified early in its course, effective treatment can assist the individual to return to a predepression state of functioning. When a disorder such as depression is not treated for several months or years, treatment may not be as effective, due to the significant negative effects of ongoing symptoms on self-esteem, socialization, work activities, schoolwork, and so on. Similarly, if a child is not identified as having ADHD, impulsive behaviors may be misinterpreted as planned and volitional. Teachers' reactions to the behaviors may be negative, and the child may respond by feeling demoralized and powerless. This can lead to power struggles and oppositional behaviors and ultimately result in a diagnosis of oppositional defiant disorder for the child.

It is clear that, for both mental health and medical disorders, preventing the disorder in the first place (primary prevention) is the ideal approach. When this is not possible, secondary prevention provides the opportunity to initiate effective treatment before the multiple repercussions of living with an untreated disorder set in.

The term early intervention refers to intervening early in the course of an illness rather than during a child's early years. If major depression begins at age 14 years, then intervention soon after the onset of symptoms would be considered early intervention. Tertiary prevention focuses on individuals who have significant and often multiple problems and who are at high risk of requiring even more intensive services. For example, an individual with severe diabetes and a history of multiple hospitalizations may require intensive out-patient services to prevent another hospitalization. An example in the mental health field would be an adolescent who has a history of multiple residential treatment interventions who deteriorates following discharge from the residential setting due to unresolved family difficulties. An example in the school setting would be a special education Setting 3 student who has a mental health disorder that is not being effectively treated, and whose behaviors are resulting in a potential referral to a self-contained Setting 4 educational placement. In the last example, tertiary prevention services would be provided through collaborative interventions that involve school personnel, the family, and community mental health agencies, with the goal of preventing a Setting 4 referral. Tertiary programs tend to be intensive and expensive. In many instances, the provision of secondary prevention early intervention activities would prevent the individual from deteriorating to the point of requiring tertiary prevention services.

POSITIVE BEHAVIORAL INTERVENTIONS AND SUPPORTS

The different types of prevention applied to school districts translate into the concepts of universal services for all students (primary), more intensive services to at-risk students (secondary), and intensive, individualized services to students who display severe problems (tertiary). Positive behavioral interventions and supports (PBIS) constitute a successful intervention that uses these three concepts.

PBIS is a decision-making framework that guides selection, integration, and implementation of the best evidence-based academic and behavioral practices, with the goal of improving academic and behavioral outcomes for all students. The major elements of PBIS are the supports of social competence and academic achievement, of decision making, and of student and staff behavior. It is based on principles of developing evidence-based behavioral and academic interventions and the use of data to guide decisions. It uses environmental manipulation to prevent problem behaviors, teaches pro-social skills and behaviors, and provides universal screening and ongoing follow-up monitoring.

PBIS provides primary, secondary, and tertiary prevention activities. PBIS implementation is provided on a continuum of services, based on student need. It uses a three-tiered model of prevention that requires that all students receive supports at the universal or primary tier. For the students who do not respond to these primary prevention interventions, secondary prevention services are provided in systems for at-risk students. These services would generally be provided within group settings in the second tier. For students who have severe problems, third-tier services are specialized and individualized.

PBIS interventions stress the need to prevent problems that otherwise would result in reactive, consequence-based strategies. When a student's problem behaviors are not responding to school-wide and classroom-wide procedures, information about the student's behavior is used to determine the function of the behavior (why it is occurring) in order to determine and strengthen more acceptable alternate behaviors, to remove antecedents and consequences that may be triggering or maintaining the problem behaviors, and to add antecedents and consequences that trigger and maintain positive acceptable alternate behaviors.

School can be a positive influence on children and adolescents, but it can also have negative impacts if staff are punitive, if they do not provide positive alternatives to inappropriate behaviors, if discipline is inconsistent, if rules are not clearly understood, or if the school setting is highly coercive. Approaches that utilize punitive responses to problem behaviors (e.g., zero tolerance policies, suspensions, referral to restrictive environments, providing aversive consequences) without a proactive, supportive school environment are associated with increased aggression, truancy, vandalism, and significant dropout rates.

PBIS is based on the concept that children and adolescents want to do well and that the majority of behavioral difficulties in the school setting can be addressed by providing clearly defined modeling of appropriate behaviors. PBIS utilizes a school-wide approach that has clearly defined expected behaviors for all and methods of skills training that teach appropriate behaviors. It defines behavioral expectations for all settings (e.g., classroom, playground, hallways, cafeteria, bathrooms) with an emphasis on maintaining a positive, safe, and respectful school environment. For example, specific behaviors are outlined for getting a teacher's attention ("Look at the teacher; raise your hand and stay calm; wait until the teacher says your name; ask your question"), for accepting criticism or consequences ("Look at the person; say 'Okay'; stay calm), for accepting "No" as an answer, and so on.

Successful individual student behavioral support is linked to host environments or school climates that are effective, efficient, relevant, durable, scalable, and logical for all students. Written goal contracts, point systems, all-class rewards, success plans, and communication with parents can be used to provide accountability and to reinforce positive behaviors.

For PBIS to be successful, it is necessary to have a continuum of services from the general population of students (universal, tier 1) to the intensive services needed by students who have severe problems (tier 3). Tier 3 students often have significant undiagnosed and untreated mental health disorders and require clinical as well as educational interventions. If PBIS is to be successful, schools need a process by which to identify these students and to ensure that clinical services are accessible to them and to their families.

MENTAL HEALTH SCREENING

Secondary prevention activities require screening tools, which are methods of identifying the presence of undiagnosed disorders. Examples in the medical field would be a skin test for tuberculosis, a mammogram for breast cancer, or a PSA blood test for prostate cancer. Unfortunately, there are no biological assays at this time that effectively detect mental health disorders. Thus, mental health screening tools rely on others' observations of behavior (e.g., parents and teachers) or self-report questionnaires.

A variety of screening tools are available for mental health screening of children and adolescents, including the Pediatric Symptom Checklist, the Behavioral and Emotional Screening System (ages 3–18 years), the Ages and Stages Questionnaire–Social Emotional, the Conners Parent-Teacher Rating Scale, and the Strengths and Difficulties Questionnaire. For a screening tool to be useful, it requires the sensitivity needed to identify the individuals who have the disorder, the specificity not to identify individuals who do not have the disorder, the validity to identify the problem for which it is designed, and the reliability to ensure that screenings done by different screeners will yield the same results. Although screening tools do not generally have 100% sensitivity, specificity, validity, and reliability, the closer to 100% that they are, the better the tool. Screening tools are not designed to diagnose a problem; they are designed to identify whether there is enough evidence that a problem exists to warrant a full evaluation.

There is considerable debate about whether schools should screen students for mental health problems and, if so, to what extent this should be done. Some mental health advocates support universal screening of all students for mental health problems such as ADHD, mood disorders, anxiety disorders, and suicide risk. There is also strong opposition to universal mental health screening, based on a variety of concerns, including privacy and confidentiality, inappropriate labeling, and the argument that mental health issues are not the purview of schools.

It is my opinion that universal mental health screening done by schools is inappropriate for a number of reasons. Any results of the screening would be part of the student's educational record, and screening may reveal very private family information that does not belong in educational records. Examples include screening that indicated evidence of fetal alcohol syndrome, or of PTSD secondary to child abuse within the home. However, it is appropriate to provide mental health screening as a part of overall health screening provided by medical personnel. Results of screening in this context become part of a medical file and are not available to the school without an information release. Given the impact of untreated mental health disorders in children and adolescents, early and periodic screening for mental health problems is very appropriate. In some cases, such as the risk of suicide, screening can save lives. (See Chapter 12 for a full discussion of diagnostic methods.)

Many physicians provide mental health as well as health screening as part of routine health checkups. In fact, all children and adolescents ages 0–21 years who are covered by Medicaid are entitled to early, periodic screening, diagnosis, and treatment (EPSDT). EPSDT screening is supposed to include a mental health screen that identifies evidence of significant social-emotional problems. If screening identifies the need for services, those services need to be paid for by Medicaid, even if they are not covered in the state's Medicaid benefit set.

Also, mental health screening can be done in the school, but not by school personnel. For example, EPSDT screening can be performed by public health nurses working in the school but hired by the county's public health department. In this scenario, information that is collected does not go to the school but remains in public health records.

The question arises about whether it is appropriate for schools to conduct a mental health screen of certain students under specific circumstances. For example, Minnesota rules mandate a mental health screen for all students being considered for special education services for Emotional Disturbance. In fact, schools routinely do mental health screening, possibly without realizing it, when they conduct a special education evaluation of a student for the Emotional Disturbance category and identify problem behaviors such as inattention, social withdrawal, hyperactivity, avoidance of peer activities, and so on. The very behaviors that are identified in special education evaluations are often also the same criteria that are used to diagnose mental health disorders. Essentially, the evaluation provides screening information that indicates evidence of a mental health disorder. Under IDEA Child Find rules, school districts are obligated to identify and evaluate all students with disabilities who may require special education services. The emotionally disturbed category of special education describes criteria such as problems forming relationships, inappropriate behaviors or feelings, pervasive unhappiness or depression, and fears or physical symptoms associated with personal or school problems. Students who have these types of chronic problems that adversely affect their educational performance are supposed to be assessed for special education. Given these characteristics, an educational evaluation essentially includes mental health screening.

For many children and adolescents who have mental health disorders, evidence of those disorders is obvious to teachers and to the other students as well. Bizarre behaviors, social isolation, agitated movements, crying in class, and many other symptoms of mental health disorders may be dramatic. Other students who have mental health disorders do not display easily recognizable evidence of these disorders, and screening tools can be quite helpful. If there is evidence of a mental health disorder, identified through either observation or the use of a screening tool, it is important for schools to have procedures and guidelines about how this information, and information about available services within the school and the community, should be communicated to parents.

Screening tools can be very helpful in identifying treatable mental health disorders. For example, several school districts have used the Columbia suicide screening tool (SAMHSA, 2016) to identify students who were at risk for attempting suicide. In the process, many high-risk students were identified, and they received treatment for major depression.

SOCIAL AND EMOTIONAL LEARNING

Many school districts are adopting social and emotional learning (SEL) programs into their curriculum. These programs focus on developing both social and emotional competencies in children and adolescents. They focus on assisting the learning process through a combination of effective classroom instruction, student engagement in positive activities in and out of the classroom, broad parent and community involvement, program planning, implementation, and evaluation. SEL is based on five clusters of student competency, developed by the Collaborative for Academic, Social, and Emotional Learning: self-awareness, self-management, social awareness, relationship skills, and responsible decision making (http://casel.org). Students learn to recognize how their emotions and thoughts influence their behaviors. They learn techniques for self-regulation of their emotions, thoughts, and behaviors and learn to work to attain academic and personal goals. They become culturally sensitive to social diversity issues and develop skills in building and maintaining positive relationships with other students. They gain mastery in making choices about their behavior and learn to assess the consequences of their actions. SEL programs promote positive academic and social behaviors while preventing negative behaviors such as bullying, violence, truancy, and drug use.

SEL is not one specific program; it defines the basic parameters of an educational approach that addresses social and emotional interventions. Common factors in instructional methods include modeling and coaching empathy skills in young children, outlining specific methods of conflict resolution, devoting classroom time to practicing group decision making, using games to promote teamwork and cooperation, teaching listening skills, and encouraging older students to mentor younger students.

Students who participate in SEL programs have better attendance records, are less disruptive in the classroom, have fewer suspensions and disciplinary actions, enjoy school more, and perform better academically than control groups that do not receive SEL programming. SEL programs benefit both students and staff. The classroom environment is less stressful and teacher-student relationships are more positive.

Examples of SEL programs include I Can Problem Solve (http://www.icanproblemsolve.info), which is a preschool through sixth grade program that is designed to enhance interpersonal cognitive processes and problem-solving skills. It uses structured lessons, classroom interactions, integration in the school curriculum, and parental involvement activities that focus on finding alternate solutions for problem solving, reducing conflict, improving the classroom climate, and improving family interactions. MindUP (http://teacher.scholastic.com/products/mindup/) is a SEL program from kindergarten through eighth grade based on research in cognitive neuroscience, evidence-based classroom pedagogy, mindfulness education, and positive psychology. It teaches regulatory strategies and skills, including focused attention and relaxation exercises. Its curriculum includes methods of learning to focus awareness, learning mindfulness of one's sensory environment, learning to focus on positive attitudes, and learning to take positive action in one's daily life.

SEL programs benefit students who do not have mental health disorders, students who are at risk of developing disorders, and students who have mental health disorders. They create a positive foundation for establishing an effective learning environment. Although they are not interventions for specific mental health disorders, they work in conjunction with interventions that are focused on the diagnosis and treatment of mental health disorders.

FAMILY-SCHOOL COORDINATORS

School districts can effectively work in partnership with community agencies that provide triage, screening, and treatment referrals as needed. A school district may be in a collaborative relationship with a county, and pooled funding (e.g., from the capture of indirect Medicaid funds) may be paying for a community nonprofit agency to provide services to families at no cost to them. The agency can hire a family–school coordinator who is available to intervene in situations where students are having significant difficulty in school. For example, the teacher or other members of the educational team could tell parents, "Your child is having problems in school including disruptiveness and off-task behaviors, and we are doing our best to identify educational reasons for these difficulties. If there are other reasons for your child's problems, you may want to take advantage of the family–school coordinator, who works with families to address these problems. There is no cost to you for these services, and whatever they identify will remain private. The school will not know about their intervention or its results unless you choose to sign a release of information allowing the information to be shared with us." At this point, if the parents agree to this plan, the family–school coordinator meets with the family to identify the problems that are contributing to the student's difficulties.

The problems may go beyond the individual student's difficulties. For example, it might be discovered through mental health screening and interviewing that the student's mother suffers from untreated major depression, or that the father was treated for ADHD as a child and now has substance use problems. There may be family social stressors including physical health problems of a family member, poverty, loss of a job, homelessness, undocumented status, and so on. The student may show evidence of ADHD as well. The family–school coordinator would then communicate concerns to the family and make referrals for diagnostic assessments as needed.

This approach addresses the bigger family picture and is more likely to be effective than a narrow focus only on the student. Parents are generally more comfortable revealing family information to a community mental health provider than to a school, as such information will go into their private files and not into their child's educational record. If the family–school coordinator makes referrals for evaluation and treatment, the school is less liable for payment because the school did not make the referral. This approach is an intermediary step in the process of identifying problems in the classroom and in intervening with diagnostic assessments and mental health treatment.

SCHOOL-LINKED MENTAL HEALTH SERVICES

The continuum of mental health services begins with universal mental health promotion and primary prevention interventions, such as positive behavior supports that serve all students. For students who have difficulty functioning in school due to emotional or behavioral problems, school social workers, psychologists, and counselors can provide counseling and skills training to help them overcome their difficulties. For students who are demonstrating evidence of significant mental health disorders, the next step on the continuum is the provision of diagnostic and treatment services by a mental health professional. These services can be provided in the community, but are often more effective and accessible when they are a component of school-linked mental health services. These services are not equivalent to school counseling, prevention services, or school-wide behavioral interventions; they are based on a medical model of diagnosis and treatment and are provided by mental health professionals within the school setting. The national principles (Weist et al., 2005) for best practice in the provision of school-linked mental health services include the following:

- All youth and families are able to access appropriate care regardless of their ability to pay.
- Programs are implemented to address needs and strengthen assets for students, families, schools, and communities.
- Programs and services focus on reducing barriers to development and learning, are student and family friendly, and are based on evidence of positive impact.
- Students, families, teachers, and other important groups are actively involved in the program's development, oversight, evaluation, and continuous improvement.
- A continuum of care is provided, including school-wide mental health promotion, early intervention, and treatment.
- Staff are held to high ethical standards, are committed to children, adolescents, and families, and display an energetic, responsive, and proactive style in delivering services.
- Staff are respectful of and competently address developmental, cultural, and personal differences among students, families, and staff.
- Staff build and maintain strong relationships with other mental health and health providers and educators in the school, and a theme of interdisciplinary collaboration characterizes all efforts.
- Mental health programs in the school are coordinated with related programs in other community settings.

- Program goals are the improvement of clinical and functional outcomes for children with a mental health diagnosis.
- Programs seek to increase accessibility for uninsured, underinsured, and culturally underserved children to co-located mental health services wherever financial, transportation, or cultural barriers exist.
- Programs are designed to improve early and appropriate identification of mental health issues in children.
- Programs serve to increase capacity of school staff to identify mental health issues and make effective adaptations in the school and classroom environment.
- Programs integrate clinical standards, diagnostic assessments, and individual outcome measurement with other promising practices at the local level to unite standards of care with systems of care.

PROVISION OF MENTAL HEALTH SERVICES WITHIN THE SCHOOL

There are strong arguments for the provision of mental health diagnostic and treatment within the school setting. Most students who have mental health disorders never receive treatment for their problems, and the disorders often have emotional and behavioral manifestations that interfere with effective learning in the classroom. Lack of access to services is a major reason for this lack of treatment; clinics often have limited evening or weekend hours, and parents may find it impossible to leave their place of employment on a weekly basis to pick up their child and bring her or him to an appointment. When parents allow an exchange of information between school personnel and community mental health providers, teachers have a better understanding of the nature of their students' difficulties and are more able to effectively provide accommodations for the students' needs. Also, when clinicians work in the school, they have a better sense of the nature of the students' difficulties within the school environment (see Chapter 15 for a discussion of collaborations between schools and county mental health programs).

As school professionals become increasingly aware of mental health problems in the student population, they grapple with determining the appropriate role of the school in providing services to these students. Many recognize that schools are in the education business, not the mental health business, yet school counselors, social workers, nurses, and psychologists all play a role in assisting these students. It may be unclear, at times, whether these services are educational in nature, or whether they constitute direct mental health treatment. In general, these school professionals provide counseling services rather than direct diagnostic and treatment services.

Counseling is the process of providing information, improving skills, and assisting a student to succeed within the school environment. Counseling is routinely provided by school social workers, psychologists, nurses, and counselors. Counseling is a mental health service that is appropriate for school professionals to provide. It differs from therapy, which is a clinical service that constitutes treatment of a disorder, such as clinical depression.

Some school professionals (e.g., licensed social workers) may have licensure that allows them to diagnose and treat children and adolescents. There are a number of different methods of providing mental health diagnostic and treatment services within the school setting. Each method has its own risks and benefits. I believe that schools should stay out of the mental health business of diagnosis and treatment, but should collaborate with other systems to ensure that students will have access to services that will result in educational gains and cost savings to the school districts.

MODELS OF SCHOOL-BASED MENTAL HEALTH SERVICES

Many children who have mental health disorders are first identified in the school setting by teachers, counselors, social workers, and so on. An educational evaluation or other interventions may identify evidence of the mental health disorder, and the student's parents may seek accessible treatment services that go beyond the typical counseling activities performed by school staff. Some schools have responded to this challenge by having their own staff provide mental health diagnostic and treatment services within the school. Professionals at a school may be interested in having mental health services available to students, but administrators may not be aware of the issues that need to be considered in setting up such a program. The following is a description of several models that can be used to ensure accessible mental health services within the school setting, with a description of each model's advantages and disadvantages.

School-Hired Professionals

Many school professionals such as school social workers have training and licensure that would allow them to set up a practice in the community and provide diagnostic and treatment services. School districts that employ these professionals to provide treatment within the school setting are, in essence, setting up that practice within the school.

This approach has advantages. It provides increased access to services by individuals who fully understand school-related issues. School administrators have control over the therapist's activities and may potentially bill Medicaid for the service and also receive special education funding for the activity if it is identified as a related service on the student's IEP. However, the approach has numerous potential problems:

• Therapists are required to document pertinent mental health information in their diagnostic and treatment notes. In the case of a school-hired therapist, all of these notes become part of the student's educational record and may include sensitive information about parents and siblings (e.g., in cases of fetal alcohol syndrome or child abuse).

• If a tragic event such as suicide were to occur, the therapist would most likely be covered by malpractice insurance (proof of which should be required by the district), but the school district could be sued for poor supervision of the therapist. School districts cannot obtain malpractice insurance and cannot necessarily rely on their errors and omissions insurance coverage to protect them. Coverage for the school district would pivot on the question of whether the supervision of mental health treatment professionals is considered an appropriate activity of a school district.

• Mental health professionals are required to be on call or to provide crisis backup coverage on evenings, weekends, and vacations.

• Schools are accustomed to billing Medicaid for IEP-related services, and frequently do. They generally don't bill private insurance, however, due to copays and deductibles that would conflict with the requirement of providing a free appropriate public education.

• In order to maximize Medicaid reimbursement for IEP mental health–related services, some school districts may be lowering the threshold for the requirement for related services by providing IEP services that would be helpful, but not necessary, to the student. The IDEA mandate requires the provision of related services that are "required to assist a child with a disability to benefit from special education." If the student were to lose Medicaid or other insurance coverage, the district would be on the hook for continuing to provide these helpful, but not required, services, as well as potentially other costly services such as residential treatment. (See Appendix 2 for additional information on providing mental health services to IEP students.)

Provision of Services Within the School by Community Mental Health or Medical Professionals

This model co-locates a community service provider such as a mental health or health clinic in the school setting. The clinic is on-site, but the school district maintains legal and financial firewalls that would not be present if the district's staff were to provide these services. The clinic leases space from the school, often at minimal or no cost, and a contractual agreement clarifies roles and responsibilities regarding indemnification, data privacy, criminal background checks, licensure, financial tasks, administrative requirements, and so on.

Although the provider in this co-located model can be an individual in private practice, I believe that it is preferable for the provider to be a community mental health or health clinic. These clinics can offer a broader array of mental health services, case consultation, psychiatric backup, and comprehensive coverage, as well as possible funding from counties or grant sources to reimburse services provided to uninsured clients.

The co-located model overcomes the problems outlined above for school-hired mental health professional services. Data are kept private, outside of the educational record. The provider can offer 24-7 crisis coverage, maximum billing capabilities, services to both general and special education students, and adequate malpractice coverage. The provider is in the school but not of the school. Its employees cannot discuss students with school staff without an information release, and the school maintains appropriate protective firewalls.

COLLABORATION OF SCHOOL-HIRED AND OUTSIDE PROFESSIONALS

The collaboration model integrates services from providers inside and outside of the school system. In some states, schools can bill Medicaid for IEP services such as skills training and skills practice. These activities are consistent with schools' mandates. Schools can partner with community mental health providers, splitting the therapy and skills training roles between them. Ongoing communication between the two systems is necessary and requires a signed parental information release.

In all of the service models described above, school-hired professionals continue to provide educationally related counseling services to students in need.

REIMBURSEMENT FOR SCHOOL-PROVIDED SERVICES

The cost of providing mental health services is an obvious hurdle for schools. Potential funding sources include private insurance and Medicaid billing for direct services; consolidated early intervening services funds; state, federal, and private grants; discretionary local government funds; and Medicaid indirect service reimbursement funds. As noted above, school districts have access to IDEA funding for mental health–related services included on IEPs. I recommend that schools carefully follow the language of IDEA, including on an IEP only those related services that are necessary and required to assist students in benefiting from special education, in order to avoid potential financial liabilities.

Ideally, on-site mental health services would be available to all students in need, regardless of the presence or type of insurance coverage. Community mental health centers generally provide this broad range of services. Co-located centers can provide similar services, and generally have a significantly lower fail and cancel rate than clinic-based services, thus improving the reimbursement for the clinic. The reduction in client load during summer vacation, however, is a major financial liability for the school-based clinics. Some clinics shift their focus during the summer to address the needs of extended school year students; some follow students throughout the summer at their own clinic headquarters; some reassign the clinicians to other tasks (e.g., mentoring) during the summer, and some have employees who take time off during the summer break.

Many programs are funded through grants, especially those serving uninsured patients and those providing nonbillable ancillary services such as teacher consultation, inservice presentations, and attendance at meetings. However, many grant-funded programs have fallen by the wayside over the years as the grants have ended. I recommend maximizing reimbursement via insurance and Medicaid and using grant funds only for start-up costs. Some states' Medicaid benefit sets include payment for many ancillary services, and some insurance companies have partnered with school districts and clinics to create a higher bundled rate for school-based mental health services that are provided to students. The programs that have remained sustainable tend to be based on partnerships between mental health care stakeholders including clinics, school districts, counties, and insurance providers.

TARGET POPULATIONS

It is my opinion that the following populations of children and adolescents who have mental health disorders should be given high priority for school-based mental health services:

• Students who have treatable disorders who are at risk for referral for a special education evaluation. As indicated above, early intervention has the best chance of producing a positive outcome for a child or adolescent who is struggling with a mental health disorder. For this reason, I recommend appropriate diagnosis and treatment at the pre-referral stage. This effort identifies treatable disorders and can prevent the need for a special education assessment in some situations.

• Students who currently receive special education services yet continue to have emotional, behavioral, and academic difficulties.

• Special education students who are at risk of referral to federal Setting 4 (self-contained at a separate school site) programs and students who are served in these restrictive placements.

PLACEMENT ALTERNATIVES

As noted above, many Setting 4 students in Emotional Disturbance behavioral programs have mental health disorders that are at least as severe as those of students in day treatment programs. Day treatment is a mental health service that is more intensive than traditional outpatient treatment. These programs often do not succeed for students who have behavior problems, oppositionality, difficulty with traditional therapeutic interventions, or other factors. A lack of appropriate therapeutic services leads to poor outcomes for this population. I recommend moving away from a fixed day treatment model that tends to avoid serving delinquent, psychiatrically disturbed students and toward a no-reject intensive, intermediate-level on-site mental health services model.

As many students who have mental health disorders also have substance use issues, co-located services would ideally address this issue as well. If co-located mental health services are to be successful, school districts must clearly define the roles of their own professionals as distinguished from the roles of co-located providers in order to avoid overlaps and gaps in services and to allay concerns about school professionals' job security. School districts that offer on-site mental health treatment services provide a significant benefit to students, their families, mental health providers, and the school system. Schools can create bridges to the mental health system while maintaining legal and financial firewalls. These services can result in educational and behavioral improvements for students and significant cost savings to school districts.

Case Consultation

Given the limited resources available for child mental health services, do you think that diagnostic and treatment services should be provided by school district employees? If so, how could the district address the multiple pitfalls outlined above? If not, how can the district ensure that students will receive the mental health services that they require?

Here are some examples of the outcomes of consultations that I have provided:

Example 1

A special education director of a small (5000-student) school district requested psychiatric consultation because of the large number of students in his district who were being referred to restrictive Setting 4 placements. A file review indicated that 85% of these students had received psychiatric diagnoses in the past, but that only 5% were receiving any mental health treatment. The director set up space in several schools for a co-located community mental health clinic to provide services. Many students received treatment for the mental health disorders that were causing their severe emotional and behavioral problems, and as a result, they were able to return to less restrictive programming. This resulted in savings of over $800,000 per year for the district.

Example 2

A large urban school district collaborated with a community mental health clinic to provide on-site mental health services in several schools. Many students were seen who otherwise would not have been able to access mental health services. As a result of this intervention, the number of behavioral incidents, suspensions, and special education referrals decreased, and overall academic indexes for the group improved.

Example 3

A school district collaborated with the crisis unit from its county to provide crisis intervention for students who were demonstrating evidence of potential danger to themselves or others. With parental permission, school social workers gave background information to county social workers, which enabled the county staff to accurately address students' risks and to arrange for appropriate interventions, including hospitalization when necessary.

CHAPTER 19

General Education, Special Education, and 504 Plan Students

AS MENTAL HEALTH DISORDERS ARE, BY DEFINITION, DIS-abilities, students who have such a disorder may qualify for specialized services to help them achieve academically. Some may benefit from additional supports in regular education programs, some may qualify for 504 plans that are designed to ensure equal treatment for students with and without disabilities, and some may qualify for special education services. This chapter describes the nature of these interventions and outlines the criteria for qualification, services that can be provided, different categories of interventions, and the types of interventions available to students who have mental health disorders.

When regular education interventions are not adequate to meet the needs of a student who has a mental health disability, the next step is to consider a 504 plan or special education services. The special education and 504 systems provide more intensive support than is generally available to students receiving educational services without them.

504 PLANS

A 504 plan stems from the Rehabilitation Act of 1973 that explicitly prohibits discrimination based on disability. It is a civil rights statute ensuring that disabled students' needs are met as adequately as are the needs of students who are not disabled.

Section 504 states, "No otherwise qualified individual with a disability in the United States, as defined in section 706(8) of this title, shall, solely by reason of her or his disability, be excluded from the participation in, be denied the benefits of, or be subjected to discrimination under any program or activity receiving Federal financial assistance" [29 U.S.C. §794(a), 34 C.F.R. §104.4(a)].

To be eligible for a 504 plan, a student must be between ages 3 and 22 years, depending on the program, and must have a disability as defined by Federal law: "An individual with a disability means any person who: (i) has a mental or physical impairment that substantially limits one or more major life activity; (ii) has a record of such an impairment; or (iii) is regarded as having such an impairment" [34 C.F.R. §104.3(j)(1)].

Note that simply having a disability doesn't mean that an individual has an impairment severe enough to qualify for services. Section 504 may include any disability, long-term illness, or other disorder that "substantially" reduces or lessens a student's ability to access learning in the educational setting because of a learning-, behavior-, or health-related condition.

In other words, the presence of a physical or mental impairment does not constitute a disability for purposes of Section 504 unless its severity is such that it results in a substantial limitation of one or more major life activities (Appendix A to Part 104, #3). The statute indicates that only physical or mental health impairments qualify, and therefore, "environmental, cultural and economic disadvantage are not in themselves covered" (Appendix A to Part 104, #3). The term "substantially limits" is based on a determination to be made by each local school district, and depends on the nature and severity of the student's disabling condition. Section 504 standards must comply with the Americans With Disabilities Act Amendments Act of 2008 that affords a broad scope of protection to eligible students. It compares these students' limitations with same-aged, nondisabled peers in the general population. Major life activities include speaking, learning, sitting, self-care, walking, manual tasks, seeing, thinking, working, interacting with others, breathing, standing, bending, lifting, and concentrating. These criteria apply to both chronic (e.g., ADHD) and acute (e.g., a broken limb) disorders. Disorders that are episodic or in remission are covered if, while they are active, they substantially limit one or more major life activities. The use of alcohol or illegal drugs is not covered or eligible under Section 504.

School districts are not automatically obligated to refer a student for a 504 evaluation based upon parent request. The district must have reason to believe that the student is in need of these services due to a disability. If the district refuses the parent's request, it must provide the parent with a notice of procedural rights. Placement decisions "are to be made by a group of persons who are knowledgeable about the child, the meaning of the evaluation data, placement options, least restrictive environment requirements, and comparable facilities" [34 C.F.R. §104.35(c)(3)]. There is no requirement to have the parents be part of the committee that decides about placement for services. The committee considers multiple sources of information (e.g., physician reports, grades, test scores, observations, disciplinary actions) in making its determination.

Students with a 504 plan are reevaluated every three years or more often if there is a significant change in placement. The 504 plan should be reevaluated on an annual basis at least to ensure that it continues to be appropriate, given the changes in educational circumstances. In most situations, students who have a 504 plan receive services in the regular classroom. However, if "the student with a disability is so disruptive in a regular classroom that the education of other students is significantly impaired, then the needs of the student with a disability cannot be met in that environment. Therefore, regular placement would not be appropriate to his or her needs and would not be required by §104.34" (34 C.F.R. §104.34, Appendix A, #24).

A wide variety of accommodations can be provided through 504 services for a student who has a mental health disorder. These are generally related to the nature and severity of the disability and the clinical manifestations that present within the school environment. Thus, a student who has ADHD and who is very distractible and disorganized could have accommodations such as a seat near the front of the class, extended time for test taking, oral rather than written tests, additional positive reinforcements, assistance with organizational skills, and so on. If a student has significant behavioral difficulties as a result of a disability, it is important to include both a behavior plan and a discipline plan in the 504 plan. Students who have a 504 plan are expected to follow school rules of conduct, but if they have behavioral difficulties, the district needs to consider the relationship between their behavior problem and their disability prior to initiating disciplinary action.

SPECIAL EDUCATION AND RELATED SERVICES

Special education is defined as "specially designed instruction," which is designated in the Individuals with Disabilities Education Act (IDEA) as follows:

Specially designed instruction means adapting, as appropriate to the needs of an eligible child under this part, the content, methodology, or delivery of instruction—

(i) To address the unique needs of the child that result from the child's disability; and

(ii) To ensure access of the child to the general curriculum, so that the child can meet the educational standards within the jurisdiction of the public agency that apply to all children. [§300.39(b)(3)]

Special education thus refers to a process of adapting the content, methodology, or delivery of instruction to a student. Adaption can be done in a variety of ways, including changes in instruction, materials, scheduling, setting, or method of student response. In addition to receiving special education accommodations and modifications, a student may receive related services. These are supportive services that are necessary for a student to be able to benefit from special education services. According to IDEA, related services (§300.34) are defined in general as: "Transportation and such developmental, corrective, and other supportive services as are required to assist a child with a disability to benefit from special education", and includes:

- Speech-language pathology and audiology services
- Interpreting services
- Psychological services
- Physical and occupational therapy
- Recreation, including therapeutic recreation
- Early identification and assessment of disabilities in children

- Counseling services, including rehabilitation counseling
- Orientation and mobility services
- Medical services for diagnostic or evaluation purposes
- School health services and school nurse services
- Social work services in schools

MENTAL HEALTH–RELATED SERVICES ON IEPS

Note that medical services are limited to diagnostic evaluation and do not include medical treatment services. In some circumstances, however, schools are obligated to provide or pay for both mental health diagnosis and treatment. Mental health–related services should be provided, just as other related services must be, if they are necessary for a student to be able to benefit from special education services. The threshold for "necessary," in terms of academic or social-emotional functioning, is a matter of significant debate between attorneys representing school districts and those representing parents. It is clear that it is not at the level of requiring services so that a student will be able to perform in an optimal manner.

Because many students who receive special education services have mental health disorders, the question arises about whether they are eligible to receive mental health services as part of their special education programming. Schools are required to be the payer of last resort for all related services, including mental health–related services. "Related services" are defined broadly in IDEA, and include psychological, social work, and counseling services. They include developmental, corrective, and other supportive services such as psychological, social work, and school nurse services designed to enable a child with a disability to receive a free appropriate public education as described in the student's IEP (see Appendix 2 for additional information).

Medical services are limited to diagnostic and evaluation services only. Medical services include the early identification and assessment of disabling conditions but do not include medical treatment provided by a physician. Counseling services are defined as services provided by qualified social workers, psychologists, guidance counselors, or other qualified personnel.

Parent counseling and training is defined as assisting parents in understanding the special needs of their child, providing them with information about child development, and helping them acquire the necessary skills to support the implementation of their child's IEP. It also applies to special services for children from birth to three years of age who have developmental delays, and who require individualized family service plans.

Home psychological services include psychological testing and assessment, consultations with school staff, and assistance in developing positive behavioral intervention strategies. Psychological services also include "planning and managing a program of psychological services, including psychological counseling for children and parents."

Social work services include preparing a social or developmental history on a child, group and individual counseling with the child and family, working in partnership with parents and others on those problems in a child's living situation that affect the child's adjustment in school, mobilizing school and community resources to enable the child to learn as effectively as possible in his or her educational program, and assisting in developing positive behavioral intervention services.

Counseling is generally considered the provision of assistance and guidance in resolving personal, social, or psychological problems and difficulties. Therapy, on the other hand, is an intervention that is intended to treat a mental health disorder. Although therapy is not defined in IDEA, case law has determined that in some circumstances, therapy needs to be included in the IEP as a related service when it is deemed necessary to support a student's education. In fact, mental health residential treatment may be the school district's responsibility to fund. If the placement is necessary for the student's education, then the program, including nonmedical care and room and board, must be funded by the school district at no cost to the parents of the child. Courts have varied significantly in decisions regarding school districts' financial liabilities in specific cases.

Many school districts are extremely reluctant to consider placing any mental health treatment services on special education students' IEPs, as doing this can create potential financial liability down the road. For example, a student might eventually require expensive mental health treatment and may not have insurance coverage that pays for it. Other school districts take the opposite approach, and include mental health treatment as related services on numerous students' IEPs. In doing so, school districts may be able to bill Medicaid for IEP related mental health services, if the treatment is both medically and educationally necessary. Educators may be unaware of the wide variations from district to district regarding this issue. Gaining an understanding of this can help put the issue in perspective for them, regarding students and the services that are available for them.

Educators may think of students' significant mental health problems as a special education issue. In fact, the vast majority of students who have mental health disorders, and even the majority of those who have severe disorders, are in the general education system. Remarkably, a significant percentage of students who receive special education services for Emotional Disturbance (called Severe Emotional Disturbance, or Emotional/Behavioral Disturbance in some states) would not have needed these services had they received appropriate pre-referral mental health interventions. Often, mental health symptoms of disorders that are untreated or inappropriately treated are the reasons for referral for special education assessments. There are also a number of students who, even when they are receiving optimal mental health services, will still require additional assistance through special education or 504 plans.

The presence of a mental health disorder does not automatically qualify a student for either special education or a 504 plan. The decision to qualify a student is made by an educational team that weighs all of the information and makes a determination as to whether the student meets the criteria for qualification. IDEA is the statute that outlines the federal criteria for special education qualification. States can add criteria to be more inclusive, but cannot reduce the federal criteria. Fourteen disability categories are defined in IDEA:

- Autism
- Deaf-blindness
- Deafness
- Developmental delay
- Emotional disturbance
- Hearing impairment
- Intellectual disability
- Multiple disabilities
- Orthopedic impairment

- Other health impairment
- Specific learning disability
- Speech or language impairment
- Traumatic brain injury
- Visual impairment, including blindness

Students who have mental health disorders could be in any one of these categories. The majority are in the emotional disturbance, other health impairment (OHI), and autism spectrum categories.

STUDENTS WITH MENTAL HEALTH DISORDERS IN GENERAL AND SPECIAL EDUCATION

Given the high percentage of child and adolescent mental health disorders in the general population, it is clear that the vast majority of students who have these disorders are receiving general education rather than special education services. Even severely emotionally disturbed students are often served in general education programs. For this reason, this book is targeted to both general and special education educators.

As prevalent as child and adolescent psychiatric disorders are in the general population, they are significantly more prevalent among students who are receiving special education services. For example, although school-based evaluations of students who qualify for services in the ASD category are considered educational and not clinical, in that they are eligibility focused rather than diagnostically focused, the criteria in many states are identical to the psychiatric DSM clinical definitions.

Although ADHD is only one of many medical conditions that can be served under the federal OHI category, in many schools it is the leading category of health problems served under OHI. Similarly, ADHD is a major leading diagnosis for students who receive Section 504 services for their medical disabilities.

Emotional Disturbance

The IDEA emotional disturbance (ED) category specifies a condition that exhibits one or more of the following characteristics over a long period of time and to a marked degree that adversely affects a child's educational performance:

- An inability to learn that cannot be explained by intellectual, sensory, or health factors.
- An inability to build or maintain satisfactory interpersonal relationships with peers and teachers
- Inappropriate types of behavior or feelings under normal circumstances
- A general pervasive mood of unhappiness or depression
- A tendency to develop physical symptoms or fears associated with personal or school problems

The term "emotional disturbance" includes schizophrenia. IDEA does not apply this term to children who are socially maladjusted unless it is determined that they have an emotional disturbance. It can be argued that impaired educational performance may include significant difficulties in the social-emotional realm at school, allowing a student who has these problems to be able to qualify for this category even if he or she is doing well academically. Note that the category not require a mental health diagnosis and that the presence of a diagnosis does not necessarily qualify the student for special education.

The vast majority of students served in the ED category either have already been diagnosed with a mental health disorder or are presenting with symptoms that strongly suggest a mental health disorder. ADHD is the most common disorder seen in these students, and referrals for special education assessments due to ongoing behaviors such as hyperactivity, impulsivity, and difficulty attending to tasks are very common.

The ED category is the only special education category that is not based on a specific disability. In many school districts there is a disconnect between the fact that a student who is receiving ED services has a diagnosed mental health disorder and that the symptoms of the disorder are the behaviors that are to be addressed in the student's IEP. When a student is receiving ED services, the diagnosed mental health disorder is not considered the student's disability per se; essentially, the category becomes the disability. In other words, it is not uncommon for school districts to acknowledge that the student may have a diagnosis, but the main issue is the student's behavior that needs to be dealt with behaviorally regardless of whether a diagnosis is present. Some districts go a step further, with the attitude that diagnosis is irrelevant and that it is inappropriate to look beyond the external behaviors to seek an underlying source of the student's problem (a mental health disorder).

According to research done by Mary Wagner (1995), the ED category has the worst outcome of all of the disability categories in absenteeism, grades, failed classes, graduation rates, employment rates, postsecondary education, unwed pregnancy, and arrest rates. Over half (58%) of ED students who graduated high school were arrested within three to five years after graduation. Among dropouts, that percentage increased to 73% by the time that they had been out of school from three to five years. According to Wagner, the primary reason for the poor outcomes was the fact that, in general, students in the ED category rarely received adequate treatment for their underlying mental health disorders.

Outcome data also indicate significant involvement with the mental health system after leaving school. The study noted that students who receive special education services for ED often have poor social skills, resulting in problematic interactions with teachers and peers.

Over the years, as health insurance companies and county social service agencies have significantly reduced placements in residential treatment facilities and have limited psychiatric hospital stays, school districts have been experiencing a dramatic increase in students who have severe mental health disorders. Many of these students are placed in the ED category. The ED category, though it is not diagnostically focused, is filled with students who have mental health disorders. In consulting with many rural, suburban, and urban school districts for the last 30 years, I have reviewed numerous files of students at the time of their first special education evaluation that led to ED placement. For example, in a consultation with an urban district, I noted that 73% of elementary and 87% of secondary ED school students had already been diagnosed with a mental health disorder. ADHD was the most common diagnosis noted, but other disorders were also prevalent, including mood disorders, anxiety disorders, psychotic disorders, ASD, attachment disorders, substance use disorder, and behavioral disorders. A history of two or more diagnoses was the norm for students receiving special education services in the ED category.

Parental divorce or separation, histories of foster care, histories of physical or sexual abuse, adoption, and parental substance use disorder are often noted in the social histories of students who are served in the ED category. Approximately half of the students at the time of their first evaluation had a history of taking psychiatric medications, and those percentages rose for students in Setting 3 (73%) and Setting 4 (93%) programs. Medications included antidepressants, stimulants, antipsychotics, lithium, antiseizure (mood-stabilizing) medications, and antianxiety medications.

The ED category of special education may contain the highest percentage of children and adolescents who have mental health disorders in the community. One study noted that the ED category had the highest percentage of students diagnosed with a mental health disorder within the previous year (70%), compared with children and adolescents in the alcohol or drug system (60%), the juvenile justice system (52%), and the child welfare system (41%) (Garland et al., 2001).

Students who receive highly restrictive services in Setting 4 placements, where they are provided educational services in separate facilities, may be placed in schools that are predominantly for behaviorally disturbed students or in programs for students who are seen as being mentally ill. Programs for the behaviorally disturbed group tend to focus on behavioral interventions, whereas the second group is provided extensive mental health services in a day treatment setting.

Ironically, when the histories of the two groups are analyzed, the behaviorally disturbed group tends to have at least as much, if not more, evidence of psychiatric disorders than the emotionally disturbed group. Histories of psychiatric diagnoses, medication and psychotherapeutic treatments, and even psychiatric hospitalization are similar for both groups. The behaviorally disturbed group tends not to fit the programs offered by mental health treatment providers, due to histories of difficulty working in traditional therapeutic settings (e.g., group therapy, individual therapy), some students' history of oppositionality and defiance, lack of parental involvement in therapy programs, and so on. As a result, students who have severe and often untreated mental health disorders are often placed in programs where they receive minimal mental health services. Their poor outcomes are tied to the fact that the E (emotional) in ED is generally not treated effectively.

Emotionally disturbed students comprise approximately 8% of the special education population, at a male-to-female ratio of 80:20. The percentage of ED students increases over the years, from approximately 4% in the 6–7-year-old group to 13% in the 16–17-year-old group. The higher percentage in secondary school reflects, for some students, late recognition of their significant emotional or behavioral disabilities. ED students are more likely to be retained in grade. Dropout rates are the highest of any special education category, with 51% of these students dropping out of school. This is twice the dropout rate of the second highest categories (learning disability, 27%; speech/language impairment, 25%). Approximately 30% of ED students are educated outside of the general education classroom for the majority of their school day. Among high school-aged ED students, 72% are expelled or suspended from school, compared to 22% of students without disabilities. ED students often lag behind their nondisabled peers by one to two grade levels in basic academic skills including reading, math, and written language. It is important to note that a significant percentage of students who receive special education services in the ED category would not have needed a referral for these services if their mental health disorders had been accurately diagnosed and effectively treated. Educators can play a major role in working with other school professionals and with parents to encourage early intervention services for at-risk students.

Other Health Impairment

The OHI category, in contrast with the ED category, is based on specific medical disabilities and can include mental health disorders as well. OHI, according to IDEA, means:

> . . . having limited strength, vitality, or alertness, including a heightened alertness to environmental stimuli, that results in limited alertness with respect to the educational environment, that (a) is due to chronic or acute health problems such as asthma, attention deficit disorder or attention deficit hyperactivity disorder, diabetes, epilepsy, a heart condition, hemophilia, lead poisoning, leukemia, nephritis, rheumatic fever, sickle cell anemia, and Tourette syndrome; and

(b) adversely affects a child's educational performance. (Individuals with Disabilities Education Act, 2004)

Some school districts interpret paragraph (a) to mean that ADHD is the only mental health disorder allowed under this category. This is not true. According to the U.S. Department of Education, in response to requests to specifically list mental health disabilities in the federal regulations:

> The list of acute or chronic health conditions in the definition of other health impairment is not exhaustive, but rather provides examples of problems that children have that could make them eligible for special education and related services under the category of other health impairment. We decline to include dysphagia, FAS, bipolar disorders, and other organic neurological disorders in the definition of other health impairment because these conditions are commonly understood to be health impairments. (71 Fed. Reg. 46550, August 14, 2006)

In other words, the major mental health disorders (e.g., ADHD, depression, bipolar mood disorder, panic disorder, obsessive-compulsive disorder, schizophrenia) are chronic health conditions, and a student who has one of these disorders and who meets the federal and state criteria for OHI, is thus eligible for special education services under this category. Often, it is the parents, and not the school district, who advocate for the OHI category for their children who have mental health disorders. Parents often see this category as less stigmatizing than the ED category and appreciate the fact that the educational team needs to have at least one member who has educational expertise in the student's mental health disorder. (Since ED is considered the disability of ED students, there is no similar requirement for a team member to have expertise in the mental health disorders that an ED student may have.) Schools may be reluctant to put a student in the OHI category, especially if the student is disruptive or aggressive, and may argue that the district only has ED-qualified teachers and not OHI-qualified teachers. As noted above, some school districts never qualify students who have chronic mental health disorders other than ADHD for the OHI category. Limited alertness is clearly a problem for many students who have clinical depression (one of the criteria is difficulty concentrating), bipolar mood disorder (one of the criteria is distractibility), schizophrenia (delusions and hallucinations clearly interfere with alertness in the educational environment), obsessive-compulsive disorder (continually having obsessional thoughts or carrying out compulsive behaviors can make it very difficult to attend to classroom information), and so on. In many school districts, ADHD is the most common medical diagnosis noted among students who are receiving OHI special education services.

Because eligibility for OHI services is based on clinical diagnosis, students receiving OHI special education services are generally more likely to have their behaviors recognized as direct manifestations of their mental health disorders than are students in the ED category.

Autism

According to IDEA, autism is a developmental disability that significantly affects verbal and nonverbal communication and social interaction that is generally evident before age 3 years and that adversely affects a child's educational performance. Other characteristics often associated with autism are engaging in repetitive activities and stereotyped movements, resistance to change in environment or daily routines, and unusual responses to sensory experiences. The term autism does not apply if the child's educational performance is adversely affected primarily because the child has an emotional disturbance. A child who shows the characteristics of autism after age 3 years could be diagnosed as having autism if the criteria above are satisfied. Interestingly, the educational definition of autism mirrors the DSM clinical diagnosis of ASD. However, even though school professionals are using these criteria in the process of doing an educational assessment that leads to placement in the autism category, school districts would generally maintain that special education eligibility rather than a clinical diagnosis is being established.

504 PLANS COMPARED WITH SPECIAL EDUCATION

There are pros and cons for parents in considering 504 versus special education services for their child. Some parents prefer a 504 plan, as they feel that it is less stigmatizing than special education placement. Other parents seek special education placement for their disabled child rather than a 504 plan, as they feel that their child will receive specialized services from a trained professional, that they will be on the decision-making team, that they would have the right to request an independent educational evaluation if they disagreed with the school's evaluation, and that they would be in a better position to advocate for their child through special education than through 504 channels.

Whether educators work in general or special education settings, they will be working with numerous students who have mental health disorders. Often, with a combination of adaptations in the general education classroom and mental health treatment provided by mental health professionals, special education referrals can be prevented. If students who have mental health disorders require more intensive services, either with a 504 plan or in special education, then it is important to ensure that these services will take into account the characteristics of their mental health disorders and their implications within the classroom.

CHAPTER 20

Effective Teaching Strategies for Students with Emotional or Behavioral Problems

"Kids are kids—you should just enjoy them.
The ones who give you the most trouble are the
ones who make you a better teacher."
—Early Childhood Special Education teacher
with over 20 years of classroom experience

NOW THAT YOU HAVE A BETTER UNDERSTANDING OF THE nature of child and adolescent mental health disorders, that knowledge can be translated into effective teaching strategies in the classroom.

Teaching approaches need to be tailored to each student's unique, individual needs. Mental health disorders are disabilities that a student may experience, but they do not define the student. Thus, it is appropriate to view a student as an individual who has a mental health disorder, rather than as a mentally ill person. A student's characteristics that are unrelated to mental health disorders are the ones that a teacher can connect with in the process of establishing a relationship.

Teachers can feel overwhelmed by the challenges of their responsibilities in working with students who have emotional or behavioral problems. Most schools provide a team meeting process in which teachers can seek help from other teachers and from counselors, psychologists, social workers, and administrators. It is especially important at the beginning of their careers for teachers to feel comfortable in seeking help and to recognize that they will be called upon in the future by other teachers as they gain more experience working with challenging students. In many districts, the least experienced special education teachers are often placed in programs serving the district's most disturbed students due to the requests of teachers with greater seniority to work with a less disabled population. It is incumbent upon the district to provide adequate guidance, backup, and support to all teachers. Even the most experienced teachers can benefit from consultation with other professionals, and the group process provides a supportive environment for all staff.

The interventions described in this chapter are grouped under different diagnostic categories for which they have the greatest application. They are not diagnosis-specific, however. They may be successful in working with students who have a variety of mental health disorders. Some may be more applicable to certain disorders (e.g., ADHD) than others, but many work for all students who have mental health problems. Providing interventions cannot be done effectively with a cookbook approach that lists specific interventions based on specific diagnoses. Each student is unique, and approaches need to be tailored to individual strengths and weaknesses.

Also, due to the high degree of comorbidity of mental health disorders, many students have multiple disorders. It is not uncommon for ADHD, anxiety disorders, mood disorders, and behavioral disorders to be present in the same individual. Even if a student only has one mental health disorder, his or her temperament, personality, and learning style will dictate the types of interventions that are likely to be most effective. Although this chapter outlines teaching strategies that can be effective with certain disorders, the reader should adopt them when they are effective for students who have other mental health disorders. They also apply to students who have not been diagnosed but show evidence of having a mental health disorder.

STRATEGIES TO PROMOTE A SENSE OF WELL-BEING IN STUDENTS

Interventions need to focus on the student's developmental age. Some students, due to their cognitive limitations or mental health disorders, are functioning significantly below their chronological age. Young children, or older students who are functioning at the level of young children, often have difficulty identifying their emotional state. They can benefit from their teacher's assistance in labeling their feelings. Statements such as, "Susan, it looks like you are feeling angry at Justin. Do you want to tell me what the problem is?" can help students identify their emotions and learn to deal with them more effectively. By labeling their internal emotional states, they can learn mastery as they develop appropriate coping strategies.

Helping the at-risk student identify negative feelings and find alternative acceptable behaviors gives them a sense of mastery over feelings and behaviors that previously were uncontrollable. Picture charts of faces expressing different emotions such as anger, sadness, or frustration can also be helpful for younger children, and for students who have ASD.

Experienced teachers learn to recognize when students are having difficulty handling their negative emotions and are at risk of becoming increasingly agitated to the point of physically acting out. Often, these students have predictable patterns of behavioral responses to stress. Teachers can learn to identify the triggers that set off these students. For example, a student may have a pattern of becoming angry if he or she is not called on first in a group discussion. This can lead to sulking or to striking out at the group's most vulnerable members. Other students may become agitated when they hear loud noises or are exposed to overstimulating environments.

Teachers who are tuned in to these patterns can be proactive with preventive interventions. Interventions can include placement in proximity to the teacher. Sometimes it is possible to distract students who are beginning to escalate by presenting them with a new, engaging activity. As boredom can lead to inappropriate behaviors, teachers need to keep students engaged in classroom activities. If students challenge the relevance of schoolwork, it is important for teachers to respond with answers that make sense to them. For example, when asked why math is important, the teacher can say that it prevents students from being taken advantage of with incorrect change when they spend money. Remaining engaged with classroom activities can be a challenge for students who have short attention spans, who have poor impulse control, or who are distracted by internal emotional states. This classroom interventions described in this chapter can assist this process.

Regardless of the types of mental health disorders that are affecting students, the primary initial goal is to earn their trust and to help them feel safe within the classroom. It can be difficult to connect with students who have depression or anxiety, as they may be withdrawn and wary of interpersonal contact. Students who have externalizing behaviors and poor impulse control may have difficulty building trust with teachers as well.

Students who have ASD often have major problems in forming relationships with others. Teachers can learn to identify methods of gaining their students' trust. Creating a safe classroom environment that is predictable, stable, consistent, and nurturing assists this process. It is helpful to use a variety of instructional strategies to engage students in the learning process and to accommodate different students' learning styles. In some cases, it may be necessary to try several different approaches until finding the ones that are successful in making positive connections.

A teacher's attitude is crucial in creating an emotional environment in the classroom in which students who have a mental health disorder feel safe and secure. Many students live in highly threatening environments where they have experienced or witnessed emotional or physical abuse. They need to get the message that the classroom is a place where no one will hurt them and where they will not hurt others. The classroom is safe and they are there to learn. When teachers display a sense of humor and are emotionally supportive and welcoming, their students feel accepted and are less likely to act out in the classroom. Teachers can build a sense of community in the classroom, and their students will feel that they are a part of an important group enterprise. They get the message that they are all in this together, working with each other on a common goal.

CLASSROOM ORGANIZATION AND DESIGN TO PROMOTE LEARNING

Alterations in the classroom environment can aid vulnerable students. Students who have a mental health disorder may have increased or decreased sensitivity to the physical aspects of their classroom that can lead to difficulties with emotional regulation, staying on task, and engaging in positive social interactions and behavior. Modifications of their sensory environments can improve their ability to function.

Students who have problems with anxiety or ASD may overreact to environmental stimuli and may respond with avoidant or agitated behaviors. Anxious students may appear to be overly vigilant, fearful, distracted, and upset. Students with ASD may also have tactile defensiveness, avoiding foods that have certain textures and wearing only soft, loose-fitting clothing.

Oversensitivity to noise may result in their seeking less stimulating places in the classroom (including crawling under a desk). Sudden loud noises such as fire drills can cause them to cover their ears and appear extremely agitated. They may have difficulty in crowded places such as lunchrooms and hallways.

Conversely, other students who have mental health disorders may be underresponsive to sensory stimuli. They may seek increased sensory stimuli, may appear hyperactive, may be clumsy due to proprioceptive difficulties, may excessively touch objects, and may generate sounds by humming, talking to themselves, and so on.

Students with over- or underresponsive sensitivities to their environment may be able to use sensory motor strategies to increase their ability to function in the classroom. Overly stimulated students may respond well to reduced light levels in the classroom. Some students, especially those with ASD, are very sensitive to fluorescent lighting and are calmer in environments with incandescent or natural lighting. Sound-deadening headphones can aid their ability to focus. Weighted blankets or vests can have a calming influence. There are several devices that provide a calming influence for students who require sensory stimulation and activity. Fidgets are malleable objects that can occupy agitated student and provide self-soothing stimulation. They may be made of rubber, silicone, plastic, clay, or putty. Examples include koosh balls, squishy hand balls, Silly Putty, twisty toys, and kneadable erasers. They are also useful for restless and hyperactive students as well. (Fidgets can turn into missiles, so it is important to gauge an agitated student's level of self-control.)

Some students may benefit from objects that they can chew, and rocking chairs and beanbags can be an effective alternative to typical school desks for some students. Being able to take movement breaks that allow standing, stretching, and walking can be helpful. Occupational therapy assessments can be beneficial in determining the best interventions for a student.

THE DIFFERENCE BETWEEN A DISABILITY AND A HANDICAP

Before looking at specific adaptations for students who have a mental health disability, it is helpful to understand the meaning of the concept of disability and the differences between the terms "disabled" and "handicapped." A disability, whether it is related to physical or mental health, refers to a condition that limits a person's movements, senses, or activities. Someone who is disabled has limited or absent abilities in a specific area. A blind person has no ability to see; a color-blind person has limited visual ability. A student who has a severe reading disability may have adequate intelligence but, because of neurological difficulties, may have significant limitations in the ability to decode written language.

A handicap, on the other hand, denotes the degree to which an individual's disabilities limit his or her ability to function in the world. This is an important distinction, because there are many people who have severe disabilities but are able to function well in life and who have minimal handicaps. Helen Keller, who was both deaf and blind, but who was a successful author, political activist, and lecturer, is an excellent example. But, there are those who have minimal disabilities but, due to a variety of factors, may be significantly handicapped. For example, a student who has a reading disability may have low self-esteem as a result of years of frustration and may be unwilling to attempt to master new skills.

The goal of educational interventions with disabled students is to maximize their abilities to succeed in school (and it is hoped in the home and community as well) and to eliminate or limit their handicaps as much as possible.

CLASSROOM INTERVENTIONS TO ADDRESS STUDENTS' MENTAL HEALTH PROBLEMS

Students who have mental health disorders are clearly disabled, many more so than those who have other medical disabilities. Unlike other medical disorders, psychiatric disorders do not present with shortness of breath, a limp, a rash, or other easily identifiable physical manifestations. Mental health disorders also may not be easily identified because many children and adolescents would rather appear to be "bad" than "sick," and thus cover up symptoms of anxiety, depression, or other mental health difficulties in order to be accepted by their peer group.

It is not nearly as straightforward a task to identify appropriate interventions to enable a student who has mental health disabilities to achieve in the educational environment as it is for students who have physical disabilities. Generally, it is easier to quantify the extent of disabilities such as hearing loss, vision impairment, muscle weakness, and so forth than to identify the extent of depression, anxiety, or inattention. Mental health symptoms may also wax and wane due to the nature of the disorder and to environmental factors. For example, an episode of depression may remit on its own. Also, environmental stresses and demands may exacerbate the severity of mental health symptoms.

It is normal practice to design accommodations and modifications that are specific to the manifestations of physical illness for students who are receiving special education services under the Other Health Impairment (OHI) category. However, many students with emotional and behavioral problems who are receiving Emotional Disturbance special education services, even when they have been diagnosed with a mental health disorder, receive generic behavioral interventions that do not focus on the nature of their underlying psychiatric disability.

This issue is a complex one, and there is considerable disagreement among both education and mental health professionals regarding the best methods of intervening with these students. In my opinion, the most practical approach is that interventions for a student who has been diagnosed with a mental health disorder and has behaviors consistent with that disorder should focus on the nature of the underlying disability and its clinical manifestations. This approach can also benefit students who have not been diagnosed but who are demonstrating evidence of an underlying mental health disorder.

What to Know First

In order to provide successful accommodations and modifications to students whose academic or behavioral difficulties stem directly from their mental health disorder, it is very useful for educators to ascertain, with parents' permission, the following information:

- The types of disorders that the student has
- Whether mental health treatment is being provided and, if so, the type of treatment (e.g., medication, psychotherapy)
- Whether treatment has just begun and symptoms are expected to improve, or whether treatment has been taking place for some time and symptoms are expected to remain at the same level
- Whether there are plans to change treatment strategies (e.g., change medications or medication dosages) and, if so, when this will be done

Some disabilities are treatable to the point that an individual is no longer handicapped by the disability. For example, someone who is near-sighted can wear glasses and no longer have visual difficulties. Similarly, some mental health disabilities are treatable to the point where no symptoms persist. For example, the symptoms of major depression, especially when treated with a combination of psychotherapy and antidepressant medication, may fully remit. Other disabilities are partially treatable, and some (e.g., individuals who have total blindness) are not treatable. The student being treated for major depression may have required a number of interventions when symptoms were significant in order to address the lack of energy, tiredness, and difficulty concentrating that are often present in this disorder. When symptoms improve, these interventions may no longer be necessary. On the other hand, a student who has ASD, even with the best treatment, will most likely continue to require a variety of educational interventions including social skills training, occupational therapy, and so forth. A student with ADHD who starts medication may demonstrate significant improvement in some areas such as reduced hyperactivity and impulsivity while continuing to have difficulty in other areas such as organizational skills.

How to Find Out

For these reasons, it is important to have open lines of communication between school staff (e.g., teachers, nursing staff, social workers), parents, and medical and mental health treatment providers. Knowing the type and stage of treatment and the student's response to treatment helps guide school staff in providing tailored interventions for students who have mental health problems. (See Chapter 17 for additional information on this issue.) Effective interventions for students who have mental health disorders go beyond the provision of accommodations and modifications. They require an appreciation that the students are as disabled as those who have physical disabilities, an understanding of the nature of the disability (its characteristics, severity, chronicity) and the use of interventions that have appropriate expectations and goals.

Setting Realistic Goals

If goals are set too low, the educational program will not be challenging enough for the student, and minimal progress will be made. On the other hand, if goals are set unreasonably high, students, parents, and teachers will be frustrated when they are not met. For example, a student may be identified as having a problem paying attention and may be on task only 20% of the time. Setting a short term goal of on-task behavior 80% of the time may, therefore, be problematic. It may be possible for some students, especially if treatment is going to be provided, but it may not be an achievable goal for other students. Ideally, goals should be set that optimally challenge but minimally frustrate the student, so that ongoing, gradual progress can be made. Behavioral interventions need to set up the student for success. If the student is repeatedly receiving negative consequences for his or her behaviors or lack of academic progress, a reassessment of the educational plan is in order.

An educational plan for a student who is color-blind would not have as its goal, "John will be able to tell the color green from the color red." A reasonable goal would be, "John will learn that when driving a car and approaching a stoplight, a glowing light on top indicates that he should stop the car, while a glowing light on the bottom indicates he should proceed." In other words, classroom interventions take into account an individual's disability and work around it to ensure success in school.

Academic interventions need to be based on the student's ability to accomplish classroom tasks. Since mental health disorders can interfere with this ability, it is important to differentiate the abilities that are measured on cognitive testing (e.g., IQ tests) and the actual abilities that students have in the classroom environment. When educators say, "I know that Johnny can do the normal classroom assignments; he's got the ability," they may not be appreciating the impact of ADHD, depression, anxiety disorders, or other mental health conditions on the student's ability to actually carry out the assignments.

Factors that can interfere with a student's ability to learn can include the specific symptoms of a mental health disorder (e.g., the distractibility of ADHD or the concentration difficulties of major depression) as well as the more generalized effects of problems with emotional regulation, difficulties in social situations, and difficulties demonstrating appropriate problem-solving skills.

SKILLS TRAINING

Skills training can be useful in assisting students who have mental health disorders to succeed in school. It can be provided by school social workers, counselors, psychologists, and, in some situations, by teachers as well. It is different from psychotherapy. Psychotherapy is an intervention that is focused on treating the student's underlying mental health disorder. Skills training, on the other hand, is an intervention that teaches the student specific skills that can be practiced and mastered in order to improve functioning in the home, school, and community environments.

Skills training is a very important component of an intervention plan for many students who have mental health disorders. There are two different populations of students who have deficits that require skills training. The first is a group of students who simply have not learned appropriate skills. This is often due to overwhelming family stressors and chaotic circumstances (e.g., homelessness, parental substance use disorder, extreme poverty). These students may have significant difficulty functioning in the educational environment due to the lack of basic skills, especially social skills.

The second group comprises students who have skills deficits that are directly due to their mental health disorder. Some mental health disorders have skills deficits by definition. Individuals who have ASD, for example, have significant deficits in social skills, and students with ASD thus have difficulty with assessing nonverbal emotional expression, with empathy, and with making appropriate decisions regarding social interactions with others. Students with AHDH may have significant difficulty with social skills, especially in regard to conversing with others without interrupting (due to the impulsivity of those who have the mixed or predominantly hyperactive forms) and in paying attention to subtle social cues from peers and adults. Other students who have mental health disorders may have intact skills, especially when the disorders manifest later in childhood or adolescence. For example, a 16-year-old who has the first onset of major depression may have excellent social skills and self-control skills and may not require any skills training if the disorder is treated promptly with good results. However, if depression continues over time, the student may require significant skills training as part of a rehabilitative program.

Skills training is based on the concept that a skill is a proficiency or ability that develops through experience or training. Skills are observable and quantifiable. They can be practiced and can be corrected in the process of training. Training differs depending on the circumstances of the student's setting (e.g., general education, special education self-contained classroom) and depending on the nature of the mental health disorder and skills deficits that are present.

Skills training may focus on any number of skill deficits. It may focus on the development of self-regulatory skills, social skills, communication skills, or the replacement of maladaptive skills with functional alternative skills. Skills training may also involve a student's parents in training, by teaching them to understand how their child processes information, responds to different environments, and so on. Parental involvement helps to generalize the acquisition of skills to both the home and school environments.

Examples of skills training include social skills training, assertiveness skills training, anger management training, and organizational skills training. Such training can help a student cope with stress, solve problems, self-monitor emotions and impulses, improve organizational scheduling abilities, and learn relaxation techniques. It can be provided in individual, group, or family settings. The goals of skills training include the development of absent, delayed, or distorted skills and assisting the family to understand their child's disorder and to be part of the training process.

Although skills training does not constitute mental health treatment, it may be a billable mental health service depending on the insurance benefit sets for Medicaid and private insurance in the student's state. School districts that can bill Medicaid for mental health services may be able to bill for skills training if it is, for example, part of a mental health treatment plan, if the skills deficits are due to the student's mental health disorder, if the provider meets certain mental health professional criteria, and if the skills training is considered medically necessary. For example, in some districts, skills training may be considered educationally necessary, may be on an Individual Education Plan (IEP) as a related service, and may also be considered medically necessary as part of a treatment plan and be billable to Medicaid. In these districts, obtaining reimbursement from both special education and Medicaid sources is not considered double dipping and may provide an additional funding stream. District administrators need to identify available funding options, given the high degree of variation between states. The American Institute for Research (https://www.air.org) is an excellent resource for providing technical support.

Skills training can be provided by school professionals in conjunction with psychotherapy, medication management, or other mental health treatment interventions provided by medical or mental health professionals in the community. It is important to understand that mental health treatment by itself does not automatically result in improvement of skills deficits and that specific skills training interventions are often necessary to complete the goals of mental health interventions. In addition to the process of teaching skills to students who have skills deficits, it is also important to work with the students over time to practice the skills that they have learned. Techniques may include reinforcement of learned skills, cueing skill-building interactions, role play, reinforcement of accomplishments, de-escalation, and the redirection of maladaptive behaviors.

Skills training is an inherent part of every teacher's daily activities. Teachers are continually shaping students' behaviors, encouraging self-control, rewarding positive social interactions, and assisting students in responding appropriately to life challenges. Skills training is often provided to students who have mental health disorders that may or may not have been diagnosed. Skills training as part of an educational plan may be done on a more formal basis, with objective measurements of baseline status, the setting of specific goals, and ongoing assessments of outcomes.

CLASSROOM ADAPTATIONS, ACCOMMODATIONS, AND MODIFICATIONS

In regard to mental health disabilities, it is generally preferable to provide treatment to lessen or eliminate symptoms than to provide adaptations for an untreated mental health disorder. This is certainly true for severely disabling disorders such as major depression or psychotic disorders.

The most effective adaptations within the school environment identify the student's actual disability and provide tailored interventions to maximize success. Adaptations, accommodations, and modifications need to be individualized for students, based upon their needs, their learning style, their interests, and the specific nature of their disabilities.

Students who have mental health or physical health disabilities may require alterations in general educational programming to meet their special needs. Adaptations for students who have mental health disorders can be most effective when the nature of the disorder and its impact in the classroom are clearly understood by educators. Ideally, interventions are provided early in the course of a mental health disorder and are continued throughout its course as necessary.

In many situations, it is possible to conduct these interventions within the regular education classroom, without requiring additional systemic interventions. A teacher may provide classroom assistance to a disabled child without any need for special education services. In fact, it is necessary to provide interventions in the classroom prior to referring a student for special education services.

Students who have mental health disorders are often impaired in multiple domains including the educational setting, at home, and in the community. They may have difficulty making and keeping friends and may have conflicts with family members. They may be experiencing significant unhappiness and anxiety, either directly as a symptom of their disorder or secondarily to the problems that they encounter in coping with their mental health difficulties. To the extent that their problems affect their educational experience, school interventions can make a significant difference not only in supporting success at school but also in boosting self-esteem as a result of these successes.

School professionals are committed to providing educational services to all students, with a focus on academic success. These services are described in a wide variety of ways, and terms are often used interchangeably. The terms services, adaptations, accommodations, modifications, supports, and interventions each have their own specific meaning.

A service is any intervention, accommodation, modification, or strategy listed on IEP and 504 plans with the intention of improving behavioral or academic performance. Adaptations are changes made to a student's learning environment, curriculum, instruction, or assessment practices that assist the student to be a successful learner. Accommodations are changes that allow a student to be able to meet the same classroom goals as the student's nondisabled classmates. They provide additional services that reduce the impact of the student's disability, allowing the student to more easily master academic requirements. For example, some students who have learning disabilities in written language may be allowed to give oral reports, take tests orally rather than in writing, or even have textbooks read out loud to them. Accommodations fall into several categories:

• Presentation accommodations change the way that instruction, assignments, or assessments are presented to the student. For example, the encouragement of making choices improves task engagement, work productivity, and accuracy.

• Response accommodations change the ways that students are permitted to respond to instruction or are organizational devices to be used by the student as an aid to formulating a response.

• Timing or scheduling accommodations are changes in the organization of or amount of time allotted for an activity or test. For example, extending time for tests for students who have ADHD tends to result in the student producing more correct answers.

• Setting accommodations are changes in the location where the student completes assignments or tests, or changes in the people who are present at that location. Providing adaptive furniture, teacher proximity, and small-group instruction can be beneficial for academics and behaviors.

Modifications, on the other hand, are changes in the curriculum taught to a student and in the schoolwork expected from the student. Modifications may provide educational materials at the reduced level at which the student is working due to the disability and may thus alter or reduce the academic expectations for the student. Both accommodations and modifications are supports, in that they support students to succeed in school to the best of their abilities.

Interventions are changes that are made through a process that focuses on developing or improving knowledge, skills, behaviors, cognitions, or emotions. An example of an intervention would be the provision of remedial math or reading services that is added to the grade-level curriculum to a student who has a learning disability, with the goal of helping the student perform at grade level.

Unfortunately, a review of the literature identifies few controlled studies that definitively demonstrate and quantify the effectiveness of classroom modifications and accommodations for mental health disorders (Lewis, Hudson, Richter, & Johnson, 2004). Harrison, Bunford, Evans, and Owens (2013) noted that over 70% of strategies for students who had ADHD that were listed on IEPs and 504 plans had no empirical grounding to support them. They also noted that the traditional approach toward interventions focused on assisting students in passing courses and graduating, rather than enhancing the competencies of students so that they could successfully accomplish age-appropriate social, behavioral, and academic expectations.

Further research is necessary to assess the effectiveness of different classroom interventions and to improve outcomes not only during the students' years at school but also once they enter the workforce as adults. Still, many educators have found the interventions described throughout this book to be successful. All are based on the premise that altered or additional services may be necessary when students' disabilities make it difficult for them to achieve in the classroom environment. The review of the literature by Harrison and colleagues (2013) indicates that academic interventions include assistance with self-management (improving classroom preparedness and skills), organizational skills, note taking (to improve quality of notes, on-task behavior, and scores on daily assignments), homework, and consultation with teachers. Interpersonal skills groups target the development of self-goals, problem-solving skills, and real-time skill practices with in-the-moment feedback. Family interventions such as family therapy, parent training, and family problem-solving communication training can reduce family tensions, including tensions related to the student's school difficulties. Some school programs offer multicomponent interventions, such as a mix of interpersonal and organizational skills training and communication with parents.

STRATEGIES FOR STUDENTS WHO HAVE ADHD

As ADHD is the most common mental health diagnosis in students who are demonstrating mental health problems in general education and in Emotional Disturbance and Other Health Impairment special education programs, it is a good starting point for illustrating methods of designing educational interventions that address the key components of a mental health diagnosis. Several of the approaches that follow are useful in working with students who have other disabilities as well.

Staff Training and Support

The first step in the process is ensuring that school staff understand that ADHD is a legitimate neurobehavioral diagnosis and that its symptoms are contributing to or causing the student's difficulty in the classroom. It is essential to ensure that educational assessments and functional behavioral assessments acknowledge that the problems that are identified in the classroom are the symptoms of the clinical disorder with which the student is diagnosed, so as not to blame the student for the disability. In other words, it is inappropriate to automatically conclude that a student who has ADHD is distractible in order to avoid schoolwork. Three external functions of behavior (avoiding tasks, seeking attention, and gaining tangible rewards) are commonly noted on functional behavioral analyses. However, a fourth function indicating that the behaviors stem from internal factors that are intrinsic to the mental health disorder can also be suggested. Of course, a student who has ADHD might be trying to avoid work or might have a combination of distractibility and avoidant behavior. It is important to attempt to clarify the degree to which a behavior is due to intrinsic factors versus external behavioral functions. The use of the Clinical-Behavioral Spectrum concept can be helpful in this regard (see Chapter 2). Teachers need to understand the symptoms of ADHD in order to appreciate that some students who have this disorder are not hyperactive and to recognize that symptoms can vary between different environments. The strategies for effective teaching of students who have ADHD are directed toward the core components of the disorder, as outlined in the DSM-5 criteria. In addition to the symptoms of the disorder itself, students may have secondary problems that stem from their previous lack of classroom success. Strategies need to address their demoralization and low expectations of themselves, if they are present.

It is important to have the classroom be well organized and to have clearly defined rules and expectations for the student. Consistency is essential. It is important to identify the student's learning style and teach accordingly. Hands-on approaches tend to be more successful than an overreliance on the student reading books and other printed materials. Engaging multiple senses helps the student master the material.

Classroom rules should be adjusted to the specific circumstances of the student. Accommodations will change over time as students master their goals. The key factor in behavioral interventions is to meet the students where they are in terms of their talents and abilities, and to challenge them to succeed with reasonable expectations. Goals need to be attainable, in order to improve the likelihood of success. Lessons may need to be modified to match the student's ability level. The level of ability reflects both cognitive abilities and other factors such as distractibility, mood shifts, and anxiety that may interfere with the student being able to utilize his or her full cognitive talents. Adjusting to these factors allows the student to succeed.

Students who have ADHD may be very disorganized and thus may have major problems being the conduit of information between the teacher and the parents. In a scenario often repeated across America, a parent asks a child, "Do you have any assignments due?" and is told "No," only to find out later that the child did not finish important coursework. It is better to have direct communication between parents and teachers via email, a website, or other communication methods to ensure that parents have accurate information about work requirements.

The practice of requiring the student to pick up an assignment sheet at the end of class to bring home is problematic, as it singles out the student in front of peers as someone who needs extra help in class. Ideally, accommodations and modifications should be as invisible to peers as is possible.

Homework often poses a major problem for a variety of reasons. Parents can help their child by setting up a consistent study time and place and creating a system for bringing homework home and returning it to school. For students who have difficulty completing tasks on time at school, it is better to adjust the work expectations of the school day rather than having the incomplete schoolwork become homework.

In some situations, it is worth considering eliminating homework for students who have significant psychiatric symptoms. Some students who have mental health disabilities may feel cognitively exhausted by the end of the school day and may have great difficulty focusing on schoolwork once they get home. If homework issues lead to ongoing power struggles that result in incomplete work and poor grades, it is worthwhile to reconsider the value of assigning the homework. Students in special education and those who have 504 plans can have accommodations and modifications that eliminate the need to do homework altogether. The upside of this plan is that it removes significant stresses for the students and their families and it reduces the stress that can otherwise exacerbate symptoms of mood and anxiety disorders. The downside is that the student may fall behind academically if assignments are not completed at home and if there is inadequate time to do them in school. It is important to weigh all factors to determine whether homework is necessary, and avoid power struggles where everyone loses. In situations where a student who has significant mental health difficulties understands the material and does well on tests, it is difficult to justify lowering grades due to incomplete homework.

Directions in class need to be clear and concise. Ideally, they should be put in writing and listed numerically. Feedback needs to continually focus on reinforcing positive behaviors, with redirection of negative behaviors provided on an as-needed basis. When consequences are necessary, they should be consistent, immediate, and pertinent to the behavior.

It is important not to draw attention to negative behaviors. It is helpful to have a subtle signal that encourages the student to redirect inappropriate behaviors. Students who have disabilities can easily become demoralized if they become the focus of attention of their classmates.

Students should be allowed as many choices as possible in order to empower them and to help them build on their success.

The teacher's attitude is crucial. It is essential to avoid taking a student's problems personally; to avoid power struggles; to remain calm and positive; and to recognize that it is the student's disability, not the student, that is the problem. This is much easier to do with students who have obvious physical disabilities than with those who have mental health disorders that can be invisible to others. It can be helpful for teachers to ask themselves how they would teach the student if he or she had a physical disability such as a traumatic brain injury or brain tumor that was causing academic, emotional, and behavioral difficulties.

Subject-Specific Strategies for Students Who Have ADHD

Students who have ADHD often have significant difficulty not only with distractibility, hyperactivity, and impulsivity, but also with more subtle deficits in executive functioning (Chan, Shum, Toulopoulou, & Chen, 2008). Executive functions are the cognitive processes that regulate, manage, and control other cognitive processes such as planning, working memory, attention, problem solving, verbal reasoning, inhibition, mental flexibility, task switching, and initiation and monitoring of actions. They require adaptations that assist them in carrying out these tasks.

Some specific strategies in math and language instruction that may be useful for teaching these subjects to students who have ADHD are listed below. Please refer to the U.S. Department of Education: "Teaching Children With Attention Deficit Hyperactivity Disorder: Instructional Strategies and Practices" (https://www2.ed.gov/rschstat/research/pubs/adhd/adhd-teaching_pg3.html) for additional information and references

Effective Math Strategies for Students with ADHD

- Have the student use columnar or graph paper to aid organization of material.
- Make copies of the problems for students who have difficulty transferring spoken or written information.
- Reduce the number of problems that the student is required to solve, since having too many problems can be overwhelming and can defeat the purpose of the assignment.
- Highlight the crucial items in the student's book.

- Clearly define the work that needs to be done by using stickers, sticky notes, and so on.
- Give work in manageable chunks, one page at a time, to avoid overwhelming the student.
- Make sure that work sheets are not too busy and full of information. Papers should have plenty of white space.
- Whenever possible, let students use aids such as calculators, multiplication charts, and so on.
- Avoid timed tests if they frustrate the student.
- Always list, clearly and concisely, what is expected of the student.

Effective Written Language Strategies for Students with ADHD

- Have consistent standards for assignment organization such as the placement of the student's name, the date, the page number, and so on.
- Anchor the paper down, as some students find that helpful, or use heavier paper.
- Use larger lined paper to facilitate written work organization.
- Allow use of computers when possible, enabling spell checks and encouraging neatness.
- Teach note-taking skills, using abbreviations and two-column note techniques. Or model note-taking.
- Promote reading comprehension using modified SQ3R (survey, question, read, recite, and review) methods. This helps the student survey the materials, look at the questions at the end of the reading assignment, highlight the work while reading, and answer questions about the reading assignment.
- Have the student engage as many senses as possible to remember and to improve learning.
- Use acronyms and mnemonics to assist memory skills.

STRATEGIES FOR STUDENTS WHO HAVE ASD

Students on the more severe end of the autism spectrum are generally served in the special education system, and some receive services in specialized, self-contained programs. However, many students who have milder forms of this disorder receive less restrictive special education services or are even served completely within general education. Many of these students have intact basic language and cognitive functions but have significant problems with social skills, environmental sensitivity, cognitive flexibility, and modulation of their emotional states. Many students who are on the milder end of the spectrum have not been diagnosed with ASD, but may appear awkward and unusual in their classroom interactions. Classroom interventions need to be tailored to each student's level of functioning. Often, there is a significant scatter of abilities, with strong abilities in some areas (e.g., rote memory) and weak abilities in others (e.g., the use of abstract language). Cognitive, speech and language, and occupational therapy assessments can help clarify a student's educational profile. This information can be used to design effective academic interventions. Given their relatively greater visual-spatial strengths compared with their receptive and expressive language skills, many students with ASD can learn and remember information better if it is presented in a visual format.

Visual aids can assist learning, self-control skills, and communication. Visual supports can help in organization of daily routines, in providing directions and instructions, and in learning new information. Visual schedules can assist students in coping with changes in their routines by helping them anticipate new activities. They can illustrate appropriate classroom behaviors and can help teach social skills. Illustrated scenarios of various social situations can assist in learning social skills.

Students who have ASD respond to positive reinforcers, but they are often different than those that are effective with other students. For example, a student who has ASD may prefer time alone, performing a favorite routine or playing with items that provide specific sensory stimulation.

As students who have ASD can be easily frustrated if they cannot succeed at an academic task, it is important to very gradually increase the level of difficulty of academic tasks. Complex tasks need to be broken down into subtasks that are reinforced in small, teachable steps. This process is applicable to life skills and social skills as well as to academic skills. As many students who have ASD are fixated on particular topics, these topics can be used to teach concepts in academic subjects. Over time, the topics can be broadened.

Sensory hypersensitivity to visual, auditory, tactile, olfactory, and taste stimuli can be addressed through the use of quiet, calming areas for relaxation and the reduction of noxious stimuli. Verbal communication skills can be taught through the use of language that is developmentally appropriate for the student. It is best to use specific, familiar, and concrete language that is simple, clear, and concise.

Teachers should pace their rate of speech to the student's ability to process language. Listening skills can be broken down into their various components such as facing the speaker, being still, and demonstrating understanding of the information being communicated. The use of concrete examples and hands-on activities can assist the process of mastering language skills. Physical, gestural, or verbal prompts can assist the learning process, but should only be used as long as they are needed so that students do not become dependent on them. Independent effort should be encouraged and rewarded.

Higher-functioning students who have ASD can learn self-management activities in which they monitor their own behavior. They can learn to identify specific behaviors and their reinforcers and to record their performance of these behaviors. This process facilitates self-mastery.

Structured play activities can facilitate attention, interaction, imitation, and social communication. They can be structured around the student's preferred activities and routines. The development of social skills requires learning specific skills such as waiting, taking turns, handling transitions, changing the topic of conversation, approaching others, and learning to be flexible in interactions with others. Students who have ASD benefit from involvement with peer mentors who model appropriate social interactions.

Assistive technology and computer applications can be very effective with students who have ASD. These are reviewed at the end of this chapter.

STRATEGIES FOR STUDENTS WHO HAVE DEPRESSION

Depression often presents with internalized symptoms that are not always obvious to educators. A student may be quietly suffering, underachieving in the classroom, and under the teacher's radar. It is helpful to assess students' social-emotional functioning as well as their academic and behavioral functioning, in order to obtain clues about whether a student may have an internalizing disorder. For example, depressed students may eat alone in the lunchroom; may not interact with peers on the playground; and may be the target of harassment, ridicule, or bullying. In the classroom, they may be unwilling or unable to contribute to classroom discussions. Other students who suffer from depression may appear irritable, angry, and oppositional. They may engage in antisocial behaviors and may begin using drugs or alcohol. It is not uncommon for parents of depressed students not to be aware that their children suffer from major depression. Educators may be the first adults to recognize the warning signs. Interventions for these students need to reflect the nature and degree, severity, and chronicity of their disorder.

If, for example, a student is newly diagnosed with major depression and is starting psychotherapy and medication treatment, he or she may have a significant sleep disturbance, may have medication side effects, and may continue to have depressive symptoms without relief for several weeks. A depressed student may have great difficulty concentrating on academic subjects and may be internally distracted by feelings of self-doubt and hopelessness. The student may require a reduced workload or even a shortened school day. As time goes on and symptoms improve, it is hoped these accommodations will no longer be necessary.

Because major depression can make it difficult for an individual to cope with everyday stressors, it is important to limit stress for depressed students as much as is reasonably possible. Assignments may need to be modified, deadlines extended, and work requirements reduced. As it may be difficult for students to formulate answers to questions in class, they may require more time to respond. Students may need to have the opportunity to go to a quiet place if they are feeling overwhelmed. Students suffering from depression are not likely to take inappropriate advantage of these interventions; generally they want to learn and to be treated like the other students. They need to understand that depression is negatively affecting their ability to do well at school, and that interventions will likely be needed only until they recover from this illness. The emotional tone of a classroom affects all students, but is especially important for students who are anxious or depressed. It is essential for teachers to ensure that the classroom environment is nonthreatening, supportive, and nurturing. Students should feel secure and comfortable taking risks with their answers, with no concerns about being ridiculed by classmates. Assignments need to be clearly defined, and feedback should be specific regarding classroom expectations.

Since depression can lead to memory difficulties and disorganization, teachers can help the student keep materials and assignments organized. They help clarify project expectations, setting timelines and understanding of the steps involved in completing the project. Students may require additional assistance in planning, decision making, and maintaining routines. Depression contributes to a negative self-image, which can lead to a vicious cycle of low self-expectations, underachievement, and feelings that one is a failure. Teachers can model positive self-talk and encourage students to build confidence in themselves. Teachers can give the message that it is all right to make mistakes and that learning from mistakes leads to a positive learning experience. Students may need coaching to learn methods of dealing with stressful social situations. Helping students set short-term, achievable goals can contribute to self-esteem and help them build on success.

It is important for parents, friends, teachers, and other school staff to construct a supportive network. It is helpful for students to be able to check in with someone every day in order to touch base and to communicate emotional concerns. This can be a school counselor, homeroom teacher, case manager, or another trusted adult. Students should be encouraged to continue their social activities as much as possible, even if they do not result in their previous level of enjoyment.

Healthy lifestyle practices should be encouraged, as they assist in the management of depression. Teachers can stress the importance of physical activity, adequate sleep, a healthy diet, and relaxation techniques. As the treatment of significant depression generally involves psychotherapy and possibly medication intervention, it is helpful to have parents sign a release of information so that school staff can communicate crucial issues about the student's mood to treatment providers, and so that the providers can apprise the school staff about the student's level of functioning and about any issues that require monitoring. It is helpful for a school mental health staff member (counselor, psychologist, social worker or nurse) to have ongoing contact with the student to provide assistance in coping with the stresses of the school environment and to assess mood. It is also important to encourage the student to be able to trust school staff and feel comfortable seeking help from them if he or she is feeling emotionally vulnerable or is experiencing suicidal thoughts.

Suicidal statements need to be taken very seriously. It is not teachers' responsibility to assess the risk of suicide, but they are responsible to alert the student's parents and school staff about it. Schools need protocols for clarifying methods of risk assessment (school staff versus crisis intervention team from an outside agency), and for possible emergency interventions including referral to a hospital emergency room.

STRATEGIES FOR STUDENTS WHO HAVE AN ANXIETY DISORDER

Many of the classroom interventions for students who have depression also apply to students who suffer from anxiety disorders. Also, as anxiety may be a symptom of a wide variety of mental health disorders, there are many approaches to addressing the educational needs of anxious students. Effective generalized approaches for all anxious students include ensuring consistency in classroom activities and expectations. Many anxious students experience a sense of relief when they know exactly what to expect in a classroom. It is very helpful for anxious students to have a place where they can touch base every day with a trusted adult professional, such as a homeroom teacher. Relationships with older cross-grade peer mentors can alleviate anxiety, especially in transition years from elementary to middle school and middle school to high school. The availability of school social workers, counselors, or psychologists with whom they can discuss anxious feelings is important as well. It is important for the school nursing staff to be sensitive to students' physical complaints that stem from anxiety, especially when students are making frequent visits to the nurse's office.

The simplest example would be a student who has a severe phobia and becomes very anxious when confronted with the phobic stimulus. A student who has a phobia of snakes may suffer a panic attack if examining a snake is part of the curriculum of a science class. Similarly, a student who has a phobia of heights may have a panic attack if asked to climb to the top of a rope in physical education class, and a student who has a phobia of enclosed spaces may have a panic attack if on a field trip for cave exploration. Often, teachers are unaware of students' phobias until the challenging situation arises. When teachers are sensitive to the possibility that some students may have great difficulty dealing with situations that leave other students unfazed, they can be on the lookout for students who are at risk of experiencing escalating anxiety and intervene appropriately. Phobic students who are repeatedly challenged by phobic stimuli beyond their emotional capacity to handle the stress can become avoidant in classes where they have been challenged, and their overall work may suffer. It is appropriate for teachers to talk with students who are experiencing this level of fear, and to allow students to avoid highly fear-producing situations if necessary. Teachers can inform parents of their observations, and ideally parents will seek help for their children if the problem is significant enough to warrant treatment.

Unfortunately, many students have experienced or witnessed abusive situations and have been traumatized as a result. It is helpful for teachers to be sensitive to this, especially when classroom activities focus on abuse-prevention topics. Referral to a school counselor, social worker, or psychologist may be necessary if the classroom discussions trigger symptoms of anxiety.

Students who have obsessive-compulsive disorder may engage in compulsive behaviors in the classroom, such as touching light switches, checking door locks, counting objects, washing hands excessively, and so on. If they are forced to discontinue these behaviors, they are likely to become significantly more anxious, and possibly to develop replacement compulsions. Teachers, with the help of school mental health staff, can work with these students to help them find methods of dealing with their obsessions and compulsions, and to avoid behaving in ways that would encourage ostracism by peers.

Students who have separation anxiety disorder or social anxiety disorder who subsequently develop school refusal can be especially challenging. They may experience significant anxiety, especially upon arriving at school, and may have great difficulty focusing in the classroom due to ongoing worries and fears. They often benefit from having a check-in time with a trusted adult when arriving at school who can help them take inventory of their feelings and can guide them in preparing for the school day. Students who have social anxiety can benefit from social skills groups, especially if other students who have a similar problem are members of the group.

STRATEGIES FOR STUDENTS WHO ARE PSYCHOTIC OR MANIC

Students who have active psychosis (e.g., delusions, hallucinations) or mania (e.g., extreme agitation, irritability, grandiosity, impaired judgment) may present with symptoms that are so severe as to make it difficult or even impossible to participate in educational activities. Both problems may present simultaneously if a student has severe enough mania to cause psychotic symptoms, or if a student has a disorder that has characteristics of both (schizoaffective disorder). If disorders are treated, symptoms will generally improve to the point that educational interventions can be successful.

Psychosis and mania share a common feature: when an individual is having severe symptoms of either, insight is lacking about one's own mental health status. Delusions are, by definition, not reversible when information to the contrary is presented to the person suffering from psychosis. An individual who has mania tends to see others as being the problem. Psychotic and manic symptoms put an individual at the clinical end of the clinical-behavioral spectrum, and he or she may respond poorly to behavioral interventions. A teacher who recognizes symptoms of psychosis or mania must communicate concerns to the student's parents, either directly or with the help of a school mental health staff member. Evidence of symptoms severe to the point that the student is in danger of harming self or others constitutes a psychiatric emergency and requires crisis interventions, including hospitalization if necessary.

In the process of treatment and recovery, students who suffer from psychosis or mania generally require an educational environment that has minimal stimulation and distraction, that is supportive and nurturing and that fosters their feeling safe and supported. It is important to avoid arguing with a student who has delusions, but it is appropriate to provide information about the actual state of affairs in a calm and caring manner. Educational interventions discussed above in the sections on depression and anxiety disorders can be helpful for these students as well. They include limiting stress, modifying assignments, and reducing workloads. It is helpful to communicate clear expectations, to assist students who have organizational difficulties, and to have a school staff member with whom students can check in on a daily basis.

Students who experience symptoms of mania are at high risk of also experiencing significant symptoms of depression, either mixed with the mania or following a manic episode. Depressive episodes in individuals who have bipolar mood disorder carry a significant risk of suicide, and these students need to be monitored closely at home and at school. Medications used to treat psychosis and mood swings may have significant side effects including sedation, confusion, abnormal body movements, headaches, dizziness, tremors, weakness, nausea, and incoordination. It is helpful for educators to work with school nurses in order to identify the specific side effect profile of the student's medications and to alert parents and treatment providers if side effects are noted.

STRATEGIES FOR STUDENTS WHO ARE OPPOSITIONAL OR DEFIANT

Some students, for a variety of reasons, are perpetually in an oppositional mode in their relationship with school and its requirements. Not surprisingly, many are oppositional with all authority figures. They may also have significant difficulty within their home environment due to their lack of compliance with rules and their continuous testing of limits. Interestingly, generalized oppositional behavior is considered normal in early childhood, and is colloquially referred to as "the terrible twos."

Oppositional behavior illustrates the difference between authority and power. An oppositional individual may have little or no authority, yet may have significant power over his or her environment as a result of the oppositional behavior. For example, a secretary who has minimal authority in a company and who works for a disrespectful boss may delay sending an important letter. Despite having little authority, the secretary has the power to significantly disrupt business activities. A toddler who is engaged in power struggles over toilet training has no authority, but has the power to disrupt parental schedules via ill-timed toileting accidents. It often baffles parents why their child will argue for hours about carrying out a task that takes only a few minutes. In fact, the child may be succeeding in demonstrating the power of capturing the parent's attention.

Oppositionality can be a powerful tool. Mahatma Gandhi and Martin Luther King Jr. advocated nonviolent resistance to oppose unfair, discriminatory laws. Rosa Parks was being oppositional when she refused to sit in the back of the bus. Oppositionality becomes problematic when it is not a focused tool, but instead is constantly and indiscriminately utilized in all situations dealing with authority figures. It then becomes self-defeating and has the potential to lead to endless power struggles, frustration, and resentment for all involved.

The behavior of many oppositional children and adolescents who continuously test limits stems from a lack of consistent limits in the home environment. The example of a "rubber fence" illustrates this phenomenon. When a farmer buys a horse and puts it in a field, the first thing that the horse does is run the fence. By doing this, the horse determines its limits. But what if the fence were rubber and changed its shape and size daily? The horse would need to test the limit daily. If the fence were to be later replaced with a solid wooden fence, the horse would test it for some time after that in order to ensure that the limit was clearly defined. Thus, if a child has parents who are inconsistent with limits, enforcing them one day but not the next, or are altering the limits continually, it is not surprising that their child, who needs limits, will continue to test them. This behavior can become habitual and can generalize to situations including school, even though limits may be clearly defined in that environment.

Another reason for ongoing oppositional behavior is that children and adolescents who have mental health disabilities may feel demoralized and powerless, and may react by engaging in power struggles. Although this behavior has no obvious goal, it does result in power over the environment by engaging authority figures in the struggle.

It is helpful, when dealing with oppositional students, to recognize that it is the oppositionality that is the problem, not the student. Experienced teachers recognize that it is essential to refrain from engaging in power struggles, because as the saying goes, "it takes two to tango." Rather than engaging in authoritarian behavior with these students, demanding compliance and threatening negative consequences if they do not comply, a more successful method is to empower the student. Offering the student choices whenever possible gives the message that he or she is a partner in the learning process.

It is important to be certain that the student is capable of completing the classroom assignments. Some students who have mental health disabilities (e.g., ADHD) are unable to complete regular classroom assignments on time due to their disorganization, poor attention span, and distractibility. They recognize their inability to complete the work, and rather than trying and failing, they may refuse to even try. If assignments were always given with appropriate modifications, the student might not have entered this cycle of continuous refusal. Unfortunately, once the cycle is entrenched, it doesn't end just because new assignments have appropriate adaptations. It may take some time to break the oppositional cycle. Some teachers become frustrated because students may have a normal IQ and may appear to them as having the capability to do the classroom work. But the teachers need to recognize that capability also includes factors other than intelligence, such as the ability to focus attention and follow through with complex assignments.

Oppositional behavior is not always due to the dynamics of underlying mental health issues; sometimes it is simply an expression of normal frustration, boredom, or attention seeking. The same approaches work with this type of oppositionality as with the types previously mentioned. The basic approach is to avoid engaging in power struggles, to offer choices as much as possible, to apply humor to the situation, and not to take the behavior personally.

Many students who are oppositional have entrenched patterns of behavior. They may use these behaviors to avoid having to demonstrate their understanding of school assignments because of the potential embarrassment from being seen as having inadequate academic skills. Experienced teachers provide these students opportunities to choose a variety of methods for demonstrating their grasp of schoolwork. A teacher might say, "Okay, you don't want to write a paper on the topic. Maybe you could draw a comic strip or make a video." By avoiding power struggles and providing different opportunities for response, teachers can break through oppositional patterns of behavior.

Whenever possible, students should be involved in the process of establishing classroom rules and expectations and in establishing logical consequences that will result if they are not followed. It is helpful to provide opportunities for recognizing students' positive contributions to the class. Activities such as teaching a skill to a peer, assisting younger or less able students, and sharing knowledge with classmates help build self-esteem and can help decrease negative, attention-seeking behaviors.

STRATEGIES FOR STUDENTS WHO HAVE CONDUCT PROBLEMS AND DISRUPTIVE BEHAVIORS

Problem behaviors are a common occurrence in classrooms at all grade levels. Children who display these behaviors in grade school have a significant risk of antisocial behaviors in adolescence. They are also at a higher risk for lower grades and poor performance on standardized tests. Their classroom behaviors require teachers' attention, make it difficult for teachers to focus on classroom instruction, and interfere with the educational experience of classmates.

Regardless of the reasons for which a student might engage in disruptive behaviors, it is necessary to maintain a stable classroom environment in which all students can learn. Teachers should display a calm attitude, focus on the positive, and ensure that classroom rules are clearly understood by all students. It is helpful to teach students the ability to recognize when they are having difficulty maintaining control of themselves and to offer them the opportunity to calm down in a safe, nonstimulating environment. It is important to avoid power struggles and to empower students with choices whenever possible. Students who have ADHD often have difficulty sitting still, and as a result their hyperactivity can be disruptive in the classroom. Students who have ASD may be disruptive when they become anxious. Self-soothing activities (e.g., engaging in a tactile activity such as playing with clay) can help a student calm down and cease his or her disruptive behavior. Tactile stimulation, use of weighted belts, seat wedges, fidget objects, or use of a large inflated ball as a seat may help many of these students calm down and can also prevent disruptive behaviors. Occupational therapy consultation can be quite helpful in providing suggestions for students with unique needs.

Although this book places considerable emphasis on addressing the underlying mental health contributors to behavioral problems, it is also important to recognize that some behavior problems do not stem from mental health disorders such as ADHD, mood disorders, anxiety disorders, or psychotic disorders. Some students fall into the behavioral or predominantly behavioral sectors of the clinical-behavioral spectrum, as described in Chapter 2. Some have distinctly antisocial attitudes; some are predatory and engage in bullying behaviors; and some engage in many other delinquent behaviors including stealing, lying, use of weapons, running away, truancy, and so on. These students may plan their antisocial behaviors and may have no remorse about harming others in the process of carrying out their delinquent behaviors. Some may have a mental health disorder but demonstrate behavior that is coincidental to the disorder and not caused by it. These students pose a special challenge to their fellow students and to their teachers.

Many schools are successfully using social and emotional learning (SEL) strategies that teach students positive alternatives to disruptive behaviors; if your school does not do this, it would be worthwhile to approach school administrators with information about SEL (see Chapter 21 for details).

Isolation timeouts in which students who are displaying severely disruptive behaviors are removed from classrooms and placed in a secluded room have been used extensively, but are controversial interventions, especially when physical restraints are part of the seclusion process. Thus it is important to identify other interventions that can be successful and that do not require harsh treatment. Stage and Quiroz (1997) identified several behavioral interventions that have proven useful in working with students who engage in disruptive behaviors:

• *Token economies* rewarding appropriate behavior have been successful for many students.

• *Overcorrection* is a process in which the disruptive student is required to restore the disrupted environment to its original state and then to practice the correct behavior. This positive practice can be used even if there was no physical disruption of the classroom; it has proven to be successful with students.

• *Differential reinforcement* is a useful technique that provides positive reinforcement for students based on the absence of disruptive behaviors during a specified time interval.

• *Group contingency procedures* provide reinforcement for group behaviors or for behaviors of individuals within a group.

• *Home-based contingencies* that rely on teachers' frequent feedback to parents regarding students' behaviors can be very helpful in providing consistency between the home and school environments.

• *Functional behavioral interventions* identify the functions of behavioral problems and the influencing antecedents that occurred prior to the behaviors. The interventions used then seek to control these antecedents in order to increase socially appropriate behaviors.

• *Stimulus cueing* is a technique in which the teacher signals the student with a neutral cue that is not detected by classmates (e.g., a predetermined chalk mark on the blackboard) that reminds the student to replace inappropriate behaviors with appropriate ones.

• *Self-management interventions* teach students methods of managing their own behaviors, rather than relying on management by external forces. Examples include self-monitoring, self-instruction, self-evaluation, and self-reinforcement training.

A review of the literature on interventions shown to be effective in reducing disruptive behaviors strongly supports the use of:

- teacher praise as positive reinforcement
- providing opportunities to respond during instruction
- using positive behavior supports including functional behavior assessments
- social skills instruction
- teaching for desired replacement behaviors and self-management
- providing positive behavior support activities on a school-wide basis (see Chapter 18 for a description of these programs)

Behavior management strategies that lead to the student's independent monitoring of behavior are preferable to those that require ongoing external monitoring. Involving students and their parents in selecting behavioral intervention strategies encourages a consistent approach for behavioral management between the home and the classroom.

STRATEGIES FOR STUDENTS WHO ARE VIOLENT

Some students engage in highly disruptive and, at times, violent behavior, and many of them have significant mental health disorders. It is important for educators to know basic techniques of de-escalation when dealing with students who are displaying these behaviors.

If the situation is out of control, with the student actively engaging in violent and destructive behaviors that endanger self and others, it may be necessary to bring in other professionals from the school, or even the police, to ensure safety for all. Educators and police need to be aware of the need to be sensitive to racial and cultural issues in order to avoid racial biases in crisis interventions. When a student is in crisis and is not demonstrating an imminent risk of violently acting out, there are steps that educators can take that will reduce the risk of further escalation that could lead to violence.

It is important to be nonthreatening to students and to give them space so that they do not feel trapped. Let the students know that the teacher or others in the school are concerned and listening. Ask how someone can help, and avoid arguing with irrational statements. Let them know that adults in the school want to help, and keep stimulation to a minimum. Have only one person do the talking while others keep some distance from the situation. Speak slowly and softly, using short, simple sentences. Avoid sudden movements, continuous eye contact, and touching the student. The student needs to know that people are there to help and to offer support.

Teachers and other school personnel can be at risk of significant injury, even with grade school students who are out of control. It is essential that they recognize this and not take any unnecessary risks. Schools should have protocols for dealing with students who are in "meltdown" mode, and all staff need to be aware of their roles in this process.

Students who have this problem on an ongoing basis tend to be referred for special education evaluations and may require more restricted placements, smaller classrooms, and even one-to-one staff. To the degree that their low frustration tolerance, acting-out behavior, difficulty with anger management, and aggressive outbursts are due to an underlying mental health disorder, treatment of that disorder can result in a reduction of these behaviors.

USE OF ASSISTIVE TECHNOLOGY

School professionals are generally familiar with the use of assistive technology (AT) to meet the needs of physically disabled and learning disabled students, but AT can also be helpful for students who are disabled with mental health disorders. AT devices are identified IDEA as "any item, piece of equipment or product system, whether acquired commercially off the shelf, modified, or customized, that is used to increase, maintain, or improve the functional capabilities of children with disabilities." The term does not include a medical device that is surgically implanted, or the replacement of such device. The term "device" includes stand-alone devices as well as hardware and software. It can include anything from low-technology devices such as a pencil grip used by a student who has a physical disability to high-technology computers programmed to deliver augmentative communication.

There is a significant degree of overlap between learning disabilities and mental health disabilities. Many students who have mental health disorders also have learning disorders. For example, according to the National Institute of Mental Health, 20–30% of students who have ADHD also have specific learning disabilities. In addition, assistive technologies that are helpful for learning disabled students may also be helpful for students who have mental health disorders and no specific learning disabilities. For example, a student who has ADHD may have difficulty reading due to problems attending to the task and may benefit from text-to-voice technology. Text-to-speech and speech-to-text technology can provide additional features such as highlighting, note taking, and word processing. The Kurzweil Educational Systems programs, for example, provide a wide range of information technology options. They can highlight in different colors (e.g., pink for headings, yellow for main ideas, green for vocabulary), find the meanings of highlighted words, extract notes and highlights, send the outline into a word processing program, and make a summary from the material.

Executive function tools help students organize materials and stay on task. They can help a person plan, organize, keep track of a calendar, list tasks, make a schedule, access contact information, and write miscellaneous notes. This allows an individual to manage, store, and retrieve information with the help of computers or handheld devices.

Free-form database software programs are helpful for students who have organization and memory disabilities. They can be used with word processing or other software, allowing the user to create and store relevant information in electronic notes that can be retrieved by typing in a fragment of the original note. Examples include the Info Select program by Micro Logic and Microsoft OneNote. The XMind program can be used to capture, organize, plan, and act on ideas, as well as encouraging visualization and creativity.

Information and data managers help students who have disabilities in the areas of organization and memory. They help students organize, plan, store and retrieve a personal calendar, a task list, contact data, and other information in electronic form. Examples include Memo to Me and WatchMinder.

The Inspiration Software program provides multiple mediums for representation, expression, and engagement, assisting students to visually organize and outline ideas to structure writing and to improve communication and expression. It helps students create visual diagrams and graphic organizers to break schoolwork into manageable selections.

Paper-based computer pens are helpful for students who have disabilities in writing, reading, memory, or listening. They record and link audio to what a student is writing, using the pen with special paper. The student takes notes while simultaneously making an audio recording of the teacher and can listen later to the portion of the presentation that is in the written notes by touching the pen to that section's handwriting or diagrams.

The Echo Smartpen by Livescribe is an example of this technology. AT can provide scaffolding for students who have learning, attention, or executive functioning problems. It is generally considered an accommodation rather than a remediation, as it fills the gaps of ability that make it difficult for a student to function. It doesn't cure the disability but allows the student to experience success in the educational process. It is a tool, just as crutches and eyeglasses are tools that provide additional help for individuals who have physical disabilities. AT bolsters existing educational plans by improving students' ability to participate in classroom activities to the best of their abilities.

AT needs to be available and accessible so that it can be used without significant interruptions in students' and teachers' activities. It also has to be accepted, primarily by the student (or it won't be used) and also by the parents, the teacher, and classmates. It is necessary to assess the student's situation in order to determine the best use of AT. The University of Kentucky Assistive Technology (UKAT) Toolkit is a research-based systematic method of delivering AT services to students. It is based on the premise that the primary goal of special education is to improve a student's ability to successfully function in schools and to successfully respond to the demands presented by the general curriculum and school environment. It encourages the consideration of non-technology and low-technology solutions before the use of high technology.

The Toolkit systematically guides IEP and AT teams in considering the use of AT from referral through implementation. The UKAT Toolkit is available for schools to download and use at no cost. Another helpful source of information is the Wisconsin Assistive Technology Initiative. AT needs to be tailored to each student's unique situation. It should not interfere with remedial work, and can be effective when skills are noted to be plateauing and the student is demonstrating minimal progress. It requires a trial period of at least 1 to 3 months, and requires training to be provided to the student and to the educational staff.

USE OF APPLICATION SOFTWARE

There are many examples of application software (apps) that provide useful adaptations for students who have mental health disabilities and specific learning disabilities. For example, AutismXpress is an app that helps students who have ASD match visual facial expressions with emotions.

The Social Express uses scenarios to teach students who have high-functioning ASD how to think about and manage social situations in order to develop meaningful social relationships. Choiceworks is an app that can help students who have organizational difficulties. Teachers and parents can use it to create visual schedules, using their own pictures or pictures from the app's library. Remind 101 sends text message reminders about homework, tests, and special events without revealing the teacher's phone number.

ClassDojo enters real-time data about student behavior by assigning points for creativity, teamwork, and other positive classroom behaviors. Information can be shared with parents and other school staff members. Dragon Dictation or Apple Dictation can be used for students who have physical impairments or learning disabilities that limit writing ability. It transcribes the human voice into words on the computer screen. ConversationBuilder-Teen helps adolescent students with verbal social skills training, teaching them appropriate methods of introducing themselves, asking questions, making verbal observations, and changing the subject of their conversation. It also teaches adolescents how to deal with sarcasm and bullying.

Phonics Genius increases phonic awareness by helping students recognize and distinguish words by sounds. Social Quest engages older elementary, middle school, and high school students in a castle adventure while helping them develop speech and language, as well as social, skills.

Quick Quest has apps that promote skills such as staying organized, having appropriate conversations, creating and maintaining relationships, developing emotional awareness, and relaxation. Social Skill Builder helps students build problem-solving skills, friendship and life skills, critical thinking, and awareness of consequences.

Everyday Speech Social Skills is designed for students who have high-functioning ASD. It teaches daily activities such as walking down the street, using a restroom, waiting in line, asking for directions or information, or joining a group. Anger Thermometer teaches anger management skills, including healthy ways to identify, understand, and control anger. Daylio is a free app that allows users to track their moods and activities over time. It analyzes the results, assisting users in detecting patterns in their mood changes.

FOR DISCUSSION

VIGNETTE: Eliot

Eliot was a very disorganized seventh grade student who had ADHD and was receiving special education services. He had significant problems with completing written assignments and great difficulty finishing tasks (one of the criteria of ADHD). He had an assignment due on a Monday and, after working very hard on it with the assistance of his parents, he finally handed it in the following Friday. The teacher noted that it was an A paper, but gave Eliot an F because the classroom rule required marking down one grade for each day that homework was late. Eliot then felt demoralized and had minimal motivation to engage in future assignments, and his parents were frustrated and angry with the teacher.

REFLECTION QUESTIONS

What could have been done differently? Would it have been appropriate for Eliot to have an accommodation that allowed papers to be handed in late without penalty? Does this accommodation address a criterion of the disorder that is a core component of the student's disability?

Would this give Eliot the message that there was no need to try to be punctual with assignments? How could this accommodation be adjusted over time, as Eliot learns organizational strategies, in order to encourage the completion of tasks?

CHAPTER 21

Evidence-Based Educational Interventions for Students with Emotional or Behavioral Problems

ACADEMICALLY FOCUSED INTERVENTIONS FOR STUDENTS who have emotional or behavior problems have recently gained attention as a particularly effective means to promote learning and reduce behavioral incidents. Specifically, the 2013 Hanover Research report, "Effective Programs for Emotional and Behavioral Disorders," asserts:

> Though teacher education geared toward emotional and behavioral disorders has historically been characterized by a focus on classroom management, social skills, and anger management, many researchers have more recently argued that academically-focused interventions—as opposed to programs focused solely on behavior—may be most effective in supporting and engaging students with conduct disorders. (Hanover Research, 2013, p. 2)

It also notes that "zero tolerance" policies, in which students are automatically suspended or expelled as a result of specific infractions, can be harmful to students with ED, insofar as such policies remove already troubled or disengaged students from the teachers and counselors who are best equipped to help them address their difficulties.

As a more effective alternative to zero tolerance policies, the preceding chapter presented a multitude of strategies that educational professionals can employ to help promote students' feelings of well-being in a safe, calm, and harmonious classroom that includes students who have emotional and behavioral problems. This chapter presents an overview of specific evidence-based classroom practices that operationalize those strategies with the goal of promoting learning and, in addition, identifies programs for effective teaching; the related literature provides detailed information about their implementation. All are flexible enough to adapt to the specific needs of each student and to take into account the nature and extent of their mental health problems.

To maximize the ability of teachers and other school professionals to use these practices and programs, schools should provide relevant in-service training, since it is likely the professionals had not previously received such training. However, excessive staff training or supervision is not required.

THE SCHOOL-WIDE AND CLASSROOM LEARNING ENVIRONMENT

A variety of strategies can be used to prevent behavioral problems and to create a classroom environment that is conducive to learning. It is essential to keep in mind that the classroom time devoted to instruction and the amount of time that students are engaged in academics are crucial factors in educational success. All too often, teachers in self-contained classrooms spend an inordinate amount of time managing students' behavioral difficulties, some of which can be prevented.

Proactive Classroom Management Techniques

Group behavioral management is more difficult than individual management because of factors such as peer contagion and the tendency of individuals to behave inappropriately in groups in ways that they would not behave on an individual basis.

Examples of proactive strategies include commonsense activities such as smiling and positively greeting students when they enter the school or classroom. Keeping the classroom organized, assuring that rules and expectations are understood by all students, setting goals, and providing feedback about performance are important. Specifically, therefore, it is useful to have cuing systems to release and regain students' attention, to provide numerous opportunities to respond to the teacher's questions, to have a visual schedule of classroom activities, to have a motivation system to reward desired behaviors, and to assure that significantly more positive than negative interactions take place in the classroom.

It is important to minimize classroom distractions, especially for students who have ADHD. Communication with students should focus on the positive, but reprimands or corrective statements, if needed, should be brief, unemotional, and nonthreatening, and be spoken in close proximity to the student.

If a student is acting out and de-escalation is necessary, teachers should speak calmly; attempt to be at the same height as the student, rather than standing over him or her; offer caring statements; and provide a way to engage in more benign behavior via alternate activities or taking a break.

Establishment of Clear Rules and Expectations

Studies have shown that it is not enough to simply establish classroom rules. No matter how obvious rules may appear to be, it is important to systematically and directly teach them to students. Research supports the traditional approaches of modeling the rules, teachers' reinforcement of the rules, and use of prompts or cues to remind students of the classroom expectations. Expanding these strategies to school-wide student support approaches increases the potential for success. Students can be included in establishing and enforcing expectations, and token systems can reinforce compliance with rules. School-wide behavioral supports can help all students learn expectations and can provide additional support to students who have behavioral problems. Expectations should be clear, concise, and explicit; positively framed; and kept to a minimum. They should be taught from the beginning of the school year and continually reviewed with the students.

Ongoing evaluation of the effectiveness of these strategies is important, and re-teaching may be necessary for students who have difficulties meeting classroom expectations. Such students include those who have attention difficulties, impulsivity, or difficulty with executive functioning. It should not be assumed that students are being "oppositional" when rules are not being followed. Often, with enough teaching and reinforcement, these students are able and willing to comply with rules and expectations.

Function-Based Interventions

Function-based interventions are designed to apply the findings of functional behavioral assessment to develop an intervention plan that addresses a student's behavioral difficulties. The key issue, in regard to students who have mental health disorders, is whether some of their behaviors stem directly from intrinsic manifestations of their disorder(s) or reflect functions such as gaining tangibles, avoiding schoolwork, or seeking attention. Sensitivity to this issue, as well as consideration of hypotheses regarding where a student's behavior falls on the clinical-behavioral spectrum, will help assure that function-based interventions will be successful for behaviorally oriented issues.

Other Classroom-Level Practices

Research indicates that that the effects of classroom practices are comparable in importance to those of students' background influences. Classroom practices include a focus on an understanding of child development and the implementation of a curriculum that is rigorous and relevant, promotes relationships, creates active participants rather than passive observers, and allows students to use their whole brain. The curriculum should be integrated and empower students to take ownership of it. It should be differentiated with respect to the content taught, the process used, the product expected, and the physical factors of the environment. Active learning should be stressed, utilizing hands-on learning principles.

ACADEMIC INTERVENTIONS

Academic Supports and Curricular or Instructional Modifications

Academic supports are designed to assist students in refining and strengthening the academic skills that are necessary for their success. Modifications involve combinations of conceptual difficulty, educational goals, and instructional methods. Content may be modified, for example, in ways that learning strategies are taught, in simplifying concepts or reading levels, and in teaching different sets of knowledge and skills. Instructional methods may be modified in various ways such as reducing distractions and presenting smaller amounts of work. Modifying curriculum to incorporate a student's personal interests can be an effective tool in managing behavior. Functional behavioral analysis can identify unique motivational features that can be incorporated into curricular modifications. For students with ongoing symptoms of mental health disorders, curriculum can be modified to take the symptoms into account in order to increase the likelihood of academic success.

Cooperative Learning

Cooperative learning (CL) is a type of classroom organization in which students work in teams on an assignment or project under conditions that satisfy certain criteria. A systemic approach requires that the team members be held individually accountable for the complete content of the assignment or project. Team requirements include members' reliance on each other to meet academic goals (positive interdependence), individual accountability, shared interactive work, use of collaborative skills, and group processing of information.

Specialized Instruction to Promote Learning and Study Skills

Specialized instruction encompasses the types of unique instructional services that are required to accomplish IEP goals and objectives. Services include modifications, alterations, and adaptations of instructional methods, techniques, materials, physical setting, media, and environment. Specialized instruction supplements the general curriculum and addresses each student's unique learning characteristics. When students have mental health disorders that interfere with their ability to engage in classroom work, specialized instruction techniques can create teaching methodologies that take these symptoms (e.g., distractibility, anxiety) into account.

Peer-Assisted Learning Strategies

Peer-assisted learning strategies have been shown to be effective in improving elementary students' reading proficiency, and the strategies show promise in the secondary school population as well. A peer-assisted learning program uses peer-mediated instruction; students work in pairs or small groups to provide tutoring in reading strategies. These could include sequencing information, generating main idea statements, and generating and evaluating predictions of academic outcomes. Program goals include improved reading accuracy, fluency, and comprehension. Peer tutors are taught to correct their partner's reading errors, to provide encouragement and feedback, and to reward correct responses. The students alternate roles as reader and tutor ("players" and "coaches"). Sessions generally last for approximately a half hour and occur three to four times a week. Students are chosen according to their needs and abilities. Pairs are changed regularly and students work on a variety of skills over time. The process allows teachers to circulate in the class, observing students and offering individual remediation. Teachers may use reading materials of their own choice.

Peer-assisted learning strategies show promise with academic subjects other than reading, and they can be adapted to the secondary school population. It is essential for teachers to be sensitive to the needs and learning styles of their students and to pair students who are compatible and cooperative with each other.

NONACADEMIC INTERVENTIONS

Social and Emotional Learning

Social and emotional learning, as defined by the Collaborative for Academic, Social, and Emotional Learning (CASEL) is "the process through which children and adults understand and manage emotions, set and achieve positive goals, feel and show empathy for others, establish and maintain positive relationships, and make responsible decisions." It focuses on self-awareness, self-management, responsible decision making, relationship skills,. and social awareness. These skills are promoted through curriculum and instruction, school-wide practices and policies and family and community partnerships.

Peer-Mediated Intervention to Promote Positive Behavioral Skills

Peer mediation can be a helpful learning tool in situations other than academic tutoring, such as the development of life skills. For example, peer-mediated intervention is effective in helping students who have autism spectrum disorder (ASD) learn appropriate social skills. Nondisabled peers are trained to implement interventions that increase and improve interactions of students who have ASD. These interventions promote the concept that learning from the very peers with whom a student is interacting on a daily basis produces an immediate, generalizable effect.

Conflict Resolution Programs

Conflict resolution is a skill that can be taught. As useful as it is for the general population of students, it is even more important for students who are impulsive and have poor social skills, mood swings, cognitive difficulties, a history of abuse or neglect, or other mental health challenges. Rather than responding to conflictual situations with anger, fear, and confusion, resulting in either aggression or frightened passivity, students learn methods of peaceful resolution of the conflict. Students learn the skills necessary to stop and think about potential responses to perceived threats and to use conflict resolution skills to deal with these challenging situations.

Social Skills Instruction as a Component of Regular Classroom Instruction

Social skills are best taught in the context of real-life classroom situations. The skills are more likely to generalize to that environment than if they are taught, for example, in a therapist's office. Social skills deficits can arise when a student had never learned appropriate social behaviors, or they can be the direct manifestation of an underlying disorder such as autism spectrum disorder.

Skills instruction includes initial training of skills, followed by ongoing practice. It encourages cooperation, interpersonal communication and listening skills, self-discipline, problem solving, and an increasing awareness of nonverbal communication. It combines a number of strategies to prevent and replace inappropriate behaviors and to increase skills that lead to social competence. Social skills instruction takes advantage of naturally occurring opportunities to teach appropriate behaviors in settings such as the cafeteria or hallways. The success of the training is measured by the ability of students to generalize their skills in a variety of settings.

Anger Management Programs

Anger management programs are focused on assisting individuals learn the skills to handle conflicts and to avoid engaging in hostile and aggressive behaviors that can stem from feelings of anger. They provide alternative choices for behavioral responses that result in increased opportunities for conflict resolution and the reduced likelihood of aggression and violence. They help the individual communicate effectively when feelings of anger arise and assert him- or herself in an acceptable manner. They teach how to respond appropriately rather than automatically react in a negative manner. Anger management skills training dovetails with social skills training, as individuals who lack social skills are often prone to misinterpret the behaviors of others, resulting in feelings of frustration and anger.

Behavior Support Management Plans

Behavior support management fosters prosocial behaviors and utilizes techniques such as respondent and operant conditioning, shaping, extinction of undesirable behaviors, redirection, and modeling of appropriate social behaviors. Interventions may include de-escalation procedures when students are agitated. Students and their parents should be fully informed about the classroom's behavior support system.

Least restrictive methods should be utilized whenever possible. They include verbal directives, redirection and prompts. More restrictive interventions include having a quiet time or time-out. Even more restrictive interventions include physical holding when a student is demonstrating evidence of danger to self or others, or the use of seclusion. School districts vary in their policies, procedures, and guidelines about restrictive procedures including touching students who are being disruptive, and educators need to be aware of them as they apply to their district. With appropriate early interventions, seclusion and restraint may be preventable.

Ideally, behavior support management for students in specialized programs for emotionally disturbed individuals should be provided within the larger context of school-wide and class-wide positive behavioral interventions and supports such as PBIS.

Pre-Correction Instructional Strategies

Pre-correction or prompting is useful in situations where the teacher reminds a student of expectations prior to activities or contexts in which there is already a history of a high risk of failure. It can be delivered via the use of gestures, statements, visual cues, modeling, or physical assistance, ideally immediately preceding the context in which the behavior is expected. For example, a student may display a pattern of disruptive behaviors when the teacher is providing one on one attention to another student. Recognizing this pattern and intervening with appropriate strategies can prevent acting-out behaviors. Prompts can begin at a minimal level, but may need to be increased in intensity if the minimal prompting is not effective. Positive reinforcement increases the likelihood of the effectiveness of prompting. When coupled with specific contingent statements of praise and increased student supervision, prompting significantly reduces inappropriate behaviors and increases appropriate behaviors.

Group-Oriented Contingency Strategy

Teachers often focus their behavioral intervention strategies on individual students, using techniques such as reinforcement (e.g., verbal praise) to increase the probability of desired behaviors. These individualized techniques, however, are difficult to practice in classrooms where there are multiple students who are manifesting inappropriate behaviors. Conversely, group-oriented techniques have proven to be as effective as individual tactics and are of practical use in classrooms where there are several students who have emotional and behavioral problems. They save the teacher's time and facilitate positive social interactions among group members. They also assist in building improved levels of appropriate behaviors.

A group-oriented contingency technique is one in which the teacher requires a specific behavior or behaviors of a group of students, and in which the presentation or the loss of a reinforcer is contingent on the performance of an individual within a group, on a subset of a group, or on the group as a whole. Group-oriented contingency strategies capitalize on peer influences, and peers, rather than teachers, are the primary change agents.

Group-oriented contingency strategies can be dependent, independent, or interdependent. Dependent contingencies are those in which all members of the group receive a reinforcement if one individual in the group meets the criterion. Independent contingencies reward the members of the group who have met the criteria for reinforcement. Interdependent contingencies require that all members of the group meet the criterion in order to receive the reinforcement.

Specific examples of targeted behaviors include talking out of turn and out-of-seat behavior. Token economies can be used as reinforcement techniques.

INDIVIDUAL PRACTICES FOR STUDENTS

Academic

Creation of Choice-Making Opportunities

Many students who have a long history of behavioral difficulties have been repeatedly told how "wrong" their behavior has been, and this can lead to feelings of powerlessness and eventual power struggles. It is essential to reframe interventions that address behavioral difficulties through the use of choice-making strategies. These strategies enable the student to have a sense of increased control over his or her life. Allowing choices promotes independence, helps students to self-monitor appropriate behaviors, gives them a sense of control, encourages active participation in appropriate activities, improves self-esteem, promotes a sense of responsibility and ultimately reduces inappropriate behaviors. Examples of choices include the choice of location where the student may work, the time that a project is worked on, and the materials used for a project. It is important to be consistent with the types and numbers of choices, to provide a variety of choices, and to reinforce choice-making opportunities that are initiated by the student.

Instruction in Self-Monitoring of Student Performance

Self-monitoring is an important component in teaching activities, especially for students who have difficulty recognizing the nature of their educational difficulties. For example, students who have attention deficits often are unaware of the nature and extent of these deficits and may feel frustrated that they continue to have academic problems despite efforts to do well in the classroom. For these students, self-monitoring by asking themselves questions such as "Am I at my desk?", "Am I doing my assignment?", "Am I listening to the teacher?", "Am I asking for help?", are more concrete than, "Am I paying attention?" Students can identify a skill that can be measured, and can graph progress of activities such as correctly spelling words on spelling tests.

Target behaviors need to be clearly defined, and baseline data need to be collected. Students are taught to self-monitor by learning the nature of the target behaviors and how these behaviors differ from other classroom behaviors, learning how to self-assess, and learning to self-record the target behaviors. Self-monitoring can alter the frequency, intensity, and duration of behaviors, and it saves teachers' time in the monitoring of students' behaviors. It provides immediate feedback, documents improvement over time, increases self-awareness, and has been demonstrated to have positive results.

Nonacademic Practices for Students
Positive Behavioral Intervention and Support

Positive behavioral intervention and support (called PBS and PBIS, discussed earlier in the text) has been shown to reduce behavioral problems and to improve academic outcomes. It is based on the premise that continual teaching, combined with feedback regarding positive student behaviors, reduces the need for discipline and promotes a climate of productivity, safety, and learning. PBIS concepts dovetail with other best practices including choice making, establishment of clear rules and expectations, proactive classroom management, and precorrection instructional strategies. Ideally, PBIS would be in place at both the secondary and the elementary school levels, with the goal of defining, teaching, and sustaining appropriate student behaviors across all school settings. It would help facilitate transition out of the programs and ideally prevent some students from requiring restrictive programming.

Peer Reinforcement to Promote Appropriate Behavior

Students who have emotional or behavioral difficulties are rejected by peers at a significantly higher rate than their nondisabled peers. Peer rejection is one of the strongest predictors of delinquency, aggressive behavior, and other negative life course outcomes. Students who have mental health disabilities often have difficulty forming and maintaining relationships, may misinterpret social cues, and may have difficulty with interpersonal problem-solving skills. These difficulties put them at increased risk for peer rejection and subsequent emotional and behavior difficulties.

Alternatively, peers can bolster self-esteem and classroom functioning. The use of peers as reinforcement agents for appropriate social and behavioral functioning of classmates, known as peer-mediated interventions, relies on peers serving as the primary change agent either directly or indirectly. Positive peer reporting utilizing praise is a simple peer reinforcement intervention in which the teacher rewards classmates for providing descriptive praise during structured daily sessions to a target child who is considered peer rejected. It is based on the premise that peers play a powerful role in the development of prosocial behaviors. Even brief daily sessions of peer praise may improve peer acceptance, social interactions, and social involvement of students who are socially withdrawn. It also can result in decreases in disruptive behaviors. Examples of positive behaviors that are reinforced by peer reinforcement include demonstrating good anger control, sharing with others, helping another classmate and working hard on assignments.

Behavior Contracts

Behavior contracts are useful for students who have persistent behavioral difficulties, who are disorganized, who fail to comply with work assignments, and who are defiant and oppositional. Contracts have the advantage of holding students accountable, providing structure and consistency, promoting responsibility, assisting in communication with parents, and improving students' grades and accountability. Contracts generally utilize daily forms that identify target behaviors, and results are reviewed with the student and sent home to parents on a regular basis. The student has the opportunity to process the behavioral data and to identify methods of behavioral improvement. Behaviors should be observable and measurable, and reinforcers should be motivating and simple to provide. Bonuses can be provided if the desired behavior is completed in a shorter period of time than expected. Contracts should be written and signed by all parties. Behaviors can be monitored by the teacher, but self-monitoring should be encouraged whenever possible.

The methodology of self-monitoring of nonacademic behaviors parallels that of monitoring for academic behaviors. In either circumstance, it is essential to identify concrete, quantifiable behaviors that the student recognizes and that can be monitored on an ongoing basis to determine improvement.

CRISIS INTERVENTION PLANNING

Classroom interventions have changed significantly over the years as misbehavior has become more serious: from the major problems in the 1940s (chewing gum, running in the hallways, talking out of turn) to today (drug and alcohol abuse, suicide, gang fights, school shootings). Today it is essential for schools to have clearly defined and understood crisis plans for situations in which students present evidence of being a danger to themselves or others. When a student makes suicidal statements or threatens to harm others, it is important for schools to have a pre-defined plan indicating which school professionals will intervene. Hennepin County in Minnesota, for example, has a crisis team that has the potential to do in-school assessments to assess the possible need for interventions such as hospitalization. Unless the relationship of the county team and the school staff is clearly agreed upon, county staff tend to defer to school professionals for crisis assessment. This process, however, can lead to school districts' assumption of unnecessary liability.

It is also essential to clarify the role of the police in the community and of police liaison officers and to define the threshold at which they will be asked to intervene. Although minor crises may be effectively dealt with by school administrative staff, counselors, social workers, and psychologists, it is important for thresholds to be defined for more intensive interventions that require community assistance. The process becomes more complex when a co-located mental health professional is working within the school setting with students and that professional's client is making statements regarding potential harm to self or others. Protocols need to be established regarding the role of the therapist in crisis assessment within the school as well as the ultimate responsibility of the school district to assure that crises are dealt with appropriately.

CHAPTER 22

Conclusions and Recommendations

THIS BOOK HAS PRESENTED USEFUL INFORMATION ABOUT child and adolescent mental health disorders, their treatment, and their implications in the classroom. It has also provided tools that teachers, school and district leaders, school psychologists, social workers, counselors, deans, and nurses can use to assist their students who have these disorders.

THE WIDE RANGE OF SCHOOL ATTENTION TO STUDENT MENTAL HEALTH ISSUES

Some educators who read this book are working in districts that have limited access to mental health services in the community and minimal or no mental health policies, guidelines, or protocols. Others work in districts that are very oriented toward identifying students' mental health needs and working in a collaborative manner with multiple types of professionals within the school system and in the community (social services, public health, corrections, mental health, and medical providers) to provide services that successfully address student needs.

It can be very frustrating for those professionals in the former category to gain knowledge about students' mental heath issues and to work within a system that does not effectively address those issues. For example, if a school district has an approach that is purely behavioral in its analysis of students' problems and in the implementation of services, it will be difficult for educators to try to address the mental health contributors to a student's behavioral difficulties in the classroom. If a district takes the approach that school professionals should never recommend that parents obtain a mental health evaluation of a student, because of concerns that the district is the payer of last resort, then a teacher may become frustrated by working with a student who may have a very treatable disorder that remains untreated. If a district's administrators have limited knowledge and understanding about mental health disorders of children and adolescents, then their decisions about interventions with students who have these disorders may be unproductive or even harmful to the students.

THE BENEFITS OF ESTABLISHING STUDENT MENTAL HEALTH POLICIES AND PRACTICES

Professionals in all positions in a school district and building who have knowledge about child and adolescent mental health disorders can make a significant difference for these students—not only within the classroom, but also within the larger context of the school system.

As members of teacher assistance teams, knowledgeable professionals can suggest interventions that are mental health focused prior to referral for special education. For example, they can work to ensure that, with parent permission, information is communicated to the student's treating professional when a student is taking medication or receiving psychotherapy. They can ask the school psychologists who perform educational assessments and functional behavioral analyses whether there is evidence that a student may have behavioral difficulties that are due to intrinsic factors stemming from a mental health disorder. They can request clarification about roles and job descriptions of the school psychologists, social workers, counselors, and nurses—and of their own roles—in terms of addressing the needs of students who have mental health disorders. Most importantly, they can shift their own attitudes and perceptions of students who have both mental health disorders and behavioral difficulties, thereby benefiting the students through their greater sensitivity, empathy, and knowledge.

With this shift, they can also be more successful in working with these students and their families. They can avoid power struggles in which they and their students become demoralized by a cycle of failure. When the mental health disorder, rather than the student, is identified as the problem, there is a significant reduction of conflict and frustration. Educators, students, and families are then more able to work together for success. This is a paradigm shift to a public health model of mental health disorders.

Educators can share information with their administrators about the various models of school mental health services that can be provided on-site within the school setting. They can help their administrators understand that schools can stay out of the mental health business of diagnosing and treating students while at the same time collaborating with community providers to ensure that at-risk students receive the help that they need.

When a school district establishes on-site, co-located mental health services, either provided by school-hired staff or by community mental health providers, educators play a vital role in ensuring the success of this intervention.

With appropriate releases of information when required, educators will be able to communicate with these providers about students' baseline behavioral presentations prior to diagnosis and during the process of treatment. In addition, they and other members of the educational team can obtain information about the nature of students' mental health disorders as they relate to the school environment. This information can be used to provide more effective educational interventions, including accommodations and modifications of curriculum. This is a similar approach to communicating with providers in the community, but is even more effective when the providers are on-site at the school.

Educators can also provide information to students about the signs and symptoms of mental health disorders and steps to take if they or their peers are experiencing them. Health teachers can advocate for expansion of the health curriculum to more effectively address such topics as mood disorders, anxiety disorders, and ADHD. Curriculum that focuses on diversity sensitivity can include the need to understand and to avoid stigmatizing students who have mental health disorders. Antibullying programs can expand their focus to recognize the increased vulnerability to victimization for students who have mental health disorders.

By being more involved in the process of identifying the key behavioral signs and symptoms of various mental health disorders and by documenting their severity, chronicity, and periodicity, educators will have an increased awareness about the nature of these disorders and of their manifestations within the classroom environment. In the process of communicating this information to treating professionals and in monitoring behavioral changes that take place following changes in treatment plans, educators become increasingly aware of the value of psychotherapeutic and medication interventions for these students.

RECOMMENDATIONS

There are many areas where mental health support for students can benefit from improvements, but I want to conclude this book by focusing on two policies that can impede both the education and treatment of students with mental health disorders. The first set of recommendations concerns, specifically, placement of students who are determined eligible for special education services because of their emotional or behavioral disabilities. The second set concerns the "payor of last resort" provision of the Individuals with Disabilities Education Act (IDEA), which makes a school district potentially responsible for its students' mental health-related costs not met through other sources and thus can impede the district's willingness to engage with a student's mental health issues.

Improved Criteria for Placement of Emotionally Disturbed Students in Special Education Classes

As indicated throughout this book, students who are determined eligible for special education services because of their emotional or behavioral disabilities present a broad and complex range of disabilities, needs, behaviors, and challenges to the public schools that serve them. Unfortunately, even with special education, these students tend to have very poor school and post-school outcomes (Wagner, 1995). The Emotional Disturbance (ED) category differs from other mental disorder categories because it is based on behavior and not on a specific, recognized disability. Indeed, a student need only demonstrate inappropriate behavior that is divergent from the behavior of peers. In other words, this becomes a tautological issue as the behavioral symptoms become the disabilities themselves.

Still, schools must make placement decisions for students with ED, just as they do for students with other diagnosed mental disorders. Without a clear definition of the student's needs and disabilities, it is difficult, and in some situations, impossible to develop and implement effective educational interventions. School staff members must try to reduce aggression, hyperactivity, or impulsivity without knowing a disability-related cause or contributing factor to that behavior.

Recommendations Regarding the ED Category

Not all students with disabilities are eligible for special education and related services under federal and state special education laws. In order to be eligible for special education and related services under federal and state law, a student must qualify under one of the 13 eligibility categories found in the Individuals with Disabilities Education Act (IDEA). Among the categories is emotional disturbance (ED), which is defined in 34 C.F.R. § 300.7(c)(4)(i) as

> a condition exhibiting one or more of the following characteristics over a long period of time and to a marked degree that adversely affects a child's educational performance: (A) An inability to learn that cannot be explained by intellectual, sensory, or health factors. (B) An inability to build or maintain satisfactory interpersonal relationships with peers and teachers. (C) Inappropriate types of behavior or feelings under normal circumstances. (D) A general pervasive mood of unhappiness or depression. (E) A tendency to develop physical symptoms or fears associated with personal or school problems.

Section 300.7(c)(4)(ii) provides that emotional disturbance "includes schizophrenia" and that "[t]he term does not apply to children who are socially maladjusted, unless it is determined that they have an emotional disturbance." Originally, the definition was created from descriptions of students made by E. M. Bower in the 1950s. He and his colleagues collected academic, emotional, and social information on over 200 students who were identified by mental health professionals as being "emotionally disturbed." Five factors were identified as separating these students from their peers. These five factors became the characteristics listed in § 300.7(c)(4)(i)(A–E). When the federal definition was originally created, it added the term serious, the stipulation that the problem adversely affected educational performance, the inclusion of schizophrenia, and the exclusion of social maladjustment unless SED (Severe Emotional Disorder) was also present. The definition neither quantifies the "long period of time," nor does it define the term "social maladjustment." The 1999 federal regulations were revised to reflect Congressional intent to remove the connotation of the term serious but not to make any substantive change.

It is important to note that, although research in children's mental health disorders has advanced significantly since the 1950s (e.g., childhood depression was not recognized as a disorder at that time), the criteria have remained essentially unchanged. While disorders from other special education categories may develop suddenly (e.g., traumatic brain injury, physical injuries resulting in the need for adaptive physical education, sudden hearing loss), the ED criteria continue to maintain the need for emotional problems having existed for a "long period of time." In fact, some children's mental health disorders such as post-traumatic stress disorder, panic disorder, mania, and so on may have sudden onset.

In explaining its position on requested changes to the ED definition during IDEA's 2004 reauthorization, the U.S. Department of Education (USDOE) comments to the final regulations state that,

> [H]istorically, it has been very difficult for the field to come to consensus on the definition of emotional disturbance, which has remained unchanged since 1977. On February 10, 1993, the Department published a "Notice of Inquiry" in the Federal Register(58 FR 7938) soliciting comments on the existing definition of serious emotional disturbance. The comments received in response to the notice of inquiry expressed a wide range of opinions and no consensus on the definition was reached. Given the lack of consensus and the fact that Congress did not make any changes that required changing the definition, the Department recommended that the definition of emotional disturbance remain unchanged. We reviewed the Act and the comments received in response to the NPRM and have come to the same conclusion. Therefore, we decline to make any changes to the definition of emotional disturbance. (USDOE, 2006)

The USDOE's comment to the final regulations shows the stalemate over the ED definition in 2006. Yet, the problems identified in this book and in previous debates in the literature continue today. It is time again to renew the debate in the current context to strive toward some consensus.

To address the fundamental weakness of the ED category in not assisting school staff to get to the heart of the child's disability, the IDEA definition could be more specifically tied to a particular disability. Forness and Knitzer (1992) proposed a revision of the definition as follows:

i. The term Emotional or Behavioral Disorder [EBD] means a disability characterized by behavioral or emotional responses in school so different from appropriate, age, cultural, or ethnic norms that they adversely affect educational performance. Educational performance includes academic, social, vocational, and personal skills. Such a disability
   a. is more than a temporary, expected response to stressful events in the environment;
   b. is consistently exhibited in two different settings, at least one of which is school related; and
   c. is unresponsive to direct intervention in general education or the child's condition is such that general interventions would be insufficient.
ii. Emotional and behavioral disorders can coexist with other disabilities.
iii. This category may include children or youth with schizophrenic disorders, affective disorders, anxiety disorders, or other sustained disorders of conduct or adjustment when they adversely affect educational performance in accordance with section.

This change is a step towards improving an understanding of ED on a national level. However, it continues to identify the ED category as being the disability, rather than mandating the identification of the student's actual disability and providing appropriate accommodations and modifications as are done within other disability categories.

Identify the Student's Disability

The following recommendations are thus directed towards identifying students' actual disabilities and addressing them appropriately within the educational setting. Some can be done by school districts, whereas others would require state or federal interventions.

- Modify financial responsibility requirements in IDEA. The potential for school districts to have to pay for costly mental health treatment including residential treatment for problems that they identify is a major factor contributing to their reluctance to address mental health disorders in special education assessments.
- Eliminate the Social Maladjustment exclusion. This is a poorly defined concept that is difficult to delineate or apply in the educational setting.
- Require mental health screening for students who are evaluated for ED placement.
- Require that screening tools are reliable, valid, sensitive and specific, and require outcome assessments to determine on a statewide level the percentages and types of disorders identified, the subsequent interventions that take place, and the academic and behavioral outcomes of those interventions.
- Funding should be made available to provide a diagnostic assessment that will clarify the problem if mental health screening identifies evidence of a psychiatric disorder that has symptoms that reflect the student's emotional or behavioral problems in the classroom. This will require funding to schools beyond their present level of reimbursement, as well as modifying potential school financial responsibilities for mental health services. Upon clarification of diagnosis, accommodations and modifications will be able to be designed to focus on the student's underlying disability. In some cases, treatment will ameliorate the problems manifested in the classroom.
- For students whose parents do not agree to allow a mental health diagnostic evaluation, even though their child is manifesting significant emotional or behavioral problems, allow an exception to the diagnostic mandate.
- Exclude from ED students who have chronic health conditions (e.g., ADHD) that are the primary cause of their emotional or behavioral problems, and address these issues in Other Health Impairment (OHI) instead. Clarify methods of determining whether the problems stem from the chronic health condition.
- Specifically identify other psychiatric disorders (e.g., Bipolar Mood Disorder, Major Depression, Panic Disorder, Obsessive-Compulsive Disorder, Post-Traumatic Stress Disorder) as being chronic health conditions.

• Expand the OHI criteria to better reflect educational manifestations of psychiatric disorders that are chronic health conditions.

Given the difficulties associated with changing federal laws and the practical reality that state laws may also be created or amended to be more specific about the nature and cause of behavior, Forness and Knitzer's (1995) recommendations, above, apply to state level changes as well. The bottom line is to ensure the student's true disabilities are identified; once done, appropriate individualized programming can occur.

Coordinate School Practices

To support policy changes, a return to the fundamental premise of individualized programming is needed. In doing so, it will be necessary to draw on the professionalism, skills, and positive attitude of parents, school staff, community partners, and students; and to set aside rigid, pre-formed, and cookie-cutter programming decisions made for groups of students. IDEA's central planning document for students is the Individualized Education Plan, and its name purposely reflects its intent.

In practice, institution of such a plan means the development and coordination of district-wide and school-wide Positive Behavior Support (PBIS) efforts, school staff training on clinical disorders, and school evaluation staff training on conducting functional behavioral assessments. It requires an understanding of how students with ED move through the school settings from being fully mainstreamed to landing in an completely segregated ED-only schools. And, it requires reviewing student files for evidence of treated and untreated mental health issues, developing appropriate community-based models for addressing student mental health, and above all, clarifying how to identify, address, track, and continually revise the student's individual plan. Important components of this plan may include school to work transition plans, consideration of IDEA's related services, planning for inclusion into school extracurricular and nonacademic activities, and other ways to make a school beneficial for an individual student. These activities could be supported by the Department of Education, or school professional- or district-led practice groups.

Monitor Education Outcomes

In order to ensure that a student's plan is working, schools and state departments of education must develop a process to track student outcomes. It is already possible to create a basic outcome-focused tracking system based on statewide and district-wide test scores, graduation rates, dropout rates, and IDEA's required individual progress reporting. With this existing information, districts could monitor the progress of students with ED on individual student, school, and district levels. These outcome reports can also be used to create a statewide picture of overall success rates with ED programming. Districts and schools with higher levels of success can assist others with lower rates and with program improvement strategies. (For a more complete discussion of education issues related to students with ED, see Stewart & Dikel, 2011).

REPEAL OF IDEA'S PAYOR OF LAST RESORT PROVISION

The Individuals with Disabilities Education Act (IDEA) ensures services to all children with disabilities by governing how states and public agencies provide early intervention, special education, and related services to infants, toddlers, children, and adolescents with disabilities. An obstacle to improving mental health services for this population is the "Payor of Last Resort" provision (IDEA Sec. 303.510, 1990), which makes the school district responsible for costs not met through other sources.

IDEA mandates that all states have mechanisms to clarify fiscal responsibilities of various public systems ("*§ 300.154 Methods of ensuring services. (3) Procedures for resolving interagency disputes (including procedures under which LEAs may initiate proceedings) under the agreement or other mechanism to secure reimbursement from other agencies or otherwise implement the provisions of the agreement or mechanism.").

However, these procedures are generally not clarified in most states for situations such as determining the fiscal responsibility for funding residential treatment services. In my opinion, to improve services to youth who have mental health disorders, the Payor of Last Resort provision that hobbles school districts because of the potential for massive financial responsibilities should be eliminated. I say that for several reasons:

1. Research indicates that approximately 18% of children and adolescents have psychiatric disorders and that 5% have a severe mental health problem, yet as few as 20% of these youth receive any mental health treatment.

2. These disorders often manifest in the school setting, especially when they result in disruptive behaviors, and can lead to an evaluation for special education services.

3. The category Emotional Disorders does not require identifying any actual disability, but is based solely on behavior. However, most students evaluated for this category show evidence of mental health problems.

4. Research indicates that the children in this category have extremely poor outcomes because their emotional problems are rarely treated. Behavioral interventions for behaviors that stem from underlying, intrinsic disorders do not tend to be successful.

5. Even when a child exhibits clear evidence of an untreated or inappropriately treated mental health disorder, school districts are reluctant to recommend mental health evaluations because they fear the potential of not only paying for the diagnostic evaluation, but the potentially massive financial responsibilities for subsequent mental health treatment services. This can cost tens of thousands or even hundreds of thousands of dollars in cases if the student is placed in residential treatment and the family's insurance does not cover the placement. Courts have decided that the students' educational needs are "inextricably intertwined" with their mental health needs, and that the district is thus responsible to pay for both educational and mental health services.

6. Across the United States, many school psychologists are under a "gag order" from their school administrators never to directly recommend that a student get a mental health evaluation. Yet, hundreds of millions of dollars are spent every year doing educational assessments to qualify these students for special education services, to provide services that are not effective. Often, students who have severe mental health disabilities (e.g., post-traumatic stress disorder resulting from trauma, mood disorders) are perceived by school

professionals simply as having behavioral problems. This only exacerbates a student's underlying disability.

7. If the Payor of Last Resort provision is eliminated, and if other funding is identified (e.g., State "High Needs Funds") that reimburses districts for special education costs exceeding a certain amount for severely disabled students, there is a greater likelihood that at-risk students would be identified, evaluated, and successfully treated. School districts would be much more willing to address students' mental health issues appropriately. They could partner with other systems (e.g., counties, physicians, mental health professionals) to more effectively serve students in a collaborative manner.

8. Unless this disincentive is removed, other interventions aimed at improving students' mental health (e.g., increasing the number of counselors in schools) will not have significant impact, as the students' underlying mental health disorders will still remain unidentified and untreated.

9. The Emotional Disturbance category of special education is a more complicated issue; it is the only disability category that is not directly tied to an actual disability (e.g., learning, developmental, physical).

The Emotional Disturbance category is a tautological category, in that it becomes the disability. For example, a student who has no mental illness, but who is delinquent and aggressive, may be placed in this category. If he or she subsequently becomes violent with a teacher or peers, even if this behavior is demonstrated to be planned and volitional, the student might not be expelled. A "manifestation determination assessment" might determine that the behavior was due to the "disability," the disability being the category itself!

In addition, the Payor of Last Resort responsibilities reduce the likelihood that an ED student will have underlying mental health disorders identified, evaluated, and treated. Perhaps this category should be eliminated and either replaced with a more functional category, or the Other Health Disability category should be used for students who have diagnosed mental health disorders that adversely affect their educational progress.

I encourage organizations that serve school administrators, school and clinical psychologists, social workers, nurses, counselors, psychiatrists, and parents to take a stand on this issue and to organize a concerted effort to eliminate the Payor of Last Resort provision when IDEA is reauthorized.

A FINAL WORD

As David Satcher (1998), a former U.S. surgeon general, said, "I'm convinced that we can shape a different future for this country as it relates to mental health." Educators, armed with knowledge and understanding about child and adolescent mental health, will be key players in making this happen.

The Diagnostic and Statistical Manual of Mental Disorders (DSM)

AN ACCURATE DIAGNOSIS REQUIRES FOUR BASIC FACTORS. It needs to be sensitive, in that the criteria need to identify the vast majority (ideally all) of the individuals who have the disorder. It needs to be specific, meaning that individuals who do not have the disorder would not be given that diagnosis. It needs to be reliable, in that, if several clinicians examined the same patient, they would reach the same diagnostic conclusion. Finally, it needs to be valid, in that it identifies individuals who actually have the disorder. Over the decades, the field of psychiatry has attempted to improve these factors in diagnosis, which has led to the criteria used today. Since the mid-1800s, the field of psychiatry has published criteria that identify the key features of mental health disorders. The Diagnostic and Statistical Manual of Mental Disorders, first edition (DSM-I), was published in 1952, followed by the DSM-II in 1968, the DSM-III in 1980, the revised DSM-III (DSM-III-R) in 1987, the DSM-IV in 1994, the DSM-IV-TR (text revision) in 2000, and the DSM-5 in 2013. Each new edition contained changes to the previous diagnostic categorizations, revising some diagnoses by either broadening or narrowing criteria, adding others, and removing ones that did not have a clear scientific basis.

All mental health disorders have significant behavioral, emotional, or cognitive disturbances, indicating abnormalities in biological, developmental, or psychological functioning. Disorders are associated with significant distress or disability, and expectable or culturally approved responses to stressors (e.g., normal grief responses) or socially deviant behaviors and societal conflicts are not mental disorders.

In May 2013, the DSM-5 was released. Major changes in the method of describing a patient's diagnosis were made from the previous edition. Since teachers may see reports from prior to and following this change, both types are described here.

The DSM-IV (1994) and DSM-IV-TR (2000) were the sources of essentially all diagnostic evaluations performed on today's K–12 students seen prior to May 2013. They utilized a multiaxial format, placing the major psychiatric diagnoses such as mood disorders, anxiety disorders, psychotic disorders, and so on, in Axis I. Axis II included mental retardation (now called intellectual developmental disorder) and personality disorders. Axis III listed physical conditions or medical disorders that might contribute to a patient's psychiatric symptoms. Axis IV defined the level of psychosocial stressors experienced by the patient, from mild to catastrophic. Finally, Axis V rated the patient's level of functioning at the time of the assessment, as well as noting the highest level of functioning experienced during the previous year.

The DSM-5 no longer uses the axial diagnosis method, and combines the former Axes I, II, and III. There is a section for separate notations for psychosocial and contextual factors that previously were the basis for Axis IV and for the degree of disability, previously noted in Axis V. As the diagnoses of many students who have mental health disorders were based on the DSM-IV-TR, this can create confusion for educators. There have been major revisions in the criteria of several disorders and elimination or incorporation into other categories of several more. For example, Asperger's syndrome is no longer a diagnosable condition, and individuals who have the history of symptoms that led to this diagnosis are now diagnosed with autism spectrum disorder.

For the purpose of clarity, the diagnostic descriptions in this book are based on DSM-5 criteria. However, some DSM-IV information is also covered to aid educators in making the transition from the fourth to the fifth edition of the manual. Not all of the diagnoses outlined below are covered in this book, but they are listed for teachers who have an interest in further exploration of mental health diagnostic and treatment issues. The following are the major changes from DSM-IV-TR to DSM-5:

In the neurodevelopmental disorder category, the term "mental retardation" is no longer used (finally!), and is replaced with "intellectual disability" (intellectual developmental disorder). Phonological disorder has been changed to speech sound disorder, and stuttering has been changed to childhood-onset fluency disorder. A new disorder, social (pragmatic) communication disorder, has been added, referring to persistent difficulties in the social use of nonverbal and verbal communication. Autism spectrum disorder, Asperger's disorder, childhood disintegrative disorder, Rett's disorder, and pervasive developmental disorder not otherwise specified have all been encompassed in the autism spectrum diagnosis. The age of onset of symptoms of Attention-deficit/hyperactivity disorder (ADHD) has been changed from being present prior to the age 7 years to being present prior to age 12 years, and the number of criteria needed for diagnosing the disorder in adults has been reduced. Reading disorder, mathematics disorder, disorder of written expression, and learning disorder not otherwise specified have been subsumed under the diagnosis of specific learning disorder.

Criteria for the category of schizophrenia spectrum and other psychotic disorders no longer have the subtypes (paranoid, catatonic, disorganized, undifferentiated, residual forms) and use a dimensional approach for rating severity of symptoms.

A number of changes were made in the Mood Disorders category. Due to concerns that bipolar mood disorder was being overdiagnosed in children and adolescents, the diagnosis of disruptive mood dysregulation disorder was added, referring to children up to the age of 18 years who exhibit persistent irritability and frequent episodes of extreme behavioral dyscontrol. Dysthymia (chronic low-level depression) was changed to persistent depressive disorder. Premenstrual dysphoric disorder (known in common terms as PMS) became a new diagnosis. Symptoms of depression in bereavement are no longer exclusionary factors for the diagnosis of depression.

In the anxiety disorders category, adults who have specific phobia or social anxiety disorder no longer need to have excessive or unreasonable anxiety for the diagnosis to be made. Separation anxiety disorder and selective mutism are now classified as anxiety disorders. PTSD and acute stress disorder are now in a new category, trauma and stressor-related disorders, and obsessive-compulsive disorder is in a new category of obsessive-compulsive and related disorders. In the latter category, hoarding disorder and excoriation (skin-picking) disorder have been added.

Feeding disorder of infancy or early childhood has been renamed avoidant/restrictive food intake disorder. The diagnosis of anorexia nervosa no longer requires amenorrhea as a criterion for females.

Gender dysphoria is a new disorder, replacing the DSM-IV-TR gender identity disorder, and separate criteria are listed for children versus adolescents and adults.

The DSM-5 chapter "Disruptive, Impulse Control and Conduct Disorders" is new, and combines diagnoses from the no-longer-present chapter "Disorders Usually First Diagnosed in Infancy, Childhood and Adolescence" and from the impulse-control chapter. The criteria for oppositional defiant disorder are now grouped into the angry/irritable mood type, the argumentative/defiant behavior type, and the vindictive type, and the exclusionary criteria of conduct disorder have been removed. Conduct disorder criteria now include descriptions of individuals who have limited prosocial emotions. Intermittent explosive disorder now includes verbal aggression and nondestructive or noninjurious physical aggression.

In the substance-related and addictive disorders category, the diagnosis of gambling disorder has been added. Regarding substances, DSM-5 no longer separates substance abuse from substance dependence. Substance use disorder criteria include criteria for intoxication, withdrawal, substance-induced disorders, and unspecified substance-related disorders.

Mental Health–Related Services on Individual Education Plans

THE MAJORITY OF U.S. STUDENTS WHO HAVE PSYCHIATRIC disorders are served in regular education programs. When students who have psychiatric disorders are identified as disabled and in need of special education, (e.g., SED/ED, OHD, ASD), it is nevertheless common for them to have severe and untreated disorders. Ideally, they would all have appropriate mental health screening and treatment through county services, public health programs, primary care, and mental health providers, but this is often not the case. Given that many students in the United States are uninsured or underinsured, and that U.S. Department of Education's Individuals with Disabilities Education Act (IDEA) mandates that schools be the payers of last resort for related services, including mental health–related services, schools face a tremendous responsibility in educating students who have mental health difficulties.

DEFINITIONS OF SERVICES

The IDEA requires school districts to provide "related services" to eligible students. Such services are defined broadly in IDEA to include psychological services, social work services, and counseling services, as follows:

[Related services include] . . . such developmental, corrective and other supportive services (including . . . psychological services, . . . social work services, school nurse services designed to enable a child with a disability to receive a free appropriate public education as described in the individualized education program of the child, counseling services . . . and medical services, except that such medical services shall be for diagnostic and evaluation purposes only) as may be required to assist a child with a disability to benefit from special education, and includes the early identification and assessment of disabling conditions in children [see 20 U.S.C. §1401(26)(A)].

The federal regulations accompanying IDEA contain guidance on the meaning of terms included in the above-cited definition, as follows:

"Counseling services" means services provided by qualified social workers, psychologists, guidance counselors, or other qualified personnel [34 CFR §300.34(c)(2)].

"Parent counseling and training" means assisting parents in understanding the special needs of their child; providing parents with information about child development; and helping parents to acquire the necessary skills that will allow them to support the implementation of their child's IEP or IFSP [34 C.F.R. §300.34(c)(8)].

"Psychological services" are defined to include not only psychological testing and assessment, consulting with other staff, and assisting in developing positive behavioral intervention strategies, but also "planning and managing a program of psychological services, including psychological counseling for children and parents" [34 C.F.R. §300.34(c)(10)].

"Social work services" is defined to include any or all of the following:

- preparation of a social or developmental history on a child,
- group and individual counseling with the child and family,
- work in partnership with parents and others on those problems in a child's living situation that affect the child's adjustment in school,
- mobilization of school and community resources to enable the child to learn as effectively as possible in his or her educational program; and
- assistance in developing positive behavioral intervention services. [34 C.F.R. §300.34(c)(14)]

The accepted definition of the term "counseling" is the provision of assistance and guidance in resolving personal, social, or psychological problems and difficulties. This definition is distinct from the accepted definition of "therapy," which is intended to relieve or heal a mental health disorder by psychological means. Therapy is not defined in IDEA, and many would argue that providing therapy to relieve or heal a psychological disorder goes beyond the supportive and corrective services to assist the child to benefit from education that are contemplated by IDEA.

STANDARD FOR PROVIDING MENTAL HEALTH-RELATED SERVICES UNDER IDEA

The determination that a related service is "necessary" is subject to varying interpretations. The United States Supreme Court articulated the standard in very practical terms, as follows: "[the student] cannot attend school unless the requested services are available during the school day."[1]

It is instructive that a Court decision rejected the multifactor test proposed by the school district, which would have permitted consideration of the need for continuous rather than intermittent care, whether existing school personnel could provide the service, the cost of the service, and the potential consequences if the service were not properly performed. The decision demonstrates the Court's view that Congress intended to ensure meaningful access to school for children with disabilities, and that a student should be provided a related service if the service is necessary for the child to be able to benefit from special education, without particular regard to the school district's financial concerns.

It is important to note that the standard mandates services that are necessary and does not mandate services that are merely "helpful" or "beneficial" to the student. In addition, the standard relates to services that are necessary to support the student's education, as opposed to other, unrelated areas of the student's life.

LIMITATIONS ON MEDICAL SERVICES

The related service definition only includes medical services that are "for diagnostic and evaluation purposes only." Other medical services are beyond the scope of IDEA-related services. For example, a school district was required to pursue medical services for diagnostic and evaluation services for a student whose unmet mental health needs were interfering with his academic and interpersonal success.[2]

Conversely, monitoring medication typically has been regarded as a medical service that goes beyond diagnosis and evaluation, and therefore excluded from a school's responsibility.[3]

CONTINUUM OF MENTAL HEALTH SERVICES

Related services provided for students' mental health needs do not necessarily neatly match the continuum of mental health services. From a mental health provider's standpoint, the continuum of services, from the least to the most intense, resembles the following:

a. A school psychologist, counselor, or social worker providing educational support and social skills training, designing positive behavioral interventions for an oppositional and defiant student, providing staff training in implementation of behavior plans, counseling (e.g., to help an anxious student benefit from educational programming), and nursing services (e.g., dispensing psychiatric medication)
b. Mental health diagnosis, outpatient therapy, or medication management
c. Day treatment
d. Residential treatment
e. Inpatient hospitalization

Traditionally, school districts have felt comfortable providing services within the first category and have considered the other services to be outside of the boundaries of school responsibility. However, a review of case law and administrative decisions reveals that school districts have been held responsible to include other kinds of services on IEPs as well.

For example, the Minnesota Department of Education found that a school district denied Free Appropriate Public Education (FAPE), which is guaranteed by IDEA, to a student because it had failed to provide psychological counseling services to address the student's unique needs. School providers and the parent all agreed that the student, who engaged in inappropriate behaviors and truancy, needed psychological counseling. The parent was unable to provide mental health services, and the state's department of education ordered the school district to arrange for mental health therapeutic counseling at district expense.[4]

OBLIGATION TO FUND
A RESIDENTIAL PLACEMENT

The most intensive (and typically the most costly) placement for students with mental health challenges is a residential placement. The federal regulations specifically contemplate residential programs for some IDEA students, as follows: "If placement in a public or private residential program is necessary to provide special education and related services to a child with a disability, the program, including non-medical care and room and board, must be at no cost to the parents of the child" (34 C.F.R. §300.104).

Courts around the country have issued decisions about a school's responsibility to fund a residential placement. The results of these cases vary widely, with some courts ordering a district to fund the costs of the program, and others finding the costs of a residential placement must be borne by another entity or the student's family.

For example, in a case involving an emotionally and behaviorally disturbed student whose behaviors included classroom disruption, profanity, insubordination, truancy, substance use, sexual promiscuity, running away, and suicide attempts, the school attempted to educate her in a day treatment setting but was thwarted by her irregular attendance. The court ordered the school to fund a residential placement, on the grounds that it was impossible to separate the student's behavior problems from the learning process, and impossible for her to make educational progress in a nonresidential setting.[5] The court declined to decide the case based upon whether the placement was prompted by "educational" concerns, stating, "What should control our decision is not whether the problem itself is "educational" or "non-educational," but whether it needs to be addressed in order for the child to learn.[6]

By contrast, in another case involving a student who engaged in running away and promiscuous behaviors, the court declined to order the school district to fund a residential placement, finding that a residential setting was not necessary to meet the student's educational needs, but was indicated due to "issues apart from the learning process, which manifested themselves away from school grounds."[7]

In another court decision, the court declined to require a school to reimburse parents for the cost of a residential placement. The court found that the student made progress in the placement offered by the public school (the school's self-contained placement included academic and emotional support in a therapeutic setting) during times he was sober, but his progress was affected when his drug problem was active. The court rejected the plaintiff's argument that the student's drug problem and disability were "intertwined," noting that acceptance of this argument would lead to the requirement that financially strapped schools fund substance abuse programs for all students who happen to be disabled, absent any legal justification. The court reasoned that "while a residential placement may have been the most effective way to treat [the student's] substance-abuse problem, that treatment was not the district's responsibility."[8]

In summary, some courts appear to rely on distinctions about the school district's mission to educate and decline to require payment for residential placements to address medical or drug related problems. Other courts inquire whether the residential setting is necessary for the child to be able to learn. While these are slightly different tests, the key to these cases appears to be whether a school district can convince the court that the student has a chance of making adequate progress in a nonresidential setting.

What constitutes adequate progress is an unpredictable and fact-specific inquiry, subject to the persuasive abilities of expert witnesses. The Eighth Circuit decided that a showing of academic progress was sufficient to demonstrate a FAPE in a case where a cahild with a behavioral disability made little behavioral progress, but progressed academically at an average rate.[9] The court stated,

> Where, as here, the record indicates that a student's behavioral problems, if unattended, might significantly curtail his ability to learn, the fact that he is learning is significant evidence that his behavioral problems have, at least in part, been attended to. Of course, we wish that [the student] had made more behavioral progress, but the IDEA does not require that schools attempt to maximize a child's potential, or, as a matter of fact, guarantee that the student will actually

make any progress at all. It requires only that the student be provided with an IEP that is reasonably calculated to provide educational benefit . . . .

PRACTICAL CONCERNS AND RECOMMENDATIONS

There is wide variability among districts regarding the threshold for defining a mental health service as a related service. This variability is understandable, given the lack of definition contained in IDEA and the discrepancies among courts.

The cost of providing services designed to address mental health needs can be expensive. In a small number of states, provisions exist in law to shift the cost of mental health services to entities other than schools. For example, Missouri[10] has capped school districts' financial responsibility limits, after which costs are borne by the state. In California, mental health–related services on IEPs were for a time the responsibility of the county rather than the school district.

In most states, however, while a school district may seek reimbursement for related services from third parties, it remains responsible if reimbursement is not available. The mandate to provide related services exists regardless of funding availability. Failure to provide a required related service can lead to responsibility for the costs of privately obtained services as well as attorneys' fees and litigation-related expenses.

The specific contractual arrangements for mental health service providers varies widely among school districts, as well. School districts may choose to have services provided by their own district-supervised staff, or through contracts with providers in the community. Each situation has its advantages and disadvantages, as indicated in Chapter 15 of this volume.

CONCLUSION

It is an inescapable fact that schools serve children whose mental health challenges affect their ability to benefit from education. Resources are scarce and mental health services can be expensive. However, it can be costly and legally indefensible to seek to avoid the responsibility to provide appropriate related services.

The authors of this appendix recommend a two-pronged approach: First, districts can enter into successful collaborative relationships with other systems (e.g., county mental health and public health programs) to assure that students' mental health needs are met through sources outside of the school setting.

Second, schools *must* educate IEP teams about the standards and requirements of the law, ensure that professionals are appropriately licensed and supervised, and seek to provide appropriate services in a cost-sensitive way.

Given the payer of last resort mandates of IDEA and the significant percentage of uninsured students, state and national school organizations should consider lobbying for changes in legislation that will result in the reduction of both legal and financial liabilities to school districts that attempt to address students' unmet mental health needs.

[1] Cedar Rapids Community SD v., Garret F., 526 U.S. 66, 72 (U.S. 1999) (availability of nursing services as a related service to ventilator-dependent IDEA student; discussion of medical services exclusion).

[2] Minnesota Department of Education Complaint No. 2101 (2005).

[3] Doe v. Shorewood School Dist., 2005 WL 2387717 (E.D. Wis. 2005); M.G. v. Sergi, 554 F.Supp.2d 201 (D. Conn. 2008).

[4] MDE Complaint No. 07-055C (2007).

[5] Independent School District 284 v. A.C., 258 F.3d 769 (8th Cir. 2001).

[6] Id. at 777.

[7] Ashland School District v. Parents of R.J., 585 F.Supp.2d 1208 (D. Ore. 2008); see also Butler v. Evans, 225 F.2d 887 (7th Cir. 2000)(where residential placement was almost exclusively for medical reasons and not for educational purposes, the court denied a parent's demand for reimbursement. Student received daily psychiatric counseling, intensive drug therapy and recreational therapy, but limited educational services).

[8] P.K. v. Bedford Central Sch. Dist., 569 F.Supp. 2d 371, 387 (S.D.N.Y. 2008).

[9] CJN v. Special School District No. 1, 323 F.3d 630 (8th Cir. 2003).

[10] http://dese.mo.gov/divspeced/Finance/HighNeedIndex.html

Note: This appendix was adapted from Sara Ruff, J.D. and William Dikel, M.D., Mental Health Related Services on IEPs, Inquiry and Analysis, November 2009.

APPENDIX 3

Special Education Evaluations of Students Who Abuse Drugs and Alcohol

SUBSTANCE USE AMONG ADOLESCENTS IS PERVASIVE, AND IT often impacts their academic progress and social-emotional functioning. (In this appendix, the term "substances" includes alcohol, illegal drugs such as cannabis or cocaine, and abused prescription drugs). However, substance use is not recognized as a "disability" under the Individuals with Disabilities Education Act (IDEA).[1] As a result, the mere fact that a student abuses substances or has been diagnosed with substance use disorder does not make the student a "child with a disability" under IDEA. Similarly, the mere fact that a student uses substances does not trigger an obligation to evaluate the student under IDEA. While these legal principles seem straightforward, they provide little solace for educators or attorneys.

In practice, complex issues arise when educators are asked to evaluate a student who is actively using, or has recently used, substances. The illegal use of drugs can mimic mental health disorders, including mood disorders (such as major depression and bipolar disorder), anxiety disorders, and even psychotic disorders. As a result, substance use can lead educators to mistakenly conclude that a student meets the eligibility criteria for special education under the category of Emotional Disorder (ED) or Other Health Impairment (OHI). Such an error can have serious consequences for the student because neither the adverse emotional effects of intoxication nor the effects of withdrawal will improve from special education and related services. Indeed, the

327

introduction of special education and related services in response to a student's substance use will compound the problem, and may even be harmful, because such services ignore the real problem and may enable the student to hide the substance use for a longer period of time.

The introduction of special education and related services in response to a student's substance use can also impair the relationship between the school district and the student's parents. When it becomes evident that such services are ineffective at addressing the student's emotional and behavioral needs, the parents may blame the school district and, ironically, may demand a greater level of service or a highly restrictive placement, such as a residential placement. In addition, when the student's substance use eventually comes to light, the parents may claim that it was "caused by" a disability or that the student was "self-medicating" because the school district failed to identify the student's disability in a timely manner. Such claims are particularly likely when the student is expelled for substance use and the parents later assert that it was a manifestation of a disability that the district allegedly failed to identify.

THE CHALLENGES IN EVALUATING STUDENTS WHO ARE USING SUBSTANCES

Active substance use can affect an educational evaluation in several respects. First, substance use can adversely affect a student's academic performance. In some cases, an undeniable correlation will exist between the onset of drug use and a decline in academic performance. Second, substance use can affect the manner in which a student functions and interacts with others in the educational environment. Third, substance use can affect a student's performance on the instruments that are administered as part of an educational evaluation. For example, active substance use can produce deficits in attention, executive functioning, problem solving, abstract reasoning, cognitive efficiency, and short-term and long-term memory.[2] Fourth, substance use can produce an inaccurate picture of a student's absolute and relative strengths and weaknesses, which, in turn, can prevent an accurate identification of the student's educational needs.

Most evaluations include parent and teacher reports of the student's educational functioning. Such reports are often obtained through interviews, checklists, and the administration of behavioral scales. Unless the parent and teacher reports are specific to the student's functioning before the substance use began, after it began, or after it ended, the reports may produce a picture of a student who has significant needs, even though such needs derive exclusively from substance use.

As stated at the outset, the substance use can mimic mental health disorders and cause educators to mistakenly conclude that a student meets the eligibility criteria for ED. Substance use can also produce symptoms such as limited endurance, inattention, inability to focus, and limited alertness, which can lead educators to mistakenly conclude that a student meets the eligibility criteria for OHI.[3] Not surprisingly, hearing officers have found that the effects of ADHD and substance use can appear similar in terms of ability to focus, complete tasks, engage in sustained effort on tasks, and demonstrating sustained interest.[4]

Obviously, the effects of substance use are most pronounced when a student is under the influence of substances at the time of the testing, observation, or interview, or when the student used substances during the 24 hours preceding the testing, observation, or interview. One hearing officer has held that if a student appears to be under the influence of a substance during the administration of an evaluation, "best practice" dictates that the educator discuss the apparent substance use with the student and the parents and then seek to obtain the student's agreement to abstain from using any substances for a specific period of time so that valid evaluation results can be obtained.[5] Unfortunately, this purported "best practice" may quickly collide with reality. Most students who are substance users will be unable to simply abstain from substance use. Moreover, as discussed below, a brief abstention from substance use may have little impact on the validity of the evaluation results.

Studies show that substance use can have lingering effects on various functions, such as short-term memory, which can negatively impact a student's overall performance. The duration and severity of the adverse effects from substance use will depend on a variety of factors, including the types of substances the student has been using and the frequency of the substance use. For example, if a substance-using student uses hardcore substances like cocaine or heroin on a daily basis, the student's performance on an educational evaluation may be impacted for weeks or even months. If the student uses a substance like methamphetamine, the student's performance may be impacted indefinitely.

SUBSTANCE USE AS AN EXCLUSIONARY FACTOR

The federal regulations implementing IDEA state that the category of ED "does not apply to children who are socially maladjusted, unless it is determined that they have an emotional disturbance."[6] Similarly, some states have adopted eligibility criteria that treat substance use as an exclusionary factor. In Minnesota, for example, the eligibility criteria for emotional or behavioral disorders (EBD) require that a student exhibit a pattern of emotional or behavioral responses that adversely affects educational performance but is not primarily a result of illegal substance use.[7] Similarly, in Wisconsin, the eligibility criteria for OHI require school districts to determine whether a student's educational performance is adversely affected as a result of a health problem. Substance use disorder is not recognized as a "health problem" for purposes of IDEA. Therefore, if a student's educational performance is adversely affected as a result of substance use, as opposed to a health problem, the student will not qualify under the category of OHI.[8]

Eligibility criteria that treat substance use as an exclusionary factor give credence to the principle that substance use disorder is not recognized as a "disability" under IDEA. But such rules do not simplify the analysis. School districts must still determine whether adverse educational performance and divergent behaviors are the result of substance use or due to a recognized disability.

SCHOOL DISTRICT DELAY IN AN EVALUATION OF A STUDENT WHO IS ACTIVELY USING SUBSTANCES

Unfortunately, federal law does not allow a school district to delay an evaluation and wait until a student stops using substances. The U.S. Department of Education has repeatedly stated that a student's substance use does not obviate a school district's child find responsibility.[9] (Schools are obligated to find all students, ages 0–21 years, who may have disabilities and who may be entitled to special education services.)

Although some states have adopted rules that treat substance use as an exclusionary factor when evaluating a student, such rules do not relieve a school district of the responsibility to conduct an evaluation in the first instance. A school district may not make a determination about the impact of a student's suspected substance use on eligibility prior to and without completing a sufficient and comprehensive evaluation.[10]

PARSING THE EFFECTS FROM SUBSTANCE USE AND A DISABLING CONDITION

The obvious challenge for an evaluation team is to identify and separate the effects of substance use from the effects of any disabling conditions that might exist. Historical data on a student can be invaluable in overcoming this challenge, particularly when the data are plotted on a time line. For instance, a precipitous decline in academic performance that correlates in time with the onset of substance use would be extraordinarily helpful information for the team to consider.[11] Data on whether the student exhibited symptoms of a disabling condition before the onset of substance use or after the conclusion of substance use would also be helpful.[12] Of course, the team will be severely hamstrung in its efforts if it lacks an accurate account of when the substance use began and, if applicable, when it ended. If the historical data cover a period of time when the student was using substances, and the onset of the substance use is unknown, it may be impossible to separate the symptoms of substance use from the symptoms of a mental health disorder.[13]

The potential for comorbidity adds to the challenge of identifying a student's educational needs. Comorbidity occurs when substance use is coupled with another disorder, such as depression or ADHD. Comorbidity does not mean that one disorder causes another; rather, it means that two disorders exist at the same time. Parents' attorneys are fond of citing studies that claim that comorbidity between substance use disorder and adolescents diagnosed with ADHD is higher than in the general population.[14] However, although the student would have had ADHD prior to abusing substances (the onset of that disorder occurs, by definition, prior to age 12 years), the ADHD symptoms may have been mild in the educational environment prior to the onset of the substance use. In this instance, it could be argued that the effect of the substances, and not the ADHD, is the culprit.

SCHOOL DISTRICTS' PROPOSAL OF A SUBSTANCE USE ASSESSMENT WHEN CONDUCTING AN EDUCATIONAL EVALUATION

IDEA does not bar a school district from proposing a substance use assessment as part of an initial evaluation or reevaluation of a student for special education. Further, some states seem to encourage the use of substance use screening or even substance use assessment as part of a special educational evaluation. In Minnesota, for example, the eligibility criteria for EBD specifically state that the evaluation may include data from substance use assessments.[15]

Caution must be exercised, however, when a school district proposes to conduct a substance use assessment as part of a special educational evaluation. Several states have data privacy laws that classify communications with a substance use counselor as "confidential" data, unless the communication relates to physical or sexual abuse of a child or a danger to self or others.[16] Parents' attorneys have argued that such laws prohibit a school district from introducing the results of a substance use assessment into evidence at a due process hearing. School districts may be able to defeat this argument by asserting that the parent voluntarily placed into controversy the physical and mental condition of the student.[17] But it is best to avoid this issue altogether. One way to avoid the issue is to inform the parent and student that the substance use assessment will not give rise to a substance use counselor-patient privilege, or any similar privilege, and to have the parent and student waive any right to assert such a privilege along with any right to assert that any part of the substance use assessment will be confidential. Parents tend to support this approach because, without a waiver, they, like the school district, may be unable to access any information the student provides to the substance use counselor.

The public policy underpinning the confidentiality of communications between a substance use counselor and a student is clear: as a society we want to encourage students to speak with substance use counselors about potential substance use problems. Unfortunately, this public policy comes at a significant cost. In practice, the shield of confidentiality may enable students to continue using dangerous substances without notice to their parents, who may be in the best position to implement the intervention that is necessary. If the students' use is endangering themselves or others (e.g., driving while intoxicated), the substance use counselor needs to recognize statutory requirements that allow communication of these concerns to the student's parents.

LEGAL ISSUES THAT CAN ARISE WHEN A SPECIAL EDUCATION STUDENT BEGINS USING SUBSTANCES

Substance use is prevalent in the student population. For example, the 2007 Minnesota Student Survey of public school students noted that 35% of male and 25% of female high school seniors reported having had five or more drinks in a row in the previous two weeks on at least one occasion. The survey also found that 28% of male and 22% of female seniors reported driving after drug or alcohol use. Further, 34% of male and 27% of female seniors reported using marijuana or its derivatives in the previous year. Although lower, the percentages for younger students are still significant and troubling.

When special education students are caught using, possessing, or distributing substances on school property, the school district may pursue expulsion if the IEP team determines that the behavior was not a manifestation of the student's disability. Many ED students have IEP goals and objectives that address impulsivity and poor choices. The parents of such students may argue that the possession, use, or distribution of substances was a manifestation of the student's disability. This argument may be highly persuasive to a hearing officer unless the school district has evidence that the student was carrying out a plan, such as a prearranged drug transaction. Of course, irrespective of the outcome of the manifestation determination, the school district would have the option of pursuing a 45-day unilateral change of placement according to IDEA regulations.

When a school district seeks to discipline a special education student for substance use, the parents may go on the offensive and argue that the district's failure to provide an appropriate program of education led to the substance use. For instance, the parents may argue that the student is self-medicating because the district failed to identify the student's needs or because the district failed to provide the services and supports that were necessary to address the student's identified needs. Hearing officers have generally rejected these arguments,[18] but school districts are well-advised to consider all the facts before reacting to such an argument.

When special education students develop substance use disorder, difficult questions can also arise in regard to the appropriateness of the student's placement. The parents may argue that the substance use disorder is the result of the student's ED, for example, and that the school district is obligated to pay for a placement in a sober school, a day treatment facility, or a residential facility that will address the student's substance use disorder. The simple response would be to provide prior written notice denying the parents' request because substance use disorder is not recognized as a disability under IDEA. However, many cases will not lend themselves to a simple response. Unfortunately, some IEPs have goals that address substance use disorder. (The following transition goal is an example: "Student will improve behaviors in his community from choosing activities involving substance use 30% of the time to choosing substance-free activities 100% of the time.") When an IEP specifically addresses substance use disorder, the school district may have a difficult time arguing that it has no obligation to further address the substance use disorder as part of a free appropriate public education.

CONCLUSION

School districts must overcome a number of challenges when conducting an initial evaluation of a student who is actively using, or has recently used, substances, and they need to be aware of the legal issues that can arise during the evaluation process. An evaluation essentially produces a snapshot of the student at a given point in time. This evaluation, combined with important historical data, can accurately depict the student's educational performance and needs, and clarify whether or not the student has a true disability as outlined in special education law.

[1] See Letter to Matsui, 49 IDELR 16 (OSEP 2007); Letter to Uhler, 18 IDELR 1238 (1992).
[2] See Independent School District No. 196, 105 LRP 43623, at Finding 100 (SEA MN July 21, 2004).
[3] Id.
[4] Id.
[5] Id.
[6] See 34 C.F.R. § 300.7(c)(4)(ii).

[7] Minn. Rule 3525.1329, subpart 2a; *see also Old Orchard Beach Sch. Dept.*, 21 IDELR 1084 (SEA Maine 1994) (state rules require ruling out any other causes; student held not EBD but truant).

[8] *See School District of Hudson*, DPI Case No. LEA-08-021 (SEA WI 2009).

[9] *See Letter to Ohler*, 18 IDELR 1238 (1992); *see also Independent School District No. 203*, 109 LRP 60322 (MN SEA Complaint Decision 09-027C Dec. 5, 2008); *Independent School District No. 196*, 105 LRP 43623 (SEA MN July 21, 2004); *In Re Child with a Disability*, 507 IDELR 388, 507 LRP 8587 (SEA M. 1986); *Lewis County School District and Iowa Dept. Ed.*, 42 IDELR 247, 105 LRP 6142 (SEA IA 2005).

[10] *See Independent School District No. 276 (Minnetonka)*, 106 LRP 26688 (MN SEA Complaint Decision Mar. 8, 2002); *see also Independent School District No. 885*, 106 LRP 28057 (MN SEA Complaint Decision Aug. 31, 1999) (concluding that district violated IDEA by delaying evaluation because of student's suspected substance use). *But see Independent School Dist. No. 11*, 28 IDELR 1144, 28 LRP 5128, at Conclusion 12 (SEA MN Aug. 26, 1998), *aff'd* 29 IDELR 311 (Oct. 2, 1998) ("However, part of the reason for delay in assessing additional areas was the Student's chemical abuse, which could affect assessment results. It was appropriate for the District to delay additional assessment [for EBD] until . . . it had assurance that the Student was not using marijuana").

[11] *See, e.g., School District of Hudson*, DPI Case No. LEA-08-021 (SEA WI 2009).

[12] *See id.*

[13] *Cf. Independent School District No. 196*, 105 LRP 43623 (SEA MN July 21, 2004) (opining that an "appropriate evaluation" can determine whether an inordinate amount of tardiness, the failure to turn in assignments, not participating in class, and failing grades were caused by marijuana use, ADHD, or another mental health disorder).

[14] *See Independent School District No. 196*, 105 LRP 43623 (SEA MN July 21, 2004).

[15] Minn. Rule 3525.1329, subpart 3.

[16] *See* Minn. Stat. §595.02, subd. 1(g); Minn. Stat. §595.02, subd. 1(i).

[17] *Independent School District No. 196*, 105 LRP 43623 (SEA MN July 21, 2004); *Board of Ed. of Oak Park Pub. Sch.*, 20 IDELR 414 (SEA Mich. Aug. 1993); *NewPort-Mesa Unified School District*, EHLR 508:263 (SEA Cal. 1986).

[18] *See Independent School District No. 196*, 105 LRP 43623 (SEA MN July 21, 2004).

Note: This appendix was adapted from Michael Waldspurger, J.D., and William Dikel, M.D., Drugs and Disabilities: Conducting Special Education Evaluations of Students Who Abuse Drugs or Alcohol, Inquiry and Analysis, July, 2010.

References

American Psychiatric Association. (2000). *Diagnostic and statistical manual of mental disorders* (4th ed., text rev.). Washington, DC: Author.

American Psychiatric Association. (2013). *Diagnostic and statistical manual of mental disorders* (5th ed.). Washington, DC: Author.

Anderson, L.S. (1976). The mental health center's role in school consultation: Toward a new model. *Journal of Community Mental Health, 12*, 83–88.

Angst, J., & Sellaro, R. (2000). Historical perspectives and natural history of bipolar disorder. *Biological Psychiatry, 48*(6), 445–457.

Barkley, R. A., & Peters, H. (2012). The earliest reference to ADHD in the medical literature? Melchior Adam Weikard's description in 1775 of "attention deficit." *J. Attention Disorders, 16*(8), 623–630.

Bower, E.M. (1969). *Early identification of emotionally handicapped children in school* (2nd ed.). Springfield, Illinois: Charles C Thomas.

Chan, R. C. K., Shum, D., Toulopoulou, T., & Chen, E. Y. H. (2008). Assessment of executive functions: Review of instruments and identification of critical issues. *Archives of Clinical Neuropsychology, 23*(2), 201–216.

Dikel, W. (2012, May). Providing mental health services in public schools— What educators need to know. Retrieved from http://www.williamdikel.com/providing-mental-health-services-in-public-schools-what-educators-need-to-know.html.

Dikel, W. (2013). The relationship between physical health and mental health. In D. C. Wiley and A. C. Cory (Eds.), *Encyclopedia of School Health.* Thousand Oaks, CA: Sage. 491–493.

Dikel, W. (2015). *Psychiatric aspects of youth violence.* Presentation for the 2015 Minnesota Correctional Education Association Conference.

Dikel, W. (2016, March/April). The case for elimination of the payor of last resort provision in IDEA. Retrieved from http://www.williamdikel.com/the-case-for-elimination-of-payor-of-last-resort-from-idea.html.

Dikel, W., Bailey, J., & Sanders, D. (1994, November 1). Community mental health support services in a special education setting. *Behavioral Disorders, 20*(1), 69–75.

Forness, S., & Knitzer, J. (1992). A new proposed definition and terminology to replace "serious emotional disturbance" in Individuals with Disabilities & Education Act. *School Psychology Review, 21*(1), 12–20.

Garland, A. F., Hough, R. L., McCabe, K. M., Yeh, M., Wood, P. A., & Aarons, G. A. (2001). Prevalence of psychiatric disorders in youths across five sectors of care. *J. American Academy of Child and Adolescent Psychiatry, 40*(4), 409–418.

Graham, S. (2013). Bullying: A module for teachers. Washington, DC: American Psychological Association. Retrieved from http://www.apa.org / education/k12/bullying.aspx?item=1

Hanover Research (2013). *Effective programs for emotional and behavioral disorders, p. 2. Retrieved from* https://www.district287.org/uploaded/A_Better_Way/EffectiveProgramsforEmotionalandBehavioralDisorde rsHanover2013.pdf

Harrison, J., Bunford, N., Evans, S., & Owens, J. (2013, September 10). Educational accommodations for students with behavioral challenges: A systematic review of the literature. *Review of Educational Research*, doi:10.3102/0034654313497517.

Individuals with Disabilities Education Act (IDEA) (1990). Sec. 303.510. Retrieved from https://sites.ed.gov/idea/

Kanner, L. (1943). Autistic disturbances of affective contact. *Nervous Child, 2*, 217–250.

Lewis, T. J., Hudson, S., Richter, M., & Johnson, N. (2004). Scientifically supported practices in emotional and behavioral disorders: A proposed approach and brief review of current practices. *Behavioral Disorders, 29*(3), 247–259.

Martin, A., Volkmar, F., & Lewis, M. (2007). *Child and adolescent psychiatry: A comprehensive textbook* (4th ed.). Philadelphia: Lippincott, Williams, & Wilkins.

MTA Cooperative Group. (1999). A 14-month randomized clinical trial of treatment strategies for attention-deficit hyperactivity disorder. *Archives of General Psychiatry, 56*(12), 1073–1086.

Nelson, E. C., Grant, J. D., Bucholz, K. K., Glowinski, A., Madden, P. A. F., Reich W., et al. (2000). Social phobia in a population-based female adolescent twin sample: Co-morbidity and associated suicide-related symptoms. *Psychological Medicine, 30*(4), 797–804.

Pastor, P., Reuben, C., & Duran, C. (2012, February 24). Identifying emotional and behavioral problems in children aged 4–17 years: United States, 2001–2007. National Health Statistics Reports, 48. Retrieved from http://www.cdc.gov/nchs/data/nhsr/nhsr048.pdf

Perou, R., Bitsko, R. H., Blumberg, S. J., Pastor, P., Ghandour, R. M., Gfroerer, J. C., . . . & Huang, L. N. (2013, May). Mental health surveillance among children United States, 2005–2011. Atlanta, GA: Division of Human Development and Disability, National Center on Birth Defects and Developmental Disabilities/CDC.

Ratwik, P. and Dikel, W. (2009, April). Bridges and firewalls: Contractual relationships for mental health services provided in school settings, *Inquiry and Analysis*. Retrieved from http://www.williamdikel.com/bridges-and-firewalls-contractual-relationships-for-mental-health-services-provided-in-school-settings.html.

Remschmidt, H. E., Schulz, E., Martin, M., Warnke, A., & Trott, G. (1994). Childhood onset schizophrenia: History of the concept and recent studies. *Schizophrenia Bulletin*, 20(4), 727–745.

Ruff, S., & Dikel, W. (2009, November). Mental health Related Services on IEPs. *Inquiry and Analysis.* 1–4

Satcher, D. (1998, April 16). Speech at the American Society of Suicidology conference.

Schlenger, W. E., Etheridge, R. M., Hansen, D. J., Fairbank, D. W., & Onken, J. (1992). Evaluation of state efforts to improve systems of care for children and adolescents with severe emotional disturbances: The CASSP (Child and Adolescent Service System Program) initial cohort study. *J. Ment. Health Adm., 19*(2), 131–142.

Stage, S. A., & Quiroz, D. R. (1997). A meta-analysis of interventions to decrease disruptive classroom behavior in public education settings. *School Psychology Review, 26*(3), 333–368.

Stewart, D., & Dikel, W. (2011, Summer). Emotional/behavioral disorders and special education: recommendations for system redesign of a failed category. *Hamline Law Review, 34*(3), 589–604.

Substance Abuse and Mental Health Services Administration (SAMHSA): National Suicide Prevention Lifeline (2104). Columbia-Suicide Severity Rating Scale (C-SSRS). Retrieved from https://suicidepreventionlifeline.org/wp-content/uploads/2016/09/Suicide-Risk-Assessment-C-SSRS-Lifeline-Version-2014.pdf

UCLA Center for Mental Health in Schools (2019). Retrieved from http://smhp.psych.ucla.edu

University of Maryland School of Medicine (2019). National Center for School Mental Health (NCSMH). Retrieved from http://csmh.umaryland.edu

U.S. Department of Health and Human Services. (2000). Report of the Surgeon General's Conference on Children's Mental Health: A national action agenda. Washington, DC: Author. Retrieved from http://www.ncbi.nlm.nih.gov/books/NBK44233/

U.S. Department of Health and Human Services. (2019). Opioids and adolescents. Retrieved from https://www.hhs.gov/ash/oah/adolescent-development/substance-use/drugs/opioids/index.html

Wagner, M. (1995). Outcomes for youth with serious emotional disturbance in secondary schools and early adulthood, *Future of Children, Critical Issues for Children and Youths, 5*(2), 90–112.

Weist, M. D., Sander, M. A., Walrath, C., Link, B., Nabors, L., Adelsheim, S., Moore, E., Jennings, J., & Carrillo, K. (2005). Developing principles for best practice in expanded school mental health. *J. Youth and Adolescence, 34*(1), 7–13.

Waldspurger, M., & Dikel, W. (2010, July). Drugs and disabilities: Conducting special education evaluations of students who abuse drugs or alcohol. *Inquiry and Analysis*. Retrieved from http://www.williamdikel.com/drugs-and-disabilities-conducting-special-education-evaluations-of-students-who-abuse-drugs-or-alcohol.html.

Suggested Reading

Dikel, W. (1999). Mental health and the schools: What educators need to know. Roseville, MN: Minnesota Department of Children, Families and Learning. Retrieved from http://www.nasponline.org/advocacy/MentalHealth.PDF

Dikel, W. (2002). Mental health and public health. *Metro Doctors, 4*(3).

Dikel, W. (2012, May). Providing mental health services in public schools. *Leadership Insider: Practical Perspectives on School Law and Policy*.

Dikel, W. (2012, December). School shootings and student mental health: What lies beneath the tip of the iceberg. National School Board Association Council of School Attorneys. Retrieved from http://www.nsba.org/SchoolLaw/Issues/Safety/School-Shootings-and-Student-Mental-Health.pdf

Dikel, W. (2013). Mental health and healthy nutrition. In D. C. Wiley & C. Cory (Eds.), *Encyclopedia of school health*. Thousand Oaks, CA: Sage. 57–59

Dikel, W. (2013). The relationship between physical health and mental health. In D. C. Wiley & A. C. Cory (Eds.), *Encyclopedia of school health*. Thousand Oaks, CA: Sage. 491–493

Dikel, W., Bailey, J., & Sanders, D. (1994). Community support services in a special education setting. *Behavioral Disorders, 20*(1), 69–75.

Dikel, W., & Ostrom, J. (2013). The behavioral/clinical spectrum. In D. C. Wiley & A. C. Cory (Eds.), *Encyclopedia of school health*. Thousand Oaks, CA: Sage.

Ratwik, P., & Dikel, W. (2009, April). Bridges and firewalls: Contractual relationships for mental health services provided in school settings. *Inquiry and Analysis*. Retrieved from http://www.williamdikel.com/bridges-and-firewalls-contractual-relationships-for-mental-health-services-provided-in-school-settings.html

Ruff, S., & Dikel, W. (2009, November). Mental health related services in IEPs. *Inquiry and Analysis*.Retrieved from http://www.williamdikel.com/mental-health-related-services-on-ieps.html

Stewart, D., & Dikel, W. (2011, Summer). Emotional/behavioral disorders and special education: Recommendations for system redesign of a failed category. *Hamline Law Review, 34*(3), 589–604.

Waldspurger, M., & Dikel, W. (2010, July). Drugs and disabilities: Conducting special education evaluations of students who abuse drugs or alcohol. *Inquiry and Analysis*. Retrieved from http://www.williamdikel.com/

drugs-and-disabilities-conducting-special-education-evaluations-of
-students-who-abuse-drugs-or-alcohol.html

Weissbrodt, D., Madeira, W., Stewart, D., & Dikel, W. (2012, Summer). Applying international human rights standards to the restraint and seclusion of students with disabilities. *Law and Inequality: A Journal of Theory and Practice, 30*(2), 287–307.

Index

medications for, 67–69
overdiagnosis of, 63
prevalence of, 11, 62–63
psychotherapy for, 66–67
schools districts lack of mental health plans
   for students with, xii
sensitivity to artificial colorings and, 159
symptom checklist for, 207
symptoms of, 63–64
teaching strategies for students with, 264–68
Tourette's syndrome and, 68
treatment of, 66–69
atypical antipsychotics, 57
for ASD, 118
AustismXPress, 285
autism
described, 113
early infantile, 113
autism spectrum disorder (ASD), 113–18, 247
behavioral interventions for, 117
case example, 118
described, 113–14, 247
DSM-IV-TR on, 113
DSM-5 on, 113
IDEA on, 247
manifestations in the classroom, 115–16
medications for, 117–18
oversensitivity to touch, sound, or light, 115–16
prevalence of, 11, 114–15
psychotherapy for, 116–17
skills training for, 117
special education services for students with,
   247
symptoms of, 114
tactile defensiveness in, 115
teachers' role in, 182–83
teaching strategies for students with, 268–70
touch sensitivity in, 115
treatment of, 116–18
types of, 114
aviophobia, 76
avoidant/restrictive food intake disorder
from feeding disorder of infancy or early
   childhood, 318

"bad drug"
"good drug" vs., 87
Baillarger, J., 50
behavior(s)
defiant, 276–78
defined, 26
described, 26
disruptive, 279–81

mental health disorders impact on, 25–41 see
   also problematic behaviors
oppositional, 276–78
peer reinforcement to promote appropriate,
   298–99
problematic see problematic behaviors
violent, 281–82 see violent behavior(s)
behavioral
defined, 26
described, 38
Behavioral and Emotional Screening System
in schools meeting challenges of students'
   mental health, 219
Behavioral category of Clinical–Behavioral Spectrum, 28–29
behavioral interventions, 152–53
for ADHD, 66–67
for ASD, 117
in substance use disorders management, 100
for youth violence and aggression, 126
behavioral problems. see problematic behaviors
behavior contracts, 299–300
behavior support management plans, 295
belief(s)
cultural, 14
benzodiazepine(s)
for GAD, 74
for separation anxiety disorder, 79
binge drinking, 91–92
prevalence of, 88
biologically based disorders
medications improving, 160–62
bipolar disorders
mood swings of, 51
bipolar II disorder
features of, 51–52
risk factors for, 52–53
bipolar mood disorder, 50–58
alcohol or drug use with, 53
alternative treatments for, 58
conditions related to, 50
described, 50
diagnosis of, 52
DMDD vs., 59
effects of, 53–54
features of, 51–52
genetics in, 52
historical background of, 50–51
lithium for, 55–56
manic episode in, 52
manic symptoms of, 51
manifestations in the classroom, 54–55
medications for, 55–58